Mastering

French

Second edition

Edward Neather
Senior Lecturer in Education
University of Exeter

with the collaboration of Isabelle Rodrigues

Betty Parr
Founding Editor

MACMILLAN

© Edward Neather 1982
© Edward Neather & Isabelle Rodrigues 1995

All rights reserved. No reproduction, copy or transmission of
this publication may be made without written permission.

No paragraph of this publication may be reproduced, copied or
transmitted save with written permission or in accordance with
the provisions of the Copyright, Designs and Patents Act 1988,
or under the terms of any licence permitting limited copying
issued by the Copyright Licensing Agency, 90 Tottenham Court
Road, london W1P 9HE.

Any person who does any unauthorised act in relation to this
publication may be liable to criminal prosecution and civil
claims for damages.

First edition 1982
Second edition 1995

Published by
MACMILLAN PRESS LTD
Houndmills, Basingstoke, Hampshire RG21 2XS
and London
Companies and representatives
throughout the world

ISBN 0–333–61429–1
ISBN 0–333–61431–3 cassettes
ISBN 0–333–61430–5 pack

A catalogue record for this book is available
from the British Library.

10   9   8   7   6   5   4   3   2   1
04   03   02   01   00   99   98   97   96   95

Typeset by ⊼ Tek Art, Croydon, Surrey

Printed in Hong Kong

The author and publishers would like to thank the
following photo sources: J. Allan Cash Ltd pp. 3, 13, 23, 24,
44, 64, 87, 92, 95, 107, 162, 173; The Mansell Collection p. 141;
Roger-Viollet pp. 12, 106, 121, 128, 140, 152, 163, 172, 184; and Helen Tyler p.

Every effort has been made to trace copyright
holders but if any have been overlooked the
publishers will be pleased to make the
necessary arrangement at the first opportunity.

The cassettes which accompany this book can be ordered from your local booksellе
in case of difficulty, from Macmillan Direct, Houndmills, Basingstoke, Hampshire,
RG21 2XS (telephone 01256 29242).

REGIONAL TECHNICAL
COLLEGE LIMERICK
LIBRARY

CLASS NO 448 NEA
ACC. NO 18137
DATE

Contents

Introduction: how to use this course

This introduction to French is intended for complete beginners in the language but it also offers a valuable refresher course for those who have previously learned a little French but now find that it has grown 'rusty'.

The book has a dual aim. Firstly, it seeks to provide a grounding in the basic skills of understanding and communicating in French for students intending to spend holidays in France, for those who are involved with business activities with French companies and for those individuals and families who participate in the expanding number of 'twinnings' between English and French communities.

Secondly, this course offers the first stages in French for students whose aims may not be solely concerned with getting by in 'survival' situations but who wish to acquire the basis of a more extensive knowledge of the grammar and structures of the language with a view to developing their language skills at a later date.

The organisation of chapters

Each chapter is organised as follows:

1. A series of *dialogues* recorded on tape and printed in the book. These dialogues concentrate on the particular function of language which is presented as the chapter heading, for example, 'Making enquiries', 'Planning a journey', and so on.
2. After the printed dialogues come the lists of useful expressions and new *vocabulary* in the chapter.
3. The *explanations* section then presents the main grammar points of the chapter.
4. *Exercises* then help you to practise the new language and situations. Firstly, the speaking skill is practised in role-play activities. The speaking exercises are then followed by reading and writing tasks. Finally there is a spontaneous dialogue recorded on tape with exercises in the book.

How to use the book

1 The key to learning a foreign language lies with developing the skill of listening. It is therefore recommended that you begin each chapter by listening to the recorded dialogues without at first following the written text, attempting to guess what is going on from your knowledge of the situation and the tones of voice.

2 Then follow the dialogues in the book, looking up new words and expressions.

3 Next, tackle the *explanations* to understand the structures of the language. This section presents the essential information about the grammar and structures used in the chapter without going into detail. Further information is given in the appropriate section of the *grammar reference section*.

4 The exercises start by giving you the chance to develop your speaking skills, and then go on to reading and writing. Many of the reading tasks are drawn from authentic French sources. Don't worry if you can't understand every word of these texts! A great deal of foreign-language reading, at all levels, consists in making sensible guesses according to the context, and not every word is essential to understanding the message. Then, the writing tasks will help you clarify your understanding of the main grammar points and fix new vocabulary in your memory.

5 Finally, the spontaneous dialogues give you the chance, from the beginning, to hear conversational French at normal speed. There will be words you have not met before, and it is always a bit of a shock, at first, to hear a foreign language at normal speed. As with the authentic reading passages, it is important to realise that you do not need to understand every word to get the message. Getting the general idea is what counts, and gradually adjusting your ear to hearing spoken French. The exercises will help you, by setting the scene and context, by giving you some of the unfamiliar vocabulary and by helping you to listen for significant points.

Chapter 20, the final chapter, is different from the others in that it consists entirely of authentic listening materials. There are many occasions when listening and understanding the foreign language are necessary skills. Information may be given over loudspeakers, on telephone answering machines, on the radio or television. This chapter gives a selection of such materials for you to listen, make notes, and then check with the translations in the *key to exercises*.

Reference material

The reference section includes a *key*, which provides answers to all the exercises, and a *grammar reference section*, which presents a summary of all the grammatical forms introduced in the book. Then there is a *guide to pronunciation*, and a short *bibliography* to guide the student in the choice of further reference material and opportunities for hearing French. Finally, *supplementary vocabularies* give further useful words on common topics, and the *glossary* lists the words introduced during the course of the book.

Edward Neather

1 Bonjour! Saying hello

Dialogues

 ### Dialogue 1

John and Mary Smith and their two children are off to spend their summer holidays in France. They drive off the ferry and a policeman of the immigration service checks their documents.

Agent: Bonjour, monsieur. Votre passeport, s'il vous plaît.
John Smith: Bonjour, monsieur. Voilà mon passeport.
Agent: Merci, monsieur. Alors, vous êtes bien John Smith?
John: Oui, monsieur. C'est bien ça. Et voilà ma femme et mes deux enfants.
Agent: Bonjour, madame.
Mary Smith: Bonjour, monsieur.
Agent: Vous restez combien de temps en France?
John: Trois semaines.
Agent: Très bien, monsieur. Alors, voilà votre passeport. Au revoir et bon séjour.
John: Merci, monsieur. Au revoir.

 ### Dialogue 2 *À l'hôtel   At the hotel*

The family drive to Caen, where they are booked into a hotel.

John: Bonjour, monsieur. Je suis Monsieur Smith. Vous avez une chambre pour ma famille.
Hôtelier: Ah, oui! Bonjour, Monsieur Smith; bonjour, Madame Smith.
Mary: Bonjour, monsieur. Et voilà nos deux enfants, Catherine et Robert.
Hôtelier: Bonjour, les enfants. Alors, monsieur, vous restez trois semaines, c'est bien ça?
John: Oui, c'est ça.
Hôtelier: Très bien, monsieur. Alors, c'est la chambre numéro cinq. Voilà votre clef.

John: Merci, monsieur.
Hôtelier: À bientôt, monsieur. Au revoir, madame.

 ### Dialogue 3

After settling in, the Smiths leave the hotel to call on Monsieur Michel Lebrun – a friend has given them a letter of introduction to him. They call at his office and are first dealt with by a secretary.

John: Pardon, madame. Est-ce que Monsieur Lebrun est là, s'il vous plaît? Je m'appelle John Smith.
Secrétaire: Ah, oui, vous êtes Monsieur Smith. Monsieur Lebrun est là. Un moment, s'il vous plaît. *(She buzzes and Monsieur Lebrun comes into the office.)*
Lebrun: Bonjour, Monsieur Smith. Très heureux de faire votre connaissance.
John: Bonjour, Monsieur Lebrun. Je vous présente ma femme, Mary, et nos deux enfants, Catherine et Robert.
Lebrun: Enchanté, madame. Bonjour, les enfants. Eh bien, est-ce que vous êtes libres ce soir? Vous pouvez dîner chez nous?
John: Avec plaisir.
Mary: Vous êtes très gentil.
Lebrun: Alors, à sept heures ce soir.
John: Merci bien, et au revoir, monsieur.
Lebrun: Au revoir, monsieur. Au revoir, madame. Au revoir, les enfants. À bientôt.

 ### Dialogue 4

The Smiths turn up for supper at 7.00 pm, as invited. Monsieur Lebrun opens the door.

Lebrun: Bonsoir, Monsieur Smith. Bonsoir, madame. Comment allez-vous?
John: Très bien, merci, monsieur. Et vous?
Lebrun: Bien, merci. Entrez, s'il vous plaît. *(He calls his wife.)* Nicole, Monsieur et Madame Smith et les enfants sont là.
Madame Lebrun: Bonsoir, Monsieur Smith. Bonsoir, Madame Smith.
John: Enchanté, madame. Et voilà nos enfants, Catherine et Robert.
Madame Lebrun: Bonsoir, les enfants.

Vocabulary

Dialogue 1

(i) Useful expressions

bonjour	good morning; good afternoon
s'il vous plaît	please
voilà	here is; this is

Caen old and new

c'est ça	that's right; that is so
c'est bien ça	
combien de temps?	how long?
au revoir	goodbye
bon séjour	have a nice stay

(ii) Nouns – masculine

le jour: day
l'agent: policeman
le passeport: passport
l'enfant: child (boy)

Nouns – feminine

la femme: wife; woman
la semaine: week
l'enfant: child (girl)

(iii) Other words

bon: good
votre: your
mon/ma/mes: my
bien: fine; well
vous restez (rester): you remain; you
   stay
en: in
France: France

trois: three
très: very
merci: thank you
alors: so; well
oui: yes
et: and
deux: two

Dialogue 2

(i) Useful expression

à bientôt   goodbye for now; see you later

(ii) Nouns – masculine   Nouns – feminine

l'hôtel: hotel   la chambre: bedroom
l'hôtelier: hotel proprietor   la famille: family
le numéro: number   la clef: key

(iii) Other words

je suis (être): I am   nos: our
vous avez (avoir): you have; you've got   c'est: it is
pour: for   cinq: five

Dialogue 3

(i) Useful expressions

je m'appelle   my name is
très heureux de faire votre connaissance   pleased to meet you; how do you do?

je vous présente   may I introduce
enchanté   delighted; it's a pleasure; how do you do?

eh bien   well now
avec plaisir   with pleasure
chez nous   at home with us
à sept heures   at seven o'clock
merci bien   many thanks; thank you very much

(ii) Nouns – masculine   Nouns – feminine

le moment: moment   la secrétaire: secretary
le soir: evening   la connaissance: acquaintance
le plaisir: pleasure

(iii) Other words

pardon: excuse me   libre(s): free
est (être): is   vous pouvez (pouvoir): you can
là: there (sometimes used for 'here' – see below)   dîner: to have supper/dinner
     avec: with
vous êtes (être): you are   gentil: kind; nice
heureux: happy; pleased   ce: this
présenter: to introduce; to present

Dialogue 4

(i) Useful expressions

bonsoir	good evening
comment allez-vous?	how are you?

(ii) Other words

entrez (entrer): come in   là: here (occasional use)
sont (être): are

Explanations

(a) 'Monsieur' and 'madame'

'Monsieur' is the equivalent of 'Mr' as in 'Monsieur Lebrun' (Mr Brown). 'Madame' is the equivalent of 'Mrs' as in 'Madame Lebrun' (Mrs Brown). In addition, 'monsieur' and 'madame' are used where English uses 'sir' and 'madam'.

French also uses 'monsieur' and 'madame' at times when English has no form of address. For example, 'bonjour, monsieur'; 'bonjour, madame'. In English we would just say 'good morning'.

(b) Conversational extras

Ordinary conversation in any language is 'oiled' by certain little expressions and words which may not add much to the meaning but which are an important part of daily communication. For example, in English we use words such as 'well' and 'now'. French uses 'alors' rather like English 'well', or 'right'. 'Bien' or 'eh bien' is used in a similar way:

Alors, vous restez trois semaines?	So, you're staying for three weeks?
Eh bien, vous êtes libres ce soir?	Well then, are you free this evening?

'Bien' usually means 'well', but it may be used to emphasise or underline a statement:

C'est **bien** ça.   That's *quite* right.

(c) Gender – masculine or feminine (grammar ref. 2.1)

All French nouns are either masculine or feminine. The best way to remember the gender of a word is to learn the word together with the correct French form for 'the' ('le', if masculine; 'la', if feminine; and 'l'', whenever a word begins with a vowel).

Masculine		Feminine	
le jour	the day	**la** femme	the woman
le passeport	the passport	**la** semaine	the week
l'enfant	the child		

(d) Plurals (grammar ref. 2.2)

le jour	the day	**les** jours	the days
la semaine	the week	**les** semaines	the weeks
l'enfant	the child	**les** enfants	the children

The great majority of French nouns form the plural, as do English nouns, by adding '-s'. In the plural, 'the' is always 'les', for both masculine and feminine words.

(e) Expressing possession (grammar ref. 3.5)

	Masculine	Feminine	Plural
my	**mon** passeport	**ma** femme	**mes** enfants
our	**notre** hôtel	**notre** chambre	**nos** enfants
your	**votre** mari	**votre** clef	**vos** enfants

(f) Questions (grammar ref. 5.11)

You will note from the dialogues that there are two main ways of putting a question:

(i) Give a rising intonation to a sentence:

Vous êtes John Smith?

Vous êtes libre ce soir?

(ii) Put 'est-ce que' in front of a statement to turn it into a question:

Est-ce que vous êtes John Smith?
Est-ce que vous êtes libre ce soir?

Exercises

● *The key to these exercises begins on p.212.*

Parlez

(Speaking exercises)

Exercise 1   Arriving at the hotel

Now it's your turn to play the part of the customer. Look at the dialogue below and use the English prompts to help you prepare your role. Then turn on the recording and practise playing the part of John Smith.

Hôtelier: Bonjour, monsieur; bonjour, madame.
John: *(Greet him, and say who you are. You can use 'je suis', or 'je m'appelle'.)*
Hôtelier: Ah oui, Monsieur Smith, vous avez une réservation. Votre passeport, s'il vous plaît.
John: *(What word do you say as you hand it over to him?)*
Hôtelier: Merci, monsieur. Alors vous restez trois semaines, c'est ça?
John: *(Confirm this, using 'c'est bien ça'.)*
Hôtelier: Alors, c'est la chambre numéro cinq. Voilà votre clef, monsieur.
John: *(Thank him.)*
Hôtelier: Bon séjour, monsieur. À bientôt.
John: *(Thank him again and say goodbye.)*

Exercise 2

Now imagine you are Mary Smith arriving at a hotel or camp-site. You will need to greet the receptionist, give your name and the length of time you are staying. You will also need to hand over your passport. Work out what you want to say and then practise. Use the following phrases to help you:

Bonjour, monsieur/madame ... Je suis / Je m'appelle... Je reste... Voilà...

Exercise 3   At Lebrun's office, John Smith introduces his wife

Now play the roles of both John and Mary Smith.

Lebrun: Bonjour, Monsieur Smith, très heureux de faire votre connaissance.
John: *(Greet him, and introduce your wife using 'je vous présente...'.)*
Lebrun: Enchanté de faire votre connaissance, madame.
Mary: *(Greet him.)*
Lebrun: Est-ce que vous pouvez dîner chez nous ce soir?
John: *(Say yes, with pleasure.)*
Lebrun: Alors, à sept heures ce soir, ça va?
John: *(Say yes, that's fine. Use 'ça va bien'.)*
Mary: *(Thank him and say goodbye.)*

Lisez et écrivez
(Reading and writing exercises)

Exercise 4

The drawings below show introductions and invitations. Read what the characters say and then fill in the gaps.

(a) Votre nom c'est?
Je ... Colette. Et ...?

(b) Anne, ... Monsieur Dupont.
Bonjour, ...
E ... ...

(c) B ..., Anne. Vous ... libre, ce soir? Vous ... dîner chez nous?
Vous ... très gentil. Avec ...

(d) Je ... Carole.

(e) Bonjour, Madame Dupont. Comment ... — ...?
Très ..., ... Et ...?

Exercise 5 Asking questions

Here are some answers. Write down what you think the questions were.

Example: If the answer is:　　Oui, je suis Monsieur Smith.
The question would be either:　Vous êtes Monsieur Smith?
　　　　　　　　　　or:　Est-ce que vous êtes Monsieur Smith?

(a)　Oui, je suis Mary Smith.
(b)　Oui, avec plaisir.
(c)　Très bien, merci. Et vous?
(d)　Oui, Monsieur Lebrun est là.
(e)　Oui, c'est bien ça.

Exercise 6

Write down the answers to the following questions using the French for 'my'. Remember to use 'mon' for 'le' words (masculine), and 'ma' for 'la' words (feminine) and 'mon' if a word begins with a vowel.

Example: C'est votre femme?
Answer: Oui, c'est **ma** femme.

    (a) C'est votre clef?
    (b) C'est votre chambre?
    (c) C'est votre enfant?
    (d) C'est votre passeport?
    (e) C'est votre famille?

Écoutez
(Listening exercise)

 Exercise 7   Spontaneous dialogue   John and Mary Smith book into their hotel

First, listen several times to the short dialogue on tape. Don't worry if you can't get every word of it, but try to understand what is going on. Then, when you have got the general idea, try answering the following questions. Either tick the box to show you recognise a key word, or answer the question in English, if there are no boxes.

(a) After giving his name, John Smith makes a further statement referring to his booking. The key word is one of the following. Tick in the box the word you hear.

        chambre   ☐
        réservation ☐
        hôtel   ☐
        famille   ☐

(b) The receptionist checks the books and confirms. How long does she say he is booked in for?

        trois jours   ☐
        deux jours   ☐
        deux semaines ☐
        trois semaines ☐

(c) What does John Smith say to confirm the period of their stay?

        oui   ☐
        c'est cela, oui ☐
        c'est ça   ☐
        voilà   ☐

(d) Mary Smith wants to check on a point about the reservation. What does she ask the receptionist?

(e) The receptionist then says to them:

Vous voulez bien remplir cette fiche, s'il vous plaît?

She is asking them to fill in a form, required whenever you book into a hotel. Which word here do you think means 'form'?

(f) What does John Smith say when he hands over the completed form?

c'est ça ☐
voilà ☐
s'il vous plaît ☐
oui ☐

(g) What room number are they told by the receptionist?

(h) What does she give them next?

(i) Finally the receptionist wishes them a good stay. What does she say?

bonjour ☐
je vous souhaite un bon voyage ☐
je vous souhaite un bon séjour ☐
bonsoir ☐

Qu'est-ce que vous prenez?
Obtaining services

Dialogues

 ### Dialogue 1   À la banque   At the bank

Already short of cash, John Smith goes along to the bank to change some money.

Employé de banque: Bonjour, monsieur. Vous désirez?

John Smith: Bonjour, monsieur. Est-ce que je peux changer cinquante livres en francs, s'il vous plaît?

Employé: Certainement, monsieur. Vous pouvez changer de l'argent liquide ou toucher un chèque. Vous pouvez aussi utiliser votre carte de crédit dans le distributeur automatique et composer votre code confidentiel. Vous obtenez ainsi de l'argent liquide. Qu'est-ce que vous préférez?

John: Je peux toucher un chèque anglais?

Employé: Vous pouvez toucher un eurochèque anglais, monsieur, si vous présentez votre carte bancaire.

John: Bien, alors voilà ma carte et voilà un eurochèque de cinq cents francs (500F).

Employé: Merci, monsieur. Est-ce que je peux voir votre passeport, s'il vous plaît?

John: Voilà mon passeport.

Employé: Merci, monsieur. Bon alors, passez à la caisse, s'il vous plaît.

 ### Dialogue 2   Au café   At the café

John meets up with his wife and children and they go for mid-morning refreshments. They take a table on the 'terrasse' of a café and the waitress comes to take their order.

Serveuse: Bonjour, monsieur. Qu'est-ce que vous prenez?

John Smith: Je voudrais un café crème.

Mary Smith: Moi, je voudrais un café noir. Et deux Oranginas pour les enfants.

Serveuse: Alors, un café crème, un café noir et deux Oranginas. C'est tout?
John: Apportez aussi deux glaces pour les petits, s'il vous plaît.
Serveuse: Oui, monsieur. Quel parfum? Il y a vanille, fraise ou chocolat.
Mary: Alors, chocolat, s'il vous plaît.
Serveuse: Bien, madame.
   (When they have finished, John asks the waitress for the bill.)
John: Mademoiselle, l'addition, s'il vous plaît.
Serveuse: Oui, monsieur. Alors, deux cafés, ça fait quatorze francs (14F), deux Oranginas, ça fait vingt francs (20F), et deux glaces vingt-quatre francs (24F). Alors, ça fait cinquante-huit francs (58F) en tout, monsieur.

John: Le service est compris?
Serveuse: Oui, monsieur. Le service est compris.
John: Eh bien, voilà. Merci, mademoiselle.
Serveuse: Merci bien, monsieur. Au revoir, monsieur. Au revoir, madame.

 ### Dialogue 3   Retour à l'hôtel   Back to the hotel

The family return to their hotel at midday to discover a slight hitch. John asks
the hotel manager for his key.

John Smith: Pardon, monsieur. Je peux avoir la clef de la chambre numéro
cinq, s'il vous plaît?
Hôtelier: Voilà, monsieur. Je suis désolé, monsieur, mais il y a un petit
problème.
John: Pourquoi?
Hôtelier: Parce que votre chambre n'est pas tout à fait prête. La femme de
chambre fait les lits.
John: Ça ne fait rien. Est-ce qu'on peut déjeuner?

Hôtelier: Je regrette beaucoup, monsieur. Le déjeuner n'est pas tout à fait prêt.
John: Ah, bon? Qu'est-ce qui se passe? Il est déjà midi et demi.
Hôtelier: Nous avons un problème d'électricité. Mais ce n'est pas grave.
John: C'est une panne, sans doute, non?
Hôtelier: Oui, mais tout remarche maintenant. Dans deux minutes, votre chambre est à vous.
John: Bien.

Vocabulary

Dialogue 1

(i) Nouns – masc.

un employé: employee
le franc: franc
le chèque: cheque
l'argent: money
de l'argent liquide: cash
le code confidentiel: personal number
le distributeur automatique: cashpoint
un eurochèque: eurocheque

Nouns – fem.

la banque: bank
la livre: pound
la carte: card
la carte de crédit: credit card
la carte bancaire: banker's card

(ii) Other words

désirer: to want; to wish
je peux (pouvoir): I can
changer: to change
cinquante: fifty
certainement: certainly
ou (alors): or (else)
vous pouvez (pouvoir): you can
toucher (un chèque): to cash (a cheque)
utiliser: to use

obtenir: to obtain
préférer: to prefer
anglais: English
mais: but
si: if
présenter: to present
bancaire: bank *(adjective)*
voir: to see
passer: to pass; to move on to

Dialogue 2

(i) Useful expressions

qu'est-ce que vous prenez?
je voudrais
ça fait
le service est compris?

what would you like?
I'd like
that comes to
is a service charge included?

(ii) Nouns – masc.

le café: coffee
le café crème: white coffee
un Orangina: fizzy orange
les petits: little ones; children
le parfum: flavour; perfume
le chocolat: chocolate
le service: service

Nouns – fem.

la terrasse: pavement café
la serveuse: waitress
la glace: ice-cream
la vanille: vanilla
la fraise: strawberry
une addition: bill

(iii) Other words

vous prenez (prendre): you take
tout: all
apporter: to bring
aussi: also
petit: small; little

quel?: which?; what?
quatorze: fourteen
vingt: twenty
vingt-quatre: twenty-four
cinquante-huit: fifty-eight

Dialogue 3

(i) Useful expressions

je suis désolé
je regrette beaucoup ⎫⎬⎭ I'm very sorry

ça ne fait rien   it doesn't matter
qu'est-ce qui se passe?   what's happening?
il est midi et demi   it's half past midday
tout remarche maintenant   everything is working again
votre chambre est à vous   your room is all yours

(ii) Nouns – masc.

le problème: problem
le lit: bed

Nouns – fem.

la femme de chambre: chambermaid
la panne: breakdown
la minute: minute

(iii) Other words

avoir: to have
il y a: there is; there are
pourquoi?: why?
parce que: because
tout à fait: completely; quite
prêt(e): ready
fait (faire): makes; is making

on: one
déjeuner: to have lunch
beaucoup: much; a lot
déjà: already
grave: serious
maintenant: now
dans: in

Explanations

(a) *Regular verbs*

préparer	*to prepare*
je prépare	I prepare / I am preparing
vous prépar**ez**	you prepare / you are preparing

changer	*to change*
je change	I change / I am changing
vous chang**ez**	you change / you are changing

If you look up 'change' or 'prepare' in the dictionary, you will find the forms 'changer', 'préparer'. This part of the verb is called the infinitive. The infinitive is also the part of the verb which is given in the vocabulary lists in this book.

The great majority of regular verbs have an infinitive with the ending '-er'. Other verbs with the infinitive ending in '-er' will have the same endings in the present tense as those shown above in the examples for 'I' and 'you'. Note that there is only one form for the present tense in French, and this can translate the English simple present (I change) or continuous present (I am changing).

(b) *Can I...? May I...?*

je peux	I can / I may
est-ce que je peux?	can I? / may I?

Est-ce que je peux changer cinquante livres? Can I change £50?
Est-ce que je peux voir votre passeport? May I see your passport?

The question may also be asked using 'Je peux ...?' and raising your voice at the end of the sentence to give it a questioning intonation:

Je peux avoir la clef de la chambre? Can I have the key to the bedroom?

Note that 'je peux' and 'est-ce que je peux?' are *always* followed by an infinitive:

je peux **changer**
est-ce que je peux **préparer?**

(c) *You can... Can you...?*

Vous pouvez changer un chèque.	You can change a cheque.
Vous pouvez dîner ce soir?	⎫ Can you have dinner this
Est-ce que vous pouvez dîner ce soir?	⎭ evening?

(d) *Giving commands and instructions*

Payez à la caisse.	Pay at the cash-desk.
Apportez deux glaces.	Bring two ice-creams.

To give an instruction, use the 'vous' form of the verb, but omit the word 'vous'. So that this does not sound too abrupt and impolite, add 's'il vous plaît' (please).

Passez à la caisse, s'il vous plaît.   Please pass along to the cash-desk.

(e) *Negatives*

Je peux avoir la clef.	I can have the key.
Je **ne** peux **pas** avoir la clef.	I cannot have the key.
Vous pouvez déjeuner.	You can have lunch.
Vous **ne** pouvez **pas** déjeuner.	You cannot have lunch.

You will see from these examples that the negative is formed by placing 'ne...pas' before and after the verb. If the verb begins with a vowel, 'ne' is shortened to 'n''.

La chambre est prête.   The bedroom is ready.
La chambre **n'**est **pas** prête.   The bedroom is not ready.
Le déjeuner **n'**est **pas** tout à fait prêt.   Lunch is not quite ready.

(f) *The indefinite article (un, une, des)*

Masculine		*Feminine*	
un chèque	a cheque	**une** serveuse	a waitress
un employé	an employee	**une** banque	a bank

In the plural, English may say 'banks' or 'some banks', 'cheques' or 'some cheques'. In French, it is not normally possible for a noun to stand alone. For the plural form you will find:

des chèques	**des** serveuses
des employés	**des** banques

(g) *What...?*

qu'est-ce que...?	what...?
Qu'est-ce que vous prenez?	What are you having?
Qu'est-ce que vous pouvez voir?	What can you see?

(h) *Why?   Because...*

pourquoi?	why?
parce que...	because...

Il y a un petit problème. **Pourquoi?**   There is a small problem. Why?
Parce que votre chambre n'est pas prête.   Because your room isn't ready.

If the following word begins with a vowel, 'que' is shortened to 'qu''.

Parce qu'il y a un problème.   Because there is a problem.

(i) *Numbers (grammar ref. 9.1)*

un	1	onze	11
deux	2	douze	12
trois	3	treize	13
quatre	4	quatorze	14
cinq	5	quinze	15
six	6	seize	16
sept	7	dix-sept	17
huit	8	dix-huit	18
neuf	9	dix-neuf	19
dix	10	vingt	20

For numbers over 20, see the *grammer reference.*

Exercises

● *The key to these exercises begins on p.213.*

Parlez

(Speaking exercises)

Exercise 1   Ordering a coffee and a vanilla ice-cream

You are placing an order at a café. Look at the dialogue below and use the English prompts to help you prepare your role. Then turn on the recording and practise playing the part of the male customer.

Serveuse: Bonjour, monsieur. Qu'est-ce que vous désirez?
Client: *(Say you would like a coffee and a vanilla ice-cream.)*
Serveuse: Un café et une glace vanille. C'est tout?
Client: *(Say yes, that's everything.)*
Serveuse: Voilà, monsieur.
Client: *(Thank her.)*
Client: *(When you have finished, call the waitress (Mademoiselle...) and ask for the bill.)*

Serveuse: Alors, un café, 7 francs et une glace, 5 francs. Ça fait 12 francs, monsieur.

Client: *(Give her the money and say thank you.)*

Exercise 2

Now decide on some items you would like to order at a café, using the vocabulary lists above and the structures in Exercise 1. Work out how you would order these items and then how you will ask for the bill.

Lisez et écrivez

(Reading and writing exercises)

Exercise 3

Practise asking 'Can I...?' / 'May I...?' by writing down the French equivalent of the questions given here in English.

Example: May I have my key?
(Est-ce que) je peux avoir ma clef?

(a) Can I have lunch?
(b) Can I go to my room?
(c) May I have a coffee?

Exercise 4

You may decide to use your credit card at the cashpoint rather than changing money at the counter. Even when you are a beginner, it's surprising how much French you can read when you can make a good guess in a particular situation. Below is the sequence of information on the cashpoint screen. See if you can answer the questions which accompany each screen.

(a)

> **BIENVENUE SUR NOTRE SERVICE.**

What do you think this polite machine is saying? Have a guess at the word 'bienvenue'.

(b)

> **COMPOSEZ VOTRE CODE CONFIDENTIEL.**
>
> **APPUYEZ SUR LA TOUCHE: VALIDE.**

This is something confidential, obviously. What are you asked to do? Then you have to give it the go-ahead. What might 'touche' mean?

(c)

| RETRAIT D'ESPECES |
| OU |
| POSITION DES COMPTES. |

Now you are being asked whether you want to take out cash or check your account. What is the word for 'cash'?

(d)

| NOUS TRAITONS |
| VOTRE DEMANDE. |

The machine is handling your request. What is the word for 'request'?

(e)

| RETIREZ LES BILLETS |
| ET |
| REPRENEZ VOTRE CARTE. |
| MERCI. |

Here are the final two instructions. What are the French words for 'banknotes' and 'card'?

Exercise 5

Here are three questions asking 'What?'. Respond to the questions, expressing your personal preference. The model answer shows you how to express a preference.

Example: Qu'est-ce que vous préférez, un café crème, un thé ou un chocolat chaud?

Answer: Je préfère un café crème, s'il vous plaît. *(Or whatever your personal preference happens to be.)*

(a) Qu'est-ce que vous préférez, un chèque ou de l'argent liquide?
(b) Qu'est-ce que vous préférez, un café ou un thé?
(c) Qu'est-ce que vous préférez comme parfum, fraise ou chocolat?

Exercise 6

Now three 'Why?' questions. Answer 'Because...' (Parce que...) using the English prompts given in brackets.

Example: Pourquoi est-ce que vous allez à la banque?
(Because you want some francs.)
Answer: Parce que je voudrais des francs.

(a) Pourquoi est-ce que vous allez au café?
(Because you want a coffee.)
(b) Pourquoi est-ce que vous allez au restaurant?
(Because you want to have lunch.)
(c) Pourquoi est-ce que la chambre n'est pas prête?
(Because there is a small problem.)

LIBRARY
REGIONAL TECHNICAL COLLEGE LIMERICK

Écoutez

(Listening exercise)

 Exercise 7   Spontaneous dialogue   Ordering drinks in a café

Now, here is a situation in a café. You'll hear the waiter greet the man and woman customers, and then they decide what they want to eat and drink. You just need to concentrate on key words such as 'chocolat', 'croissant'. Don't be too concerned about bits of the dialogue which you can't yet understand. The exercises will help you recognise the key words, and some of the language you have already met in the earlier texts of this chapter.

(a) How does the waiter ask what they want?

Mesdames, messieurs, bonjour, qu'est-ce que vous voudriez? ☐
Mesdames, messieurs, bonjour, qu'est-ce que vous prenez? ☐
Mesdames, messieurs, bonjour, qu'est-ce que vous désirez? ☐
Mesdames, messieurs, bonjour, qu'est-ce que vous voulez boire? ☐

(b) Tick items from the list below which you think are ordered by the couple.

Woman	*Man*
un café au lait	un café au lait
un café noir	un café noir
un grand chocolat chaud	un grand chocolat chaud
un thé	un thé
une limonade	une limonade
un pain au chocolat	un pain au chocolat
un pain aux raisins	un pain aux raisins
un croissant	un croissant
une glace	une glace

(c) The man asks for the bill. (He says, 'Je vous dois combien?', meaning 'How much do I owe you?'.) Enter the price of each item on the list below and the total of the bill stated by the waiter.

un café   ? francs
un grand chocolat   francs
deux croissants   francs

Total   francs

(d) What does the man ask when he pays?

REGIONAL TECHNICAL COLLEGE LIMERICK LIBRARY   448 NEA   CLASS NO   ACC. NO 18137   DATE

QU'EST-CE QUE VOUS PRENEZ?   21

③ Pour aller à . . .?
Directions

Dialogues

 Dialogue 1   Au syndicat d'initiative   At the tourist information centre

John Smith: Bonjour, madame. C'est la première fois que nous sommes à Caen. Est-ce que vous avez des renseignements sur la ville, s'il vous plaît?
Dame: Avec plaisir, monsieur. Voilà un plan de la ville et voilà le guide officiel. Vous voulez des renseignements sur les monuments principaux?
John: Oui, s'il vous plaît.
Dame: Eh bien, sur le plan vous voyez ici le château. Devant l'entrée principale du château, vous voyez l'église Saint-Pierre.
Mary Smith: C'est l'église avec une grande flèche?
Dame: Oui, c'est bien ça, madame. Alors, suivez la rue Saint-Pierre et la rue Écuyère, traversez la place Fontette et l'église Saint-Étienne est sur la gauche.
John: Ah oui, elle est très connue. Et près de l'église, qu'est-ce que c'est?
Dame: C'est l'Hôtel de Ville. Vous pouvez visiter aussi le port de Caen.
Mary: Il y a un port ici, à Caen?
Dame: Oui, madame, il y a un port très important. Le Jardin des Plantes est aussi très intéressant.
John: Très bien. Alors merci beaucoup, madame.
Dame: Je vous en prie, monsieur. Bon séjour à Caen.

 Dialogue 2

They decide to go first to the church of Saint-Étienne but manage to get lost despite the plan. John Smith stops a passer-by.

John Smith: Pardon, monsieur, pour aller à l'église Saint-Étienne, s'il vous plaît?
Passant: L'église Saint-Étienne, eh bien, vous allez tout droit, vous traversez la place Fontette, vous prenez la première rue à droite et l'église est sur votre gauche.

A 'syndicat d'initiative' in Burgundy (top)
and another in the Rhône Valley (foot)

John: C'est loin d'ici?
Passant: Ah non, monsieur. Dix minutes à pied, seulement.
John: Merci beaucoup, monsieur.
Passant: De rien.

 ### *Dialogue 3*

Having looked round the church, they decide to go to the castle.

John Smith: Pardon, monsieur, pour aller au château, s'il vous plaît?
Passant: Au château. C'est assez loin, monsieur.
John: Ah bon?
Passant: Oui, à pied il faut une demi-heure, au moins, surtout avec les enfants. Prenez l'autobus.
John: C'est une bonne idée. Où est l'arrêt d'autobus?
Passant: Là, devant l'Hôtel de Ville.
John: Merci, monsieur, vous êtes bien aimable.
Passant: Je vous en prie, monsieur.

The castle walls at Caen

Dialogue 4

They get on the bus. Most passengers getting on seem to have tickets already. John speaks to the driver.

John: Deux adultes et deux enfants, s'il vous plaît.
Conducteur: Vous allez où, monsieur?
John: Au château.
Conducteur: Alors douze francs quarante (12F 40). Merci. N'oubliez pas d'oblitérer vos billets. Voilà votre monnaie.
John: Merci, monsieur.

 Dialogue 5

After visiting the castle, they decide to take the children to see the ships in the port of Caen.

John: Pardon, monsieur. Vous savez, où est le port de Caen?
Passant: Je regrette, monsieur, je ne sais pas. Je ne suis pas d'ici.
John: Pardon, madame, pour aller au port, s'il vous plaît?
Dame: Vous allez tout droit, vous traversez la place Courtonne et le bassin Saint-Pierre est sur votre droite.
John: Merci, madame. C'est loin d'ici?
Dame: Non, pas du tout. À deux cents (200) mètres, environ.
John: Merci, madame.
Dame: De rien, monsieur.

Vocabulary

Dialogue 1

(i) Useful expressions

sur la gauche	on the left
qu'est-ce que c'est?	what's this?
merci beaucoup	thanks very much
je vous en prie	don't mention it; you're welcome

(ii) Nouns – masc.   **Nouns – fem.**

les renseignements: information	la fois: time
le plan: plan	la ville: town
le guide: guide	une entrée: entrance
le monument: monument; public building	une église: church
	la flèche: spire
le château: castle	la rue: street
un Hôtel de Ville: town hall	la place: square
le port: port	la plante: plant
le jardin: garden	

(iii) Other words

premier (première): first
nous sommes (être): we are
à: to
sur: on
de: of; from
officiel(le): official
vous voulez (vouloir): you want
principal(e): main; principal
vous voyez (voir): you see
ici: here

devant: in front of
grand(e): big; tall
suivez (suivre): follow
traversez (traverser): cross
connu(e): well-known
près de: near
visiter: to visit
important(e): important
intéressant(e): interesting

Dialogue 2

(i) Useful expressions

pour aller à...?
tout droit
à droite
à pied
de rien

how do I get to...?
straight ahead
to the right
on foot
don't mention it; you're welcome

(ii) Noun – masc.

le pied: foot

(iii) Other words

vous allez (aller): you go
loin (de): far (from)

dix: ten
seulement: only

Dialogue 3

(i) Useful expressions

ah bon?
il faut une demi-heure
au moins

oh really?
you need half an hour
at least

(ii) Nouns – masc.

un autobus: bus
un arrêt: stop

Nouns – fem.

une demi-heure: half an hour
une idée: idea

(iii) Other words

assez: quite
surtout: above all; especially
bon (bonne): good

où?: where?
aimable: nice; kind

Dialogue 4

(i) Nouns – masc.

un adulte: adult
le billet: ticket

Nouns – fem.

la monnaie: small change

(ii) Other words

douze: twelve
quarante: forty

oublier: to forget
oblitérer: to stamp; to cancel a ticket

Dialogue 5

(i) Useful expressions

je ne suis pas d'ici
sur votre droite
pas du tout
à deux cents mètres:

I don't come from here
on your right
not at all
two hundred metres away

(ii) Nouns – masc.

le bassin: dock

(iii) Other words

vous savez (savoir): you know
je ne sais pas (savoir): I don't know

environ: approximately; about

Explanations

(a) *Asking the way*

> Pardon, monsieur/madame, le château s'il vous plaît?
> Pardon, monsieur/madame, où est le château, s'il vous plaît?
> Pardon, monsieur/madame, pour aller au château, s'il vous plaît?

These three possibilities for asking the way all have the same meaning. You can use whichever you find easiest to remember.

In reply to your question you will hear the following replies:

(vous) allez tout droit
(vous) prenez la première rue à droite

go straight on
take the first street on the right

(Make sure you distinguish between 'tout droit' (straight on) and 'à droite' (on the right).)

Note also the following expressions:

sur votre **gauche**   on your left
sur votre **droite**   on your right

(b) 'à'

à + le = **au** (to the)	Vous allez **au** château.
	You are going to the castle.
à + la = **à la**	Vous allez **à la** gare.
	You are going to the station.
à + l' = **à l'**	Vous allez **à l'**église.
	You are going to the church.
à + les = **aux**	Vous allez **aux** églises.
	You are going to the churches.

In the above examples, 'à' has the meaning 'to'. There are other possible meanings some of which you have met already.

With the name of a town, 'à' may mean 'to', 'at', 'in':

à Caen; à Paris.

Note the phrases:

à droite / à gauche	on the left / on the right
à pied	on foot
à deux cent mètres	two hundred metres away

(c) 'de'

de + le = **du** (of the)	l'entrée **du** château
	the castle entrance (= entrance of the castle)
de + la = **de la**	la porte **de la** banque
	the door of the bank
de + l' = **de l'**	la porte **de l'**église
	the door of the church
de + les = **des**	le Jardin **des** Plantes
	the Botanical Garden (= garden of the plants)

The usual meaning of 'de' is 'of' or 'from', and it is the usual way in French of expressing possession, as in the following examples. Notice that English has various ways of showing possession whereas French nearly always makes use of 'de':

le port **de** Caen	the port of Caen
L'Hôtel **de** Ville	the town hall
le mari **de** Madame Smith	Mrs Smith's husband

(d) *Adjectives (grammar ref. 3)*

Adjectives are the words which are used to describe appearances or characteristics. In French, the adjective usually comes *after* the noun it describes.

Masculine		Feminine	
le guide officiel	the official guide	la brochure officie**lle**	the official brochure
le port principal	the main port	l'entrée principal**e**	the main entrance
un jardin intéressant	an interesting garden	une église intéressant**e**	an interesting church

The feminine form of the adjective usually adds '-e'. Sometimes there are other slight changes, as with 'officiel/officielle' in the example above, and 'bon/bonne' below. If the adjective already ends in '-e' (e.g. une personne aimable), there is no change. Often, as with 'principal/principale', there is no change in pronunciation.

A small number of very common adjectives come *before* the noun:

Masculine		Feminine	
un **bon** repas	a good meal	une **bonne** promenade	a good walk
un **petit** enfant	a little child	une **petite** église	a little church

To form the plural of an adjective, you usually add '-s' to the singular form:

Masculine		Feminine	
les jardins **intéressants**	the interesting gardens	les brochures **officielles**	the official brochures

(e) *Giving instructions*

Chapter 3 has more examples of the imperative, the form used for giving instructions and commands:

Suivez la rue!   Go down the street!
Traversez la place!   Cross the square!
Prenez la première rue à droite!   Take the first street on the right!

Note also: N'oubliez pas!   Do not forget!

N'oubliez pas d'oblitérer vos billets!   Don't forget to stamp your tickets!

Here are some more examples of how to make instructions negative (Do not...!):

Traversez la rue!	→	**Ne** traversez **pas** la rue!
Allez au port!	→	**N'**allez **pas** au port!

(f) 'Qu'est-ce que c'est? C'est...'

To ask the name of something, point and say, 'Qu'est-ce que c'est?'. The answer is 'C'est un/une...':

> Qu'est-ce que c'est? C'est un château.
> Qu'est-ce que c'est? C'est une église.

(g) 'Il y a' and 'voilà'

Use 'il y a' to make a general statement and 'voilà' when you can actually point at the object:

Il y a un château à Caen.	There is a castle in Caen.
Voilà le château.	There is the castle. *(pointing to it)*
Il y a un arrêt d'autobus devant l'Hôtel de Ville.	There is a bus stop in front of the town hall.
Voilà l'arrêt d'autobus.	There is the bus stop. *(pointing to it)*

Exercises

● *The key to these exercises begins on p.214.*

Parlez
(Speaking exercises)

Exercise 1   Directions

Now it is your turn to ask the questions. Look at the dialogue below and use the English prompts to help you prepare your role as the female visitor getting directions from a passer-by (un passant). Then turn on the recording and practise playing your part.

Visitor: *(Ask how you get to the castle.)*
Passant: Au château, alors, vous êtes à pied?
Visitor: *(Say yes, you are on foot.)*
Passant: Alors, vous allez tout droit, vous prenez la deuxième rue à droite et le château est devant vous.
Visitor: *(Ask if it is far from here.)*
Passant: Oui, madame, assez loin.
Visitor: *(Ask if there is a bus.)*
Passant: Oui, madame, en bus c'est à trois minutes.
Visitor: *(Ask where the bus stop is.)*
Passant: Là, devant l'Hôtel de Ville.
Visitor: *(Thank him.)*
Passant: De rien, madame.

Exercise 2

Now imagine that you want to go to the following places in Caen. Make up different phrases to ask the way, using any of the expressions given in the *explanations* section.

le château
le port de Caen
l'église Saint-Pierre

le Jardin des Plantes
l'église Saint-Étienne
l'Hôtel de Ville

Lisez et écrivez
(Reading and writing exercises)

Exercise 3

You are on holiday in a French town and you want to get some information about the region. Which of the following signposts do you follow?

< *Commissariat de Police*

Chambre de Commerce >

< *Agence de Voyage*

Syndicat d'Initiative >

Exercise 4

Write answers to the following questions using the example as a model. For each answer choose a different adjective from the list below.

Example: Vous allez au château?
Answer: Oui, c'est un château intéressant.

(a) Vous allez au port? (Oui, c'est...)
(b) Vous allez à l'église? (Oui, c'est...)
(c) Vous allez au château? (Oui, c'est...)
(d) Vous avez le guide? (Oui, j'ai...)
(e) Vous voyez l'entrée? (Oui, je vois...)

Choose appropriate adjectives from this list and remember to add the ending for feminine words:

intéressant
important
principal

officiel
connu

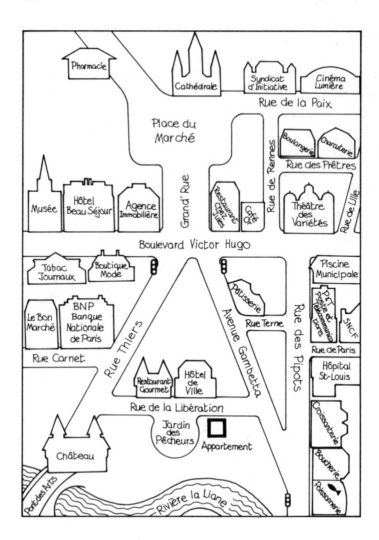

Exercise 5

You are staying with friends in France. Their flat is next to the Jardin des Pêcheurs on the town plan above. You return to find a note asking you to join them at a particular building (bâtiment) and giving directions where to find them. But they have forgotten to name the building where you are meeting! Read the directions, look at the map and decide where they want to meet you.

En sortant de l'appartement, prenez à droite. Au bout de la rue, tournez à gauche. Remontez l'avenue jusqu'aux feux. Traversez le boulevard et prenez la rue juste en face. Allez jusqu'à la place. Nous attendons là devant le bâtiment.

Écoutez

(Listening exercise)

Exercise 6   Spontaneous dialogue   Asking for information at the 'syndicat d'initiative'

In this dialogue, a woman asks for information at the 'syndicat d'initiative'. She begins by saying: 'Je voudrais savoir où se trouve le château', meaning, 'I would like to know where the castle is' ('où se trouve' is often used to mean the same as 'où est'). Try to pick out the instructions of the official and tick the boxes in (b) below.

(a) The woman asks where the castle is. What does the official use to make his explanation clear?

(b) Listen carefully to the directions given on tape and choose the correct instructions from those given below:

vous tournez à gauche   ☐
vous tournez à droite   ☐
première à gauche   ☐
première à droite   ☐

(c) What does the woman ask after she has been given the instructions?

(d) What is also worth visiting in the same area? Tick the appropriate box.

une très belle église   ☐
un port très intéressant   ☐
une très belle cathédrale   ☐
un jardin très intéressant   ☐

(e) He gives her instructions for finding this second place of interest. He begins: 'Vous sortez du château...' (You go out of the castle...). What does he tell her to do next?

(f) The official says goodbye and then says:

Je vous souhaite une excellente journée.

Have a guess at what you think this last sentence might mean, choosing from the following possibilities:

I hope you have an excellent day   ☐
I wish you an excellent day   ☐
I hope you have an excellent stay in Caen   ☐
I wish you a pleasant stay in Caen   ☐

C'est ouvert?
Making enquiries

Dialogues

John Smith makes a number of telephone calls while planning visits in the area.

 ### Dialogue 1

Monsieur au téléphone: Allô, ici la piscine municipale de Caen.
John: Bonjour, monsieur. Quand est-ce que la piscine est ouverte?
Monsieur: Ce matin, monsieur, la piscine est ouverte de neuf heures à midi.
John: Et l'après-midi, c'est ouvert aussi?
Monsieur: Oui, monsieur. L'après-midi la piscine est ouverte de deux heures à six heures.
John: Les heures d'ouverture sont les mêmes tous les jours?
Monsieur: De lundi à vendredi les heures sont les mêmes. Le samedi la piscine est ouverte jusqu'à neuf heures du soir, et le dimanche de dix heures moins le quart jusqu'à cinq heures et demie.
John: Merci beaucoup, monsieur.

 ### Dialogue 2

John: Allô, c'est le Musée du Débarquement?
Monsieur: Allô, oui, monsieur, ici c'est le Musée du Débarquement à Arromanches.
John: Alors, je voudrais savoir, monsieur, quand est-ce que le musée est ouvert?
Monsieur: Le musée est ouvert tous les jours de neuf heures à midi et de quatorze heures à dix-neuf heures.
John: Merci bien, monsieur.

DEVINEZ OÙ IL PUISE SON BON GOÛT.

Suc des Vosges
BONBONS
SÈVE DE PIN
RUCHER LA VOSGIENNE
LV
LA VOSGIENNE
NATURALLY FLAVOURED DROPS · 125 g ℮ 4½ OZ

TELECARTE 50

 Dialogue 3

Dame au téléphone: Allô, syndicat d'initiative à Lisieux.

John: Bonjour, madame. Je viens à Lisieux avec ma famille et je voudrais savoir s'il y a une visite guidée de la basilique Sainte-Thérèse.

Dame: Oui, monsieur, il y a des visites accompagnées tous les jours de neuf heures à midi et de quatorze heures à seize heures trente.

John: Bien. Et quand est-ce qu'il y a le spectacle Son et Lumière à la basilique?

Dame: Le spectacle Son et Lumière est donné tous les soirs, sauf le vendredi, à vingt et une heures trente.

John: Merci, madame.

Dame: De rien, monsieur.

 Dialogue 4

Mary goes to the theatre box-office to book seats.

Mary: Bonjour, madame. Est-ce que vous avez deux places pour la représentation de mardi soir?

Dame à la caisse: Je suis désolée, madame. Mardi, c'est complet.

Mary: Quel dommage! Et mercredi?

Dame: Mercredi aussi. Je regrette, mais c'est complet. Il reste des places libres jeudi soir à cent vingt francs (120F).

Mary: Bien. Et à quelle heure commence la pièce?

Dame: À sept heures et quart, madame. Il y a un entr'acte à neuf heures moins le quart.

Mary: Vous prenez la carte Visa?

Dame: Certainement, madame.

Vocabulary

● *Note that all numerals and days of the week are to be found in grammar ref. 9.1 and 9.2.*

Dialogue 1

(i) Useful expressions

les heures d'ouverture — the opening times
tous les jours — every day

(ii) Nouns – masc. / Nouns – fem.

le monsieur: man; gentleman — la piscine: swimming pool
le téléphone: telephone — une heure: hour
le matin: morning — l'ouverture: opening
l'après-midi: afternoon
le quart: quarter

(iii) Other words

allô: hello (only on telephone) — même: same
municipal(e): municipal — jusqu'à: until
quand?: when? — moins: less
ouvert(e): open

Dialogue 2

(i) Nouns – masc.

le musée: museum
le débarquement: landing

(ii) Other word

savoir: to know

Dialogue 3

(i) Useful expressions

tous les soirs — every evening

(ii) Nouns – masc. / Nouns – fem.

le spectacle: show; performance — la dame: lady
le son: sound — la visite: visit
la basilique: basilica
la lumière: light

(iii) Other words

je viens (venir): I come; I am coming
guidé(e): guided

donné(e): given; presented
sauf: except (for)

Dialogue 4

(i) Useful expressions

quel dommage!
il reste des places libres

what a pity!
there are some seats left

(ii) Nouns – masc.

un entr'acte: interval
le théâtre: theatre

Nouns – fem.

la place: seat (at theatre or cinema)
la pièce: play
la carte Visa: Visa credit card

(iii) Other words

complet (complète): full up
commencer: to begin

certainement: of course

Explanations

(a) *Times (grammar ref. 9.2(e))*

(i) 'Quelle heure est-il?'   What's the time?

Il est une heure.	It's one o'clock.
Il est deux heures.	It's two o'clock.
Il est trois heures et demie.	It's half past three.
Il est cinq heures et quart.	It's quarter past five.
Il est sept heures moins le quart.	It's quarter to seven.

(ii) 'Quand...?'   When?   'À quelle heure...?'   (At) What time?

Quand est-ce que vous venez au théâtre?	When are you coming to the theatre?
Quand est-ce que le spectacle commence?	When does the show start?
À quelle heure est-ce que le spectacle commence?	At what time does the show start?

at one o'clock	à une heure	(1h)
at two o'clock	à deux heures	(2h)
at three o'clock	à trois heures	(3h)
at half past four	à quatre heures et demie	(4h 30)
at half past five	à cinq heures et demie	(5h 30)
at half past six	à six heures et demie	(6h 30)
at quarter past seven	à sept heures et quart	(7h 15)
at quarter past eight	à huit heures et quart	(8h 15)
at quarter to nine	à neuf heures moins le quart	(8h 45)
at quarter to ten	à dix heures moins le quart	(9h 45)
at ten past eleven	à onze heures dix	(11h 10)
at twenty past eleven	à onze heures vingt	(11h 20)
at ten to ten	à dix heures mois dix	(9h 50)
at twenty-five to nine	à neuf heures moins vingt-cinq	(8h 35)
at ten past twelve (midday)	à midi dix	(12h 10)
at twenty to twelve (midnight)	à minuit moins vingt	(11h 40)

(iii) The 24-hour clock

The 24-hour clock is normally used for times of train departures and arrivals, and sometimes with opening times, to avoid any confusion.

14h = quatorze heures = 2.00 pm
14h 30 = quatorze heures trente = 2.30 pm

Heures d'ouverture: de 14h à 19h   from 2 pm until 7 pm
(= de quatorze heures à dix-neuf heures)
Heures d'ouverture: de 19h 30 à 21h 45   from 7.30 pm until 9.45 pm
(= de dix-neuf heures trente à vingt et une heures quarante-cinq)

(b) Days of the week

Lundi, je vais à la piscine. On Monday I'm going to the swimming pool.
Mardi, je vais au théâtre. On Tuesday I'm going to the theatre.
Mercredi, je visite le château. On Wednesday I'm visiting the castle.
Jeudi, je visite le musée. On Thursday I'm visiting the museum.
Vendredi, je vais à la plage. On Friday I'm going to the beach.
Samedi, je fais des courses. On Saturday I'm going shopping.
Dimanche, je vais à l'église. On Sunday I'm going to church.

As you see from these examples, you use the names for the days of the week in French without any word to translate the English word 'on'. Note that they do not start with a capital letter except at the beginning of a sentence.

(c) 'Je veux...' I want... 'Je voudrais...' I would like...

'Je voudrais' is rather more polite than 'je veux'.

Je veux...	I want...
Je voudrais...	I would like...
Je veux savoir...	I want to know...
Je voudrais savoir...	I would like to know...
Je voudrais savoir s'il y a une visite...	I would like to know if there is a visit...
Je voudrais savoir quand le musée est ouvert.	I would like to know when the museum is open.
Je voudrais visiter le château.	I would like to visit the castle.

Exercises

● *The key to these exercises begins on p.215.*

Parlez
(Speaking exercises)

Exercise 1   A telephone enquiry

Can you make an enquiry by telephone? Look at the telephone conversation below and use the English prompts to help you prepare your role (male enquirer). Then turn on the recording and practise making enquiries.

Dame au téléphone: Allô, syndicat d'initiative, bonjour.
You: *(Greet her and ask her when the castle is open.)*
Dame au téléphone: Le château est ouvert de 9h à 12h et de 14h à 18h 30.
You: *(Ask her if there are guided visits.)*
Dame au téléphone: Oui, monsieur, il y a des visites guidées tous les jours à 10h et à 15h.
You: *(Ask if there is a 'Son et Lumière' show at the castle.)*
Dame au téléphone: Oui, monsieur, tous les soirs sauf le dimanche et le vendredi, à 21h 30.
You: *(Thank her.)*
Dame au téléphone: De rien, monsieur. Au revoir, monsieur.

Exercise 2

Now imagine that you are booking tickets at the theatre box-office. Think of how many seats you want, and the evening and time of the play you want to see. Use the following cues to help you:

Est-ce que vous avez deux/trois/quatre places...
C'est pour jeudi/vendredi/samedi soir...
Quand est-ce que la pièce commence?

Lisez et écrivez

(Reading and writing exercises)

Exercise 3

Put the following times into French. Use the 12-hour clock. Write complete sentences, as in the example. If you need more help, look back at the *explanations* to find other examples of expressing the time.

Example: Il est trois heures cinq. (3.05)

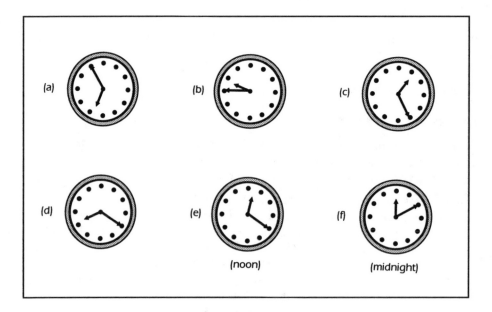

Exercise 4

For your diary, make a list of the places you plan to visit during a week's holiday. Write down the days of the week and opposite each put a place you could visit.

Example: lundi – le château

Exercise 5

You are in the town of Chinon for a few days in January. One afternoon, you decide to visit the castle and you read the times of opening posted at the entrance.

(a) Will you be able to visit this afternoon?
(b) If there is any problem this afternoon, when will you be able to visit?

CHATEAU DE CHINON

XIe, XIIe, XIIIe, XVe Siècles

Cadre mémorable de l'entrevue de Jeanne d'Arc
et de Charles VII (8 mars 1429)

OUVERT AU PUBLIC

Le matin	du 1er janvier au 31 décembre	10h à 12h
L'après-midi	du 15 mars au 30 septembre	14h à 19h
	du 1er octobre au 31 octobre	14h à 18h
	du 1er novembre au 15 mars	14h à 17h

Exercise 6

Think of a place that you would like to visit and then write down things you would like to see and do there.

Example: Je voudrais visiter Bayeux. Je voudrais visiter la cathédrale. Je voudrais voir la tapisserie.
Je voudrais visiter Monte Carlo. Je voudrais voir le casino. Je voudrais aller sur la plage.

Écoutez
(Listening exercise)

Exercise 7   Spontaneous dialogue   Going to the cinema

Here, a couple are making up their minds which film to go and see – and all of them star Gérard Depardieu! You might recognise the film titles but, to help you, they are written down below. You will also need to listen out for times of performance.

(a) First you hear a tape-recorded message giving you the cinema programme. The list below is not correct. Match up each screen with its film:

Screens	**Films**
Salle 1	*Germinal*
Salle 2	*Manon des Sources*
Salle 3	*Cyrano de Bergerac*

(b) There are four separate showings of each film. What time does each showing begin?

(c) The man and woman discuss which film they want to see. What is the man's preference? You will have to listen carefully, because he shortens the title to one word, and speaks it quickly!

(d) They discuss the time of the showing they want to see. When do they decide to go?

5 Midi et demi, ça va? Making arrangements

Dialogues

 Dialogue 1   Au petit déjeuner   At breakfast

While having a leisurely breakfast at the hotel, the Smiths are visited by their friend Michel Lebrun.

Lebrun: Bonjour, tout le monde. Bon appétit. Comment ça va?

John: Bonjour, Michel. Quel plaisir de vous revoir. Ça va très bien, merci. Et vous?

Lebrun: Très bien, aussi. Comment se passe votre séjour à Caen?

Mary: Très bien. Nous sommes ravis de notre visite.

Lebrun: Bien. Alors, excusez-moi de déranger votre petit déjeuner, mais qu'est-ce que vous prévoyez pour aujourd'hui?

John: Ce matin, nous allons faire des courses.

Mary: Oui, ce matin nous voulons acheter des vêtements pour les enfants. Après cela, nous ne savons pas encore.

Lebrun: Si vous êtes libres à midi, je vous invite à déjeuner au restaurant avec ma femme et moi.

John: Avec plaisir. Vous êtes très gentil. Les enfants aussi?

Lebrun: Mais bien entendu! Alors, nous allons déjeuner aux *Cultivateurs* près de l'avenue du Six Juin. Vous connaissez la rue?

John: Oui, je connais la rue, mais où est le restaurant?

Lebrun: Eh bien, prenez la rue en direction de la rivière, et le restaurant est sur votre droite au quai de Juillet. À quelle heure est-ce qu'on se retrouve?

John: Nous sommes à votre disposition.

Lebrun: Alors, midi et demi, ça va?

John: Oui, ça va très bien.

Lebrun: Alors, à plus tard. Au revoir.

John: Au revoir et merci.

A street in Caen

 ### Dialogue 2

John Smith pauses to chat to the hotelier as he hands in his key, on the way out after breakfast.

Hôtelier: Vous aimez ce temps, monsieur?

John: Ah non! Nous n'avons pas de chance. Il pleut encore. Est-ce qu'il ne fait jamais beau à Caen?

Hôtelier: Mais si, monsieur! Généralement il fait beau en été. Il fait même très chaud quelquefois. Mais la mer n'est pas loin, vous savez; c'est un climat maritime, comme chez vous en Angleterre, et il pleut de temps en temps.

John: Vous croyez qu'il va faire beau plus tard?

Hôtelier: C'est possible. Le temps change vite ici. Regardez! On voit déjà un peu de ciel bleu. Le soleil va revenir, vous allez voir.

John: Vous êtes optimiste, monsieur. Mais je crois que nous allons acheter des coupe-vent pour les enfants quand même. On ne sait jamais, c'est vrai.

Hôtelier: Bonne chance, quand même, monsieur. Amusez-vous bien!

Vocabulary

Dialogue 1

(i) Useful expressions

tout le monde	everybody
bon appétit	have a good meal; enjoy your meal
comment ça va?	how are you?
quel plaisir de vous revoir	how nice to see you again
comment se passe votre séjour?	how is your visit going?
excusez-moi	excuse me; forgive me
faire des courses	to go shopping
je vous invite	I invite you
bien entendu	of course
en direction de	in the direction of
à quelle heure est-ce qu'on se retrouve?	when shall we meet?
à votre disposition	at your disposal
à plus tard	see you later

(ii) Nouns – masc.

le petit déjeuner: breakfast
un appétit: appetite
les vêtements: clothes
le restaurant: restaurant
le cultivateur: farmer
le quai: quay

Nouns – fem.

une avenue: avenue
la rivière: river
la direction: direction
la disposition: disposal; disposition

(iii) Other words

nous sommes (être): we are
ravi(e): delighted
déranger: to disturb
vous prévoyez (prévoir): you foresee; you have in mind
pour: for
aujourd'hui: today
nous allons (aller): we are going
nous voulons (vouloir): we want
acheter: to buy

après: after
cela: this; that
nous savons (savoir): we know
encore: yet
inviter: to invite
vous connaissez (connaître): you know
je connais (connaître): I know
plus: more
tard: late

Dialogue 2

(i) Useful expressions

il fait beau	the weather is fine
de temps en temps	from time to time
il va faire beau	the weather will be fine
le soleil va revenir	the sun will be back
même	even
quand même	all the same; nevertheless
bonne chance!	good luck!
amusez-vous bien!	enjoy yourselves!

(ii) Nouns – masc.   Nouns – fem.

le temps: weather; time

l'été: summer

le climat: climate

un peu: a little

le ciel: sky

le soleil: sun

le coupe-vent: anorak; windcheater

la chance: luck

la mer: sea

(iii) Other words

aimer: to like

il pleut (pleuvoir): it's raining

encore: again

jamais: never

si: yes (see *explanations*)

généralement: generally

chaud(e): warm; hot

quelquefois: sometimes

maritime: maritime

comme: like

vous croyez (croire): you think

possible: possible

vite: quickly

regarder: to look (at)

peut-être: perhaps

on: one

bleu(e): blue

optimiste: optimistic

vrai(e): true

Explanations

(a) *Greetings and good wishes*

Bon appétit	Enjoy your meal
Bon séjour	Have a nice stay
Bon voyage	Have a good trip
Bonne chance	Good luck
Ça va?	How are you? / How are things?

'Ça va?' is the most common way of asking people how they are. The answer is usually the same as the greeting:

Ça va?	How are you?
Ça va, merci.	I'm fine thanks.

You hear the little word 'ça' in many everyday expressions, such as 'c'est ça', meaning 'that's right'. Also, if you don't know the French word for something in a shop, you can point to it and say, 'ça, s'il vous plaît'.

(b) *Going to...*

Nous allons We are going	visiter to visit	le château. the castle.
Nous allons We are going	faire to do	des courses. some shopping.

Note also:

Il va faire beau.   It's going to be fine.

(c) *'Je crois que...'   I think that...*

Je crois qu'il va faire beau.   I think it's going to be fine.

(You could also say, 'Il va faire beau, **je crois**'.)

Je crois que I think (that)	nous allons acheter we are going to buy	des coupe-vent. some anoraks.

Note that the word 'that' can be left out in English, but you must *always* use 'que' in the French sentence.

(d) *'Quel temps fait-il?'   What's the weather like?*

(i)

Il fait beau.	It's fine.
Il fait mauvais.	It's bad weather.
Il fait chaud.	It's hot.
Il fait froid.	It's cold.

(ii)

Il y a du soleil.	It's sunny.
Il y a du vent.	It's windy.

(iii)

Il pleut.	It's raining.
Il neige.	It's snowing.

(e) 'Ne...jamais' Never

Il **ne** fait **jamais** beau. It's never fine.
On **ne** sait **jamais**. One never knows. / You never know.

The word 'jamais' can stand by itself, for example:

Vous allez au théâtre? – **Jamais**! Do you go to the theatre? – Never!

(f) 'Oui' OR 'si'

The French for 'yes' is usually 'oui', but 'si' is used to contradict a negative question or statement:

Il ne fait jamais beau? – (Mais) **Si**! Is the weather never fine? – Oh, yes!

Exercises

● *The key to these exercises begins on p.215.*

Parlez
(Speaking exercises)

Exercise 1 What are you doing today?

You are talking with a French acquaintance about your programme for the day. Look at the dialogue below and use the English prompts to prepare your role. Then turn on the recording and practise playing your part.

Ami français: Alors, vous avez prévu quelque chose pour aujourd'hui?
You: *(Say that this morning (ce matin) you are going to visit the castle.)*
Ami français: Ah, oui, c'est très intéressant. Et après?
You: *(Say that you are going to lunch at a restaurant. Ask him if he knows (connaître) a good restaurant.)*
Ami français: Oui, certainement, il y a *le Coq d'Or* tout près du château. S'il fait beau vous pouvez manger à la terrasse. C'est très joli.
You: *(Say that's a good idea. Ask if he thinks it is going to be fine.)*
Ami français: Oui, je suis sûr qu'il va faire beau aujourd'hui. Et après le déjeuner? Vous allez visiter autre chose?
You: *(Say that after lunch you think you are going to do some shopping in town.)*
Ami français: Alors, bonne journée.
You: *(Thank him and say goodbye.)*

Exercise 2

Here is your diary for a week's stay in Caen. Think of how you will say what you are going to do on each day of the week to answer the question 'Qu'est-ce que vous allez faire?'. For example, if someone says to you 'Qu'est-ce que vous allez faire lundi?', you will answer, 'Lundi matin, je vais visiter le château.' You can use expressions such as 'je vais visiter...'; 'je vais voir...'; 'je vais aller à...'.

	lundi	mardi	mercredi	jeudi	vendredi	samedi	dimanche
matin	le château	le port	la basilique	Musée du Débarquement	faire des courses	la piscine	l'église Saint-Étienne
après-midi		le musée		la tapisserie de Bayeux	déjeuner au restaurant		
soir			le théâtre		le cinéma	dîner chez des amis	

Exercise 3

Then imagine you are in Caen with a partner or your family and try saying 'nous allons...' instead of 'je vais...'.

Exercise 4

Read the following weather forecast. Then tick to show whether the statements are *true* or *false* (T or F).

Aujourd'hui

Temps frais, couvert et pluvieux le matin, avec quelques éclaircies l'après-midi.

Vent : sud-ouest modéré le matin, faible l'après-midi.

Températures minimales : 13 à 16°

Températures maximales : 17 à 20°

Demain La matinée est encore pluvieuse mais les éclaircies reviennent plus franchement ensuite.

Vent : sud-ouest modéré.

Températures minimales : 13 à 16°

Températures maximales : 18 à 21°

Today (Aujourd'hui)

(a) It will rain this morning. T☐ F☐
(b) It will be very windy. T☐ F☐
(c) There will be some sunshine in the afternoon. T☐ F☐

Tomorrow (Demain)

(d) There will be blue sky in the morning. T☐ F☐
(e) The wind will not be very strong. T☐ F☐
(f) Maximum temperatures up to 21°. T☐ F☐

Exercise 5

Here are a number of statements about the weather. Write sentences to express the idea that you *think* this is what the weather *will be* like.

Example: Il fait beau.
Answer: Je crois qu'il va faire beau.

    (a) Il fait mauvais.
    (b) Il fait froid.
    (c) Il pleut.

Écoutez

(Listening exercise)

Exercise 6   Spontaneous dialogue   Talking about the weather

Mark and Amanda are walking in the countryside during their French holidays. The weather looks a bit uncertain, so when they pass through a village they stop to check their way with a lady working in her garden and ask her whether she thinks it is going to rain. Listen to the tape and try to pick out the key words which will help you answer the questions below.

(a) Listen carefully to the tape. Try to match pronunciation to spelling and say which of the following places they are walking to:

      Manasset   ☐
      Maljasset   ☐
      Massenet   ☐
      Malasset   ☐

(b) How much longer do you think they need to get there?

      encore plus d'une heure   ☐
      encore une heure et demie   ☐
      encore une heure   ☐
      encore moins d'une heure   ☐

(c) Amanda responds 'si long que ça' when she hears they have an hour to go. What does the tone of her voice indicate? Surprise? Resignation? What do you think 'si long que ça' might mean?

(d) Listen for the key word in the lady's reply when Amanda asks if it is going to rain. When does she think it is going to rain?

      not at all   ☐
      tomorrow   ☐
      later in the day   ☐
      soon   ☐

(e) What reason does the lady give for the fact that it rains a lot in this region? (Compare what the hotelier says in Dialogue 2 above.)

(f) In talking about the weather, the lady says 'on s'y habitue'. Which of the following do you think this might mean?

It gets to be a habit. ☐
You have to put up with it. ☐
It mustn't get you down. ☐
You get used to it. ☐

(g) Why does Amanda refer to England and the English?

(h) You hear the lady say 'tempéré', which looks just like the English word 'temperate'. What do you think she might be saying?

(i) Mark thinks that one thing is particularly important when you go walking. What do you think he is saying?

(j) Try repeating the way you wish someone a 'good walk'. Try writing it down and check your spelling with the *key*.

6 ⬡ Vous aimez ça?
Shopping

Dialogues

 Dialogue 1   On achète des vêtements   Shopping for clothes

Vendeuse: Bonjour, monsieur. Bonjour, madame. Vous désirez?
Mary: Où sont les vêtements pour enfants, s'il vous plaît, mademoiselle?
Vendeuse: Par ici, madame. Qu'est-ce que vous cherchez?
Mary: Je voudrais des coupe-vent pour nos deux enfants.
Vendeuse: Oui, madame. Alors, nous avons des coupe-vent de toutes les tailles et de toutes les couleurs. Est-ce que la fillette préfère un coupe-vent bleu, rouge ou vert?
Mary: Pour elle, un coupe-vent rouge, je crois.
Vendeuse: Et pour le garçon?
Mary: Pour lui, un coupe-vent bleu. Oui, c'est ça.
Vendeuse: Voilà, madame. C'est la taille exacte pour lui et pour elle, je crois. Vous aimez ça?
Mary: Oui, très bien.
Vendeuse: C'est tout, madame?
Mary: C'est tout pour eux. Mon mari cherche un pullover.
Vendeuse: Les pullovers sont au rayon messieurs.
John: Bien, alors. J'y vais. À plus tard.

 Dialogue 2   On achète des vêtements (suite) *Shopping for clothes* (continued)

Mary: Moi, je voudrais un imperméable.
Vendeuse: Oui, madame. Voilà un imperméable rouge. Il est très chic. Ou alors, un imperméable jaune, si vous préférez. Vous voulez essayer le jaune?
Mary: Oui, pour moi c'est préférable, je crois. Je ne porte jamais de rouge.
Vendeuse: Ah oui, madame. Il est très bien.
Mary: Alors je prends les deux coupe-vent et l'imperméable. Ça fait combien?

52 *MASTERING FRENCH*

Vendeuse: Le coupe-vent de la fillette fait cent vingt francs (120F) et le coupe-vent du garçon fait cent quarante francs (140F). L'imperméable fait quatre cent cinquante francs (450F), alors sept cent dix francs (710F) en tout. Payez à la caisse, s'il vous plaît, madame.

Mary: Oui. Où est la caisse?

Vendeuse: Là-bas, madame, près de l'entrée.

Mary: Merci bien. Ah, voilà mon mari.

Vendeuse: Vous avez votre pullover, monsieur?

John: Non, rien. Il n'y a rien pour moi. Je ne trouve jamais de vêtements à ma taille. Des pullovers énormes et des pullovers minuscules, mais pas un pullover de taille normale, comme moi!

Vendeuse: Je suis désolée, monsieur.

John: Ce n'est pas de votre faute, mademoiselle. Ce n'est rien. Les coupe-vent des enfants sont jolis et l'imperméable de ma femme est joli aussi.

Mary: Tu aimes mon imperméable?

John: Oui, beaucoup.

Dialogue 3 Retour à l'hôtel *Return to the hotel*

Hôtelier: Alors, vous voyez, monsieur. Il ne pleut plus. C'est fini le mauvais temps. Vous allez avoir de la chance aujourd'hui, quand même. Il va faire beau, je crois.

John: Oui, heureusement. Après le déjeuner nous allons faire un petit tour en voiture, peut-être.

Hôtelier: Ah oui, vers la mer peut-être. Les plages de la région sont très belles. Vous aimez aller au bord de la mer, madame?

Mary: Oui, beaucoup. Et les enfants adorent ça, quand il y a du soleil.

Hôtelier: Amusez-vous bien, alors.

Vocabulary

Dialogue 1

(i) Useful expressions

par ici	this way; over here
de toutes les tailles	in all sizes
j'y vais	I'm going there; I'm on my way

(ii) Nouns – masc.

Nouns – fem.

le garçon: boy

le pullover: pullover

le rayon: department

le rayon messieurs: the men's department

la vendeuse: sales assistant

la taille: size

la couleur: colour

la fillette: little girl

(iii) Other words

chercher: to look for

rouge: red

vert(e): green

exact(e): exact

Dialogue 2

(i) Useful expressions

ça fait combien?	what does that come to?
à ma taille	in my size
ce n'est pas de votre faute	it's not your fault
il n'y a rien pour moi	there's nothing for me
ce n'est rien	it doesn't matter

(ii) Nouns – masc.

Nouns – fem.

un imperméable: raincoat

le mari: husband

la suite: continuation

la faute: fault

(iii) Other words

chic: smart
jaune: yellow
essayer: to try
préférable: preferable
porter: to wear
je prends (prendre): I take; I'll take
payer: to pay
là-bas: over there

rien: nothing
trouver: to find
trop: too
énorme: enormous
minuscule: tiny
normal(e): normal
joli(e): pretty

Dialogue 3

(i) Useful expressions

il ne pleut plus
au bord de la mer

it's not raining any more
at the sea-side

(ii) Noun – masc.

le tour: tour; trip

Nouns – fem.

la voiture: car
la plage: beach

(iii) Other words

fini(e): finished
mauvais(e): bad
heureusement: luckily; happily

vers: towards
beau (belle): beautiful
adorer: to love; to adore

Explanations

(a) Likes and dislikes

j'aime	I like; I love
j'aime beaucoup	I like very much

Vous **aimez** le tennis?
Oui, **j'aime** le tennis.
Oui, **j'aime beaucoup** le tennis.

Do you like tennis?
Yes, I like tennis.
Yes, I like tennis very much.

Vous **aimez** la région?
Oui, **j'aime** la région.
Oui, **j'aime beaucoup** la région.

Do you like the region?
Yes, I like the region.
Yes, I like the region very much.

When used with a verb, 'aimer' is always followed by the infinitive:

J'aime	**aller**	à la plage.
I like	going	to the beach.

J'aime faire les courses.	I like going shopping.
J'aime beaucoup faire les courses.	I like going shopping very much.
J'aime jouer au tennis.	I like playing tennis.
J'aime beaucoup jouer au tennis.	I like playing tennis very much.

(b) *For him, for her, for me, etc. (grammar ref. 4.1(f))*

C'est pour qui?	*Who is it for?*
pour moi	for me
pour toi	for you (*familiar*)
pour lui	for him
pour elle	for her
pour nous	for us
pour vous	for you
pour eux	for them (*masc.*)
pour elles	for them (*fem.*)

For example, in the text of Chapter 6 you will find:

Pour **moi**, c'est préférable.
Pour **lui**, un coupe-vent bleu.
C'est tout pour **eux**.

The same forms are used after other prepositions, such as 'avec' (with):

Avec qui?	*Who with?*
avec moi	with me
avec toi	with you (*familiar*)
avec lui	with him
avec elle	with her
avec nous	with us
avec vous	with you
avec eux	with them (*masc.*)
avec elles	with them (*fem.*)

(c) *'Être'   To be*

je suis	I am
tu es	you are (*familiar form*)
il est	he is
elle est	she is
nous sommes	we are
vous êtes	you are (*polite form*)
ils sont	they are (*masc.*)
elles sont	they are (*fem.*)

Notes:

(i) French has two words for 'you': 'tu' is familiar, and is the form used to children, close friends, family and animals; 'vous' is the polite form used in all normal conversation between strangers or colleagues. For a foreigner it is safest to stick to the polite form 'vous'.

(ii) French has two words for 'they', depending on whether one is talking about a group of males (ils), or a group of females (elles). If a group is mixed gender, the masculine form 'ils' is used.

(d) 'On'

'On' is commonly used to mean 'they', 'you', 'people', 'one', as in the examples below:

On ne sait jamais.	You never know. / One never knows.
On voit déjà un peu de ciel bleu.	You/One can already see a bit of blue sky.

Very often, 'on' is used to mean the same as 'nous' (we). Both the following sentences mean 'What are we going to do today?'

Qu'est-ce qu'**on** va faire aujourd'hui?
Qu'est-ce que **nous** allons faire aujourd'hui?

(e) *Possession*

French has no equivalent to the English 'apostrophe s', and always shows possession by using 'de' (of):

le coupe-vent **de** la fillette	the girl's anorak
l'imperméable **de** ma femme	my wife's raincoat
le coupe-vent **du** garçon	the boy's anorak
les coupe-vent **des** enfants	the children's anoraks

(f) *'C'est'   It is / this is / that is*

*Qu'est-ce que **c'est**?*	*What is it? / What is this?*
C'est le château.	It's the castle.
C'est un climat maritime.	It's a maritime climate.
C'est possible.	It's possible.
C'est vrai.	That's true.
C'est tout?	Is that all?
C'est de votre faute.	It's your fault.

(g) *More about negatives*

(i) | ne...rien   nothing |

Il **n'**y a **rien** pour moi.   There's nothing for me.

When there is no verb, 'rien' can stand alone:

Vous avez votre pullover,   Have you got your pullover,
monsieur? Non, **rien**.   sir? No, nothing.

(ii) | ne...plus   no longer / not any more |

Il **ne** pleut **plus**.   It's not raining any more. / It's no longer raining.

(h) *Uses of 'en'*

(i) *Seasons*

en été	in summer
en automne	in autumn
en hiver	in winter

(ii) *Countries*

en Angleterre	in England
en France	in France
en Normandie	in Normandy

(iii) *Transport*

| en voiture | by car |
| en avion | by plane |

(i) *Use of 'y' (there)*

J'**y** vais.	I'm going there.
Est-ce que vous **y** allez?	Are you going there?
Nous **y** allons tous les jours.	We go there every day.

(j) *'Tout'   Everybody / everything / all*

(i) When 'tout' means 'everything', it never changes its form:

C'est **tout**? Is that everything?

(ii) When 'tout' comes before the noun and means 'all' or 'every' or 'the whole', it has four possible spellings, depending on whether the noun is masculine or feminine, singular or plural.

masculine singular	**tout** le monde	everybody
masculine plural	**tous** les jours	every day
feminine singular	**toute** la famille	the whole family
feminine plural	**toutes** les couleurs	every colour

(k) *More about adjectives*

> Vous voulez essayer **le jaune**?   Do you want to try the yellow one?

You will see from this example that French does not translate the English 'one' in this sort of expression. Note these further examples:

Vous préférez **le bleu**?	Do you prefer the blue one?
Vous aimez **le rouge**?	Do you like the red one?
Apportez deux glaces pour **les petits**.	Bring two ice-creams for the children (the little ones).

Exercises

● *The key to these exercises begins on p.217.*

Parlez

(Speaking exercise)

Exercise 1 Talking about the weather

Now see if you can take part in a conversation with a shopkeeper (commerçant) about the weather. Look at the dialogue below and use the English prompts to help you prepare your role (male customer). Then turn on the recording and practise playing your part.

Commerçant: Bonjour, monsieur. Il fait encore mauvais aujourd'hui.

You: *(Say yes, the weather is bad again. Ask him if he thinks it is going to be fine later.)*

Commerçant: Peut-être, monsieur. On ne sait jamais. Mais il pleut aussi chez vous en Angleterre, non?

You: *(Say yes, it rains a lot in England. Say that you are out of luck, but perhaps there will be (il va y avoir) some sunshine later.)*

Commerçant: Ah oui, monsieur. Je suis optimiste. Mais n'oubliez pas votre imperméable.

You: *(Say one never knows. Tell him you think you will be visiting a museum today.)*

Commerçant: C'est vrai. Quand il pleut, un musée, c'est très bien. Alors, bonne journée!

You: *(Thank him and say goodbye.)*

Lisez et écrivez

(Reading and writing exercises)

 ## Exercise 2

In list (a) below is a collection of various items or places. In list (b) is a collection of people and places. Show which things belong to each other by linking items from each list with 'de', 'de la', 'de l'', 'du', 'des'. (If you need more help here, look back at the *explanations* in Chapter 3.)

Example: l'imperméable **de** l'enfant.

(a) le pullover		(b) la chambre
le port		le château
l'entrée	**de**	les hommes
la voiture	**de la**	la ville
la clef	**de l'**	Monsieur Lebrun
le numéro	**du**	Caen
l'imperméable	**des**	l'enfant
la piscine		le monsieur
les vêtements		

Exercise 3

You are in a department store and you need articles (a)–(f) listed below. Read the list of departments and indicate in the box where you will find the articles you want. Write **1** for 1st floor (premier étage), **2** for 2nd floor (deuxième étage), **3** for 3rd floor (troisième étage), **SS** for basement (sous-sol) and **RC** for ground floor (rez-de-chaussée). First of all, try to do the exercise by guessing the meaning of the words you don't know. You can check your guesses with the key and by looking words up in the *glossary*.

3e Étage	Tout pour le jardin
2e Étage	Disques/Jouets/Librairie/Cafétéria
1er Étage	Chaussures/Confection(Dames)/Confection(Hommes)
Rez-de-chaussée	Droguerie/Parfumerie/Électro-ménager/Vaissellerie
Sous-sol	Alimentation

(a) a cookery book ☐
(b) washing powder ☐
(c) bread and cheese ☐
(d) a cardigan ☐
(e) a garden sunshade ☐
(f) a toaster ☐

Exercise 4

You are asked the following series of questions about your personal likes and dislikes. Choose answers which give your own opinions from the list of possible replies given, and write out a response. You can either write out a full-length reply, for example, 'Non, je n'aime pas faire les courses'; or you can give a short answer making use of 'ça', for example, 'Non, je n'aime pas ça'; 'Oui, j'adore ça'.

Questions	*Possible answers*
(a) Vous aimez le sport?	Non, je n'aime pas...
(b) Vous aimez le tennis?	Oui, j'aime...
(c) Vous aimez le beau temps?	Oui, j'aime beaucoup...
(d) Vous aimez faire les courses?	Oui, j'adore...
(e) Vous aimez visiter les musées?	Comme ci comme ça. (So so.)
(f) Vous aimez déjeuner au restaurant?	Ça dépend. (It all depends.)
(g) Vous aimez aller au théâtre?	
(h) Vous aimez aller à la piscine?	

 ## Exercise 5

Complete the sentences following the examples given:

Example: Le coupe-vent rouge, c'est pour Catherine?
Answer: Oui, c'est pour **elle**.
Example: Les deux enfants sont avec leur père?
Answer: Oui, ils sont avec **lui**.

(a) L'imperméable jaune, c'est pour Mary? (Oui,...)
(b) Le pullover bleu, c'est pour John? (Oui,...)
(c) Le coupe-vent bleu, ce n'est pas pour le garçon? (Mais si,...)
(d) Monsieur Lebrun est avec ses amis? (Oui, il est...)
(e) John est avec sa femme? (Oui,...)
(f) Mary est avec les enfants? (Oui,...)

Écoutez
(Listening exercise)

 ## Exercise 6   Spontaneous dialogue   Buying a bathing costume

Silvie is in a shop, buying a bathing costume. There will be words you don't know, but the exercises try to help you make the right guesses. Listen carefully, trying to guess the words from the context and also to think about how the unknown words are *written*. One of the problems with French is that the written word often looks quite different from the way it sounds.

(a) How does the shop assistant offer to help the customer:

     Bonjour, madame. Vous désirez?   ☐

     Bonjour, madame. Je peux vous aider?   ☐

     Bonjour, madame. Vous cherchez quelque chose?   ☐

     Bonjour, madame. Vous désirez quelque chose?   ☐

(b) Silvie is shopping for a bathing costume (un maillot de bain). What do you think the shop assistant's next question means? (Focus on the key words 'une pièce' and 'deux pièces'.)

     Vous voulez un maillot une pièce ou un maillot deux pièces?

(c) Which of these does Silvie want? Do you understand the reason she gives for her choice? This is what she says. You could look up in the *glossary* the key word 'nager'.

     Je voudrais un maillot pour nager.

(d) The shop assistant points out where the shopper can find the costumes. What directions do you hear?

(e) Silvie is astonished. Why? These are her words. The key word is 'choix'. Does it remind you of an English word?

     C'est fou. Il y a un choix incroyable.

(f) The shop assistant enquires about colour. All the following questions are about the colour of the costume: Does it have stripes?, Is it all one colour?, etc. Guess at the meaning of these questions.

    (i) Vous voulez quelle couleur?

    (ii) Vous préférez l'uni?

    (iii) Vous voulez les rayures...

    (iv) ...ou des imprimés peut-être?

(g) Which of these does the shopper choose? And she wants 'une couleur sombre'. What do you think this means, bearing in mind that she makes this choice because it will be more slimming – 'ça amincit!'.

(h) The assistant shows her something suitable, and asks her what size she is. (Vous faites quelle taille?) What is the answer?

(i) The shopper asks if she can try it. The key word is 'essayer' (to try). How is the whole question phrased?

(j) She is directed to 'les cabines d'essayage'. What do you think these might be?

Qu'est-ce que vous allez manger?
Eating out

Dialogues

 Dialogue 1   Au restaurant   In the restaurant

John Smith: Ah, les voilà. Bonjour, Michel, bonjour, Nicole.
Michel Lebrun: Bonjour, mes amis.
Nicole Lebrun: Bonjour, tout le monde. Asseyez-vous, je vous en prie.
Michel: Alors, vous allez prendre un petit apéritif avant de manger?
Mary: Oui, avec plaisir. Pour moi, un kir, s'il vous plaît.
John: Et pour moi, un pernod.
Michel: Bien. Vous voyez, ma femme et moi, nous aussi, nous aimons
  beaucoup le kir. Et pour les enfants, des jus de fruits?
John: Oui, des jus d'orange.
Michel: Garçon! Un kir, un pernod et deux jus d'orange, s'il vous plaît.
Garçon: Oui, monsieur.
Michel: On peut avoir le menu, s'il vous plaît?
Garçon: Certainement, monsieur. Le voilà.

 Dialogue 2   Au restaurant (suite)   *In the restaurant* (continued)

Michel: Alors, qu'est-ce que vous allez prendre comme hors d'œuvre? Mary, si
  vous voulez goûter une spécialité régionale, je vous conseille un pâté
  normand, ou même des moules marinière.
Mary: Je vais goûter le pâté normand, alors.
John: Moi, je vais essayer les moules marinière.
Michel: Et toi, chérie, qu'est-ce que tu prends? Le pâté, les moules ou autre
  chose?
Nicole: Je vais prendre des escargots.
Michel: Moi aussi, je vais prendre des escargots. Et les enfants?
Mary: Pour les enfants? Eh bien, on fait un menu enfant, sans doute.

Garçon: Voilà vos apéritifs, messieurs-dames. Un kir pour madame, un pernod pour monsieur et deux jus d'orange pour les petits. Et qu'est-ce que vous allez prendre comme hors d'œuvre?

Michel: Alors, pour commencer, nous prenons les escargots pour deux personnes, les moules marinière pour une personne, un pâté normand, et une assiette de charcuterie pour les deux petits.

Garçon: Bien, monsieur. Et ensuite?

Michel: Nous n'avons pas encore choisi.

Garçon: Bien, monsieur. Je reviens dans quelques minutes, alors.

 ### Dialogue 3 *Au restaurant* (suite) *In the restaurant* (continued)

Michel: Comme plat principal? Vous voulez encore prendre une spécialité régionale, Mary? Il y a l'escalope normande, ou alors les tripes à la mode de Caen.

Mary: Je n'aime pas beaucoup les tripes. Pour moi, c'est un peu trop gras. Mais je voudrais bien essayer l'escalope.

Michel: Vous avez raison. C'est délicieux ici.

John: Moi, j'aime beaucoup le steak au poivre.

Michel: Vous aimez votre steak saignant ou bien cuit?

John: Saignant. C'est meilleur, je crois.

Michel: Et toi, chérie, qu'est-ce que tu vas prendre?

MENU

HORS D'ŒUVRES

Araignée de Mer Mayonnaise	78F
Langoustines Mayonnaise	80F
6 Huîtres Farcies Florentine	75F
Soupe de Poisson	38F
Galantine de Saint-Jacques	43F
Terrine de Foie de Volaille	38F
Jambon Cru de Pays	40F
Assiette de Charcuterie	30F
Artichaut Vinaigrette	22F
Pâté Normand	32F
Assiette de Saumon Fumé	43F
Pamplemousse Glacé	18F
Melon Glacé	18F
Moules Marinière	35F
6 Escargots	35F

POISSONS

Darne de Lieu Meunière	42F
Friture de Scampi Milanaise	40F
Maquereau au Vin Blanc Grillé	40F
Sole Meunière	75F
Suprème de Turbot Sauce Crème	70F

VIANDES

Escalope de Dinde Pannée Viennoise	42F
Noix d'Entrecôte Béarnaise	55F
Coq au Vin	46F
Steak au Poivre	50F
Canard à l'Orange	52F
Escalope Normande	48F
Tripes à la mode de Caen	40F

DESSERTS

Plateau de Fromages	22F
Corbeille de Fruits	18F
Glaces	18F
Pêche ou Fraises Melba	25F
Crème Caramel	18F
Café Express	7F

Nicole: J'hésite entre l'escalope et le canard à l'orange. Ils sont tous les deux très bons ici, mais l'escalope est peut-être meilleure, alors, l'escalope pour moi aussi.

Garçon: Vous avez choisi, messieurs-dames?

Michel: Oui, alors nous allons prendre: deux escalopes, un steak au poivre et un canard pour moi. Et les enfants?

Mary: Catherine aime les œufs, alors une omelette pour elle. Robert, lui, n'aime pas les œufs, mais il adore la viande. Est-ce que vous faites des menus enfants?

Garçon: Bien sûr, madame. Au menu enfant il y a steak haché frites ou omelette frites en plat principal et une glace en dessert.

Mary: C'est parfait. Alors une omelette et un steak haché bien cuit, s'il vous plaît.

Michel: Et comme boisson, une grande bouteille d'eau minérale non-gazeuse, s'il vous plaît. Et on va prendre quand même une bouteille de vin pour fêter votre séjour en France, non? Alors apportez-nous une bouteille de bordeaux maison.

 Dialogue 4 *Au restaurant (suite et fin)* **In the restaurant** *(continued and concluded)*

John: Quel repas délicieux!

Mary: Oui, alors. Vraiment excellent!

Michel: Et ce n'est pas encore fini! Vous prenez bien un peu de fromage?

Mary: Ah oui, c'est vrai. En France, on mange le fromage avant le dessert.

Nicole: Oui, les Français préfèrent quelque chose de sucré à la fin du repas. Vous savez, ici en Normandie nous avons les meilleurs fromages du monde. Le camembert, le livarot, le pont l'évêque.

John: Je ne connais pas le livarot.

Michel: C'est le roi des fromages, mais plus fort que le camembert. Voilà le plateau de fromages. Vous pouvez choisir. Et après comme dessert?

Mary: Moi, je vais prendre une glace, tout simplement. Et des fruits pour les enfants.

John: Moi aussi, je vais prendre un fruit.

Michel: Monsieur!

Vocabulary

Dialogue 1

(i) Useful expressions

tout le monde	everybody
asseyez-vous	sit down

(ii) Nouns – masc.   **Noun – fem.**

un apéritif: aperitif   une orange: orange
le kir: white wine with a dash of
    blackcurrant liqueur (cassis)
le jus (de fruit): (fruit) juice
le jus d'orange: orange juice
le menu: menu

(iii) Other words

s'asseoir: to sit down   manger: to eat
avant: before (time)

Dialogue 2

(i) Useful expressions

je vous conseille   I recommend (to you)
je vais goûter   I'll try (taste)
autre chose   something else
sans doute   probably
pour commencer   to start
nous n'avons pas encore choisi   we've not yet chosen

(ii) Nouns – masc.   **Nouns – fem.**

les hors d'œuvres: hors d'œuvres;   la région: region
    starters   la moule: mussel
le pâté: pâté   la spécialité: speciality
un escargot: snail   une assiette: plate
                                          la charcuterie: cold meats

(iii) Other words

vous voulez (vouloir): you want   autre: other
goûter: to taste   ou: or
normand(e): Norman   ensuite: next
marinier (marinière): marine (but   choisir: to choose
    here, a way of serving mussels)   quelques: some; a few
chéri (chérie): dear; darling   je reviens (revenir): I return

Dialogue 3

(i) Useful expressions

à la mode de   after the fashion of; in the style of
c'est délicieux   it's delicious

(ii) Nouns – masc.

le plat: dish
le steak: steak
le poivre: pepper
le canard: duck
un œuf: egg
le menu enfant: children's menu
le steak haché: minced steak
le dessert: dessert

Nouns – fem.

une escalope: cutlet
les tripes: tripe
la mode: fashion
une omelette: omelette
la viande: meat
les frites: chips
la bouteille: bottle
l'eau minérale: mineral water

(iii) Other words

prendre: to take
gras: fat; fatty
avoir raison: to be right
délicieux (délicieuse): delicious
saignant: bloody; rare (meat)
cuit(e): cooked
meilleur: better

hésiter: to hesitate
entre: between
parfait(e): perfect
gazeux (gazeuse): sparkling
non-gazeux (non-gazeuse): still
fêter: to celebrate

Dialogue 4

(i) Useful expressions

quel repas délicieux!
quelque chose de sucré
à la fin du repas
plus fort que le camembert
tout simplement

what a delicious meal!
something sweet
at the end of the meal
stronger than camembert
quite simply

(ii) Nouns – masc.

le repas: meal
le fromage: cheese
le Français: Frenchman
le roi: king
le plateau: tray
le plateau de fromages: cheese board
le fruit: fruit

Nouns – fem.

la Française: Frenchwoman
la fin: the end

(iii) Other words

vraiment: really; truly
excellent: excellent

fort: strong

Explanations

(a) *Regular verbs*

In Chapter 2 you were introduced to regular verbs with the infinitive ending in '-er'. The great majority of French regular verbs follow the '-er' pattern. There are two other types of regular verbs which you can recognise from the ending of the infinitive, and there are examples in this chapter:

chois**ir**	to choose
attend**re**	to wait for

You will find the full present tense of these verbs in *grammar ref. 5.1(a)*.

(b) *Making comparisons*

Le livarot	est	**plus fort**	que	le camembert.
Livarot	is	stronger	than	camembert.
Catherine	est	**plus petite**	que	son frère.
Catherine	is	smaller	than	her brother.

As you see in the examples above, the usual way of making comparisons in French is to use the adjective preceded by 'plus' (more).

A very few common adjectives are irregular and do not follow this pattern. The ones you are likely to meet are 'meilleur' (better) and 'pire' (worse).

When the definite article 'le' or 'la' is used with this form of the adjective, you form the French superlative, that is the English form in '-est', such as 'biggest', 'smallest', 'strongest'.

les meilleurs fromages	the best cheeses
Catherine est **la plus petite**.	Catherine is the smallest.
le fromage **le plus fort**	the strongest cheese

(c) *Adjectives and adverbs*

Adjective		*adverb*	
heureux	happy	heureusement	happily
général	general	généralement	generally
certain	certain	certainement	certainly
simple	simple	simplement	simply

Adverbs in English very often have the ending '-ly' added to the adjective, as in the examples above. In French, the *feminine* form of the adjective often adds '-ment', as in the examples. There are sometimes small spelling changes in the French adverbs, for example:

évident → évidemment
patient → patiemment

The form of the adverb never changes.

(d) *Emphasising the pronouns*

In Chapter 6 you met the pronouns 'moi', 'toi', 'lui', 'elle', 'nous', 'vous', 'eux', and 'elles', which are used in expressions such as 'avec moi', 'pour lui'. The same pronouns are frequently used in French for emphasis. In similar circumstances English makes the emphasis with the voice:

Moi, je prends une escalope.	*I'll* take a cutlet.
Toi, qu'est-ce que tu prends?	What would *you* like?
Moi, j'aime beaucoup le steak.	*I'm* very fond of steak.

This is a very characteristic way of expressing oneself in French, and you will hear it often. To make it stronger still you might add 'aussi':

Moi aussi, je vais prendre un fruit.	*I'll* have a fruit *too*.
Nous aussi, nous aimons le kir.	*We* like kir *as well*.

(e) *Use of the definite article (grammar ref. 1.1)*

French sometimes uses the definite article 'le', 'la', 'les' in places where you would not expect it in English.

Catherine aime **les** œufs.	Catherine likes eggs.
Moi, j'aime beaucoup **le** steak.	I like steak very much.
Le fromage est bon à manger.	Cheese is good to eat.

In all these examples, French uses the definite article because the words 'œufs', 'steak' and 'fromage' are used in a general sense.

(f) *Verbs without a following preposition*

Some French verbs do *not* have a following preposition, unlike their equivalents in English:

Je	cherche	un pullover.
I	am looking *for*	a pullover.
Ils	attendent	l'autobus
They	are waiting *for*	the bus.

Exercises

● *The key to these exercises begins on p.218.*

Parlez
(Speaking exercise)

Exercise 1   Ordering a meal

Now it's your turn to play the part of a female customer in a restaurant. Look at the dialogue below and use the English prompts to help you prepare your role. Then turn on the recording and practise playing the customer's part.

Garçon: Bonjour, madame. Vous désirez?
Customer: *(Order an apéritif and ask to see the menu.)*
Garçon: Voilà votre apéritif, madame. Et maintenant, qu'est-ce que vous aimeriez prendre?
Customer: *(Start with the hors d'œuvres (comme hors d'œuvres je voudrais), and then order the whole meal, going through main course, cheese board and dessert, using the menu on p. 65.)*
Garçon: Bien, madame. Et comme boisson?
Customer: *(Order a bottle of red or white wine, or mineral water, or whatever suits your taste.)*
   (At the end of the meal call over the waiter and ask him for the bill.)

Lisez et écrivez
(Reading and writing exercises)

Exercise 2

RESTAURANT
'Les Vieux Amis'
Menu touristique: 68^F TTC
Hors d'œuvres (au choix)
Assiette de Charcuterie
Potage du jour
~
Plat Principal (au choix)
Poulet au vin
Entrecôte Forestière
Sole dieppoise
~
Fromages ou Pâtisserie
~
Boissons en sus
Service Compris (15%)

Read the menu, then tick to show whether the statements are *true* or *false* (T or F).

(a) You can have cheese and dessert.   T☐ F☐

(b) You have to add 15% service charge.   T☐ F☐

(c) Drinks are included in the price.   T☐ F☐

(d) Soup is one of the starters.   T☐ F☐

Exercise 3

You are in Paris and you are choosing a restaurant to suit your taste. Read the descriptions of restaurants, and put the appropriate number (1, 2, 3 or 4) in the box opposite the statements of preference (a)–(d).

1

> **LA CLOSERIE DES LILAS (cuisine traditionnelle).** 3, rue Littré (6e). Le Gotha du show-bizz et des arts affectionne le bar, l'excellente cuisine et la superbe terrasse de verdure de cette institution de Montparnasse. (env 160 F t.c. à la brasserie).

3

> **TAVERNE KRONENBOURG (Alsace),** 24, bd des Italiens (9e). On aime cette taverne pour ses grillades et de belles spécialités alsaciennes. Orchestre le soir. Formule à 69 F.

2

> **L'ENTRECOTE DE PARIS (grillades),** 29, rue de Marignan (8e). Aux Champs-Elysées, la célèbre formule: salade aux noix, faux-filet grillé avec sa fameuse sauce et pommes allumettes. Unique formule à 79 F.

4

> **JULES VERNE (hors catégorie).** Tour Eiffel, Champ de Mars (7e). Tout Paris à vos pieds vu du haut de la Tour Eiffel, dans un cadre raffiné d'une éclatante sobriété. Cuisine de grande classe: fricassée de homard, escalope de foie gras au radis noir confit, croustillant de turbot roti.

(a) You want to try regional cooking. ☐

(b) You want to dine outside in a pretty setting. ☐

(c) You want to have a superb view over Paris. ☐

(d) You just want a grilled steak and chips. ☐

Exercise 4

Write sentences to make comparisons. Start with the phrase given, then complete the sentence by choosing a phrase from Box 1 and a phrase from Box 2.

Example: Le théâtre est plus intéressant que le cinéma.

(Remember that before a vowel, 'que' changes to 'qu'', e.g. 'qu'en'.)

(a) Le climat français
(b) Le Jardin des Plantes
(c) La couleur rouge
(d) Dans le Midi il fait
(e) Le livarot
(f) Le théâtre
(g) Mon imperméable
(h) Catherine

Box 1	Box 2
est plus fort que	en Angleterre
est plus beau que	le port
est plus chic que	votre coupe-vent
est plus chaud que	le cinéma
est plus belle que	son frère
est plus délicieux que	le camembert
est plus intéressant que	la couleur jaune
est meilleur que	le climat anglais

Écoutez

(Listening exercise)

Exercise 5   Spontaneous dialogue   Celebrating in a restaurant

Silvie and Patrick celebrate Silvie's birthday by eating out at a restaurant. They decide on an apéritif, then they order their meal. Listen and see if you can tick off on the list below the items which they order. As always, listen for the key items and try to find them in the list. Quite a lot of their chat will be difficult for you at this stage, but it will help you get used to the rhythms of French speech and it doesn't affect your understanding of key items.

(a) What does the waitress ask, after she has greeted them:

Vous aimeriez manger tout de suite? ☐
Vous aimeriez un apéritif avant le repas? ☐
Qu'est-ce que vous aimeriez prendre? ☐
Qu'est-ce que vous aimeriez boire? ☐

(b) Which of the following do they decide to drink before the meal?

un pernod ☐
un martini ☐
un kir royal ☐
un dubonnet ☐

(c) From the following list, tick the items that are chosen by the couple:

Hors d'œuvres
araignée de mer ☐
saumon fumé ☐
les escargots ☐
soupe de poisson ☐
crevettes grillées ☐
6 huîtres ☐
moules marinière ☐

Plat principal
darne de lieu ☐
sole meunière ☐
escalope de dinde ☐
coq au vin ☐
blanquette de veau ☐

(d) They have to solve the problem of the colour of the wine they want to order. What is the solution? Tick the right box below. Note that 'une bouteille' is 'one bottle' and 'une demi-bouteille' is 'a half bottle'.

une bouteille de rouge ☐
une bouteille de blanc ☐
une bouteille de rouge et une demi-bouteille de blanc ☐
une bouteille de blanc et une demi-bouteille de rouge ☐

8 Vous venez d'où? Talking about yourself and others

Dialogues

 Dialogue 1   Un sondage   A public opinion poll

John Smith has paid an early call to the 'syndicat d'initiative' to pick up more information about the excursion they are planning for today. As he leaves he is stopped by a young woman conducting some market research on tourism in Normandy.

Demoiselle: Excusez-moi, monsieur. Est-ce que vous êtes en vacances ici?

John: Oui.

Demoiselle: La municipalité de Caen fait un sondage sur le tourisme dans la ville et dans la région. Est-ce que vous avez quelques minutes pour répondre à des questions?

John: Mais oui. Je ne suis pas pressé.

Demoiselle: Bien, alors, vous venez d'où, monsieur?

John: Je viens d'Angleterre.

Demoiselle: Vraiment? Vous parlez bien français. Et comment vous appelez-vous, monsieur, votre prénom et votre nom de famille?

John: John Smith.

Demoiselle: Est-ce que je peux vous demander si vous êtes seul ici ou avec votre famille?

John: Je suis avec ma famille.

Demoiselle: Vous êtes combien de personnes en tout?

John: Nous sommes quatre. Il y a ma femme, mon fils, ma fille et moi.

Demoiselle: Et où est-ce que vous logez pendant votre séjour, au camping ou à l'hôtel?

John: Pendant notre séjour à Caen nous sommes dans un hôtel. Mais on a l'intention de se promener quelques jours dans la région, et pour cette excursion, on va faire du camping.

Demoiselle: Vous restez combien de temps à Caen?

John: Nous sommes ici depuis quatre jours, et nous allons rester encore quinze jours avant de rentrer.

Demoiselle: Et quelle est votre profession?

John: Je suis professeur de français dans une école secondaire.

Demoiselle: Ah, c'est pour ça que vous parlez si bien français. Donc, ce n'est pas votre première visite en France?

John: Oh non, bien sûr. Je viens en France chaque année, si possible.

Demoiselle: Et vous connaissez bien la Normandie?

John: Pas du tout. En général, on passe les vacances dans le Midi ou à Paris. C'est notre première visite à Caen.

Demoiselle: Et quelles sont vos impressions?

John: Nous sommes tout à fait ravis de notre visite. Nous aimons beaucoup la ville, les gens sont très aimables.

Demoiselle: Comment est-ce que vous occupez votre temps? Qu'est-ce que vous faites dans la journée?

John: Eh bien, d'habitude, on se lève assez tard – ce sont les vacances après tout. Après le petit déjeuner, ça dépend. Quelquefois on se promène en ville, on visite les monuments, ou alors on va passer la journée à la plage. Il y a beaucoup d'endroits à visiter et tellement de choses à voir.

Demoiselle: Vous êtes satisfait, alors?

John: Oui, à part le temps. Aujourd'hui, il y a encore beaucoup de vent et le temps reste gris.

Demoiselle: Qu'est-ce que vous prévoyez pour aujourd'hui?

John: C'est aujourd'hui le jour de marché à Dives-sur-Mer, et je crois que le vieux marché de Dives est très intéressant.

Demoiselle: Vous avez raison. C'est très intéressant. Bien, alors, monsieur. C'est tout. Je vous remercie beaucoup.

John: Mais de rien. Au revoir, mademoiselle.

Dialogue 2   Retour à l'hôtel   Return to the hotel

John Smith returns to the hotel and to a problem. As he enters, the manager tells him that his son is lost and Mrs Smith has called the police.

Hôtelier: Ah, Monsieur Smith! Vous voilà enfin! Votre petit garçon est perdu et votre femme est très inquiète.

John: Ah, mon Dieu! Où est-elle?

Hôtelier: Elle est dans le salon avec un agent de police.

$\star\star\star$

Agent: Calmez-vous, madame. Votre fils ne peut pas être loin. Faites-nous une description détaillée de lui, s'il vous plaît. Il a quel âge?

Mary: Il a huit ans. Il a les cheveux noirs, il est de taille moyenne pour son âge. Il porte un pullover rouge, une chemise bleue et un pantalon court.

Agent: Il s'en va souvent comme ça?

Mary: Ah non! Il reste toujours près de nous, surtout à l'étranger. Je ne comprends pas du tout.

Agent: Et il n'est pas dans sa chambre, vous êtes sûre?

Mary: Mais oui, j'en suis certaine.

Agent: Il est absent depuis combien de temps?

Mary: Une demi-heure, à peu près.

John: Il faut faire quelque chose. Je vais chercher dans le quartier. Il est peut-être tout près de l'hôtel.

Agent: Calmez-vous, monsieur, et asseyez-vous, je vous en prie. La police cherche déjà votre fils ... Regardez! Voilà mon collègue qui arrive avec lui. Vous voyez?

John: Dieu merci!

Agent: Ce n'est pas difficile de se perdre dans une ville inconnue, surtout quand on est petit.

Vocabulary

Dialogue 1

(i) Useful expressions

vous venez d'où?	where do you come from?
je viens de	I come from
nous sommes quatre	there are four of us
nous sommes ici depuis quatre jours	we've been here for four days
encore quinze jours	another fortnight
bien sûr	of course
dans le Midi	in the South of France
d'habitude	usually
ça dépend	it all depends
ou alors	or else
il y a tellement de choses à faire	there are so many things to do
je vous remercie	thank you

(ii) Nouns – masc.

le sondage: public opinion poll
le tourisme: tourism
le prénom: first name
le nom de famille: surname
le fils: son
le camping: camping (site)
le professeur: teacher
les gens: people
un endroit: place
le vent: wind
le marché: market
le jour de marché: market day

Nouns – fem.

les vacances: holidays
la municipalité: municipality
la question: question
la fille: daughter
une intention: intention
une excursion: excursion
une profession: profession
une école: school
une année: year (see *grammar ref. 9.2(f)*)
une impression: impression

(iii) Other words

répondre à: to answer

pressé(e): in a hurry

demander: to ask

seul: alone

loger: to stay; to put up at

pendant: during

se promener: to go for a walk;
    to go for a ride

depuis: since

rentrer: to return (home)

secondaire: secondary

donc: then; therefore

occuper: to occupy; to spend (time)

chaque: each; every

je viens (venir): I come

parler: to speak

général(e): general

tout à fait: completely

se lever: to get up

satisfait(e): satisfied

à part: except for

gris(e): grey

vieux (vieille): old

Dialogue 2

(i) Useful expressions

mon Dieu!

il a quel âge?

il est de taille moyenne

comme ça

à l'étranger

j'en suis certain(e)

tout près

Dieu merci

good heavens!

how old is he?

he is of average height

like this; like that

abroad

I'm sure of it

very close

thank God

(ii) Nouns – masc.

le salon: sitting room; lounge

un âge: age

un an: year

les cheveux: hair

le pantalon: trousers

le quartier: district

le collègue: colleague

Nouns – fem.

la police: police

la description: description

la chemise: shirt

(iii) Other words

enfin: at last

perdu(e): lost

inquiet (inquiète): worried; anxious

se calmer: to calm down

détaillé(e): detailed

court(e): short

s'en aller: to go away

souvent: often

toujours: always

comprendre: to understand

sûr (sûre): sure

certain(e): certain; sure

absent(e): absent

à peu près: about; approximately

arriver: to arrive

se perdre: to lose oneself

inconnu(e): unknown

Explanations

(a) *Reflexive verbs (grammar ref. 5.3)*

Here is an example of a reflexive verb:

se laver	*to wash oneself*
je **me** lave	I wash **myself**
tu **te** laves	you wash **yourself**
il **se** lave	he washes **himself**
elle **se** lave	she washes **herself**
nous **nous** lavons	we wash **ourselves**
vous **vous** lavez	you wash **yourself/yourselves**
ils/elles **se** lavent	they wash **themselves**

From this example you will see that the main feature of a reflexive verb is the *reflexive pronoun*, shown in **bold type** in the French example. In the text of the chapter you met the infinitive of the reflexive verb 'se perdre' (to lose oneself):

Ce	n'est pas	difficile	de se perdre	dans une ville inconnue.
It	is not	difficult	to lose oneself	in an unknown town.

There are a number of verbs which are reflexive in French but *not* in English. This means that you use them with the reflexive pronoun in French, but this has no equivalent in English, for example:

je **me** promène   I walk OR I go for a walk
on **se** promène   we go for a walk
on **se** lève   we get up
je **m'**appelle   I am called OR my name is

When someone asks you what your name is, they will use the reflexive verb 's'appeler' and ask one of the following questions:

Comment vous appelez-vous?
Comment est-ce que vous vous appelez?

The extra 'vous' is the reflexive pronoun.

When giving commands or instructions you follow the pattern explained in Chapter 2 with the addition of the reflexive pronoun.

Calmez-vous! (from 'se calmer')   Calm down!
Asseyez-vous! (from 's'asseoir')   Sit down!

(b) *Use of the prepositions 'en' and 'à'*

With names of countries	
Je suis en France.	I am in France.
Je vais en Angleterre.	I am going to England.

With names of towns	
Nous sommes à Caen.	We are in Caen.
Nous allons à Paris.	We are going to Paris.

(c) *Questions*

(i)

Quel?	What? / Which?
Quel parfum?	Which perfume?
Quelle profession?	What profession?
Quels parfums?	Which perfumes?
Quelles professions?	What professions?

Although 'quel' changes its form to agree with the noun when it is plural or feminine, there is no difference in the *spoken* form of all the four examples above.

All are pronounced to sound like 'kel'. The only time when pronunciation varies is where a plural word begins with a vowel, and you can hear the final '-s' run onto the following vowel, for example:

Quelles églises?   Which churches?

(ii) Here are two ways of asking questions which you have already learned:

Vous allez au château?
Est-ce que vous allez au château?

Vous voulez une glace?
Est-ce que vous voulez une glace?

There is another possibility which you meet sometimes, where the order of verb and subject is reversed:

Allez-vous au château?
Voulez-vous une glace?

When asking someone their name, you can reverse the order of subject and verb in this way with the reflexive verb 's'appeler':

Comment vous appelez-vous?

(d) *Uses of 'on'*

Notice how common it is to use 'on' in French, often when you could equally well say 'nous' (we):

On se lève tard, **on** se promène en ville, **on** visite les monuments.
We get up late, we go for a walk round town, we visit the sights.

(e) *'C'est...' / 'Ce sont...'*

C'est le château.   It's the castle.
Ce sont les vacances.   It's the holidays.

(f) *'Il faut'   It is necessary... / We've got to... / We must...*

Il faut faire quelque chose. $\begin{cases} \text{It is necessary to do something.} \\ \text{We've got to do something.} \end{cases}$
Il faut parler français.   We've got to speak French.
Il faut chercher le garçon.   We must look for the boy.

(g) *Using 'avoir' to express age*

Quel âge **avez-vous**?   How old are you?
Il a quel âge?   How old is he?

J'ai trente ans.   I am 30 (years old).
Il a huit ans.   He is 8.

(h) *Definite article with countries and regions*

Vous connaissez bien **la** Normandie?   Do you know Normandy well?
J'aime beaucoup **la** France.   I like France very much.

The definite article is used with the names of countries and provinces, as in the examples above, *except* after the prepositions 'en' and 'de':

Je viens souvent **en** France.   I often come to France.
Je viens **d'**Angleterre.   I come from England.

(i) *Singular or plural?*

Some words are singular in one language and plural in another. There are two examples in this chapter:

les cheveux hair
le pantalon trousers

(j) *The use of 'vieux/vieille'*

The adjective 'vieux' comes in front of the noun and has an irregular feminine form:

un vieux marché an old market
une vieille ville an old town

Exercises

● *The key to these exercises begins on p.219.*

Parlez

(Speaking exercise)

Exercise 1   Taking part in a poll

You are asked by a researcher ('chercheur' or 'chercheuse') to answer a few questions in a 'sondage'. Look at the dialogue below and use the English prompts to help you prepare your role as the man being asked the questions. Then turn on the recording and practise playing your part.

Chercheuse: Excusez-moi, monsieur, est-ce que vous avez quelques minutes pour répondre à des questions?
You: *(Say yes, with pleasure, you are in no hurry.)*
Chercheuse: Vous êtes en vacances ici?
You: *(Say yes, it's your first visit to Caen.)*
Chercheuse: Vous venez d'où, monsieur?
You: *(Say you are from England.)*
Chercheuse: Vous êtes au camping municipal?
You: *(Say no, you are staying at a hotel.)*
Chercheuse: Vous êtes seul ici?
You: *(Say that you are here with your wife and two children.)*
Chercheuse: Quelle est votre profession?
You: *(Give your profession.)*
Chercheuse: Comment est-ce que vous passez votre temps ici?
You: *(Say that you go for walks in town, visit public buildings and so on.)*
Chercheuse: Et quelles sont vos impressions de la ville?
You: *(Say that you are delighted, and your wife also. The people are friendly and you like the town.)*
Chercheuse: C'est tout, monsieur. Merci bien.
You: *(Say don't mention it and goodbye.)*

Lisez et écrivez

(Reading and writing exercises)

Exercise 2

Read the advertisement below and see if you can get enough information to answer these questions.

- (a) Do you need a special licence to hire a boat?
- (b) Which part of France will you travel through?
- (c) What is the distance between Redon and Angers?
- (d) How many people can this sort of boat accommodate?
- (e) What will you discover on the way?
- (f) When you stop, which sports are available?

TOURISME FLUVIAL DANS LES PAYS DE LA LOIRE

LOUEZ VOTRE BATEAU HABITABLE SANS PERMIS

OÙ ?

Des châteaux de la Loire à l'Océan Atlantique, partez à la découverte des rivières de la région. Plus de 350 km de paysages sans cesse renouvelés entre Angers et Redon.

QUAND ?

Du printemps à l'automne pour 1 semaine, 1 week-end ou 1 mini-semaine (du lundi au vendredi).

COMMENT ?

En famille ou entre amis, louez l'un des 158 bateaux SANS PERMIS (de 2 à 12 personnes) proposés par 11 sociétés de locations. Vous découvrirez le plaisir de la navigation, les châteaux, manoirs, abbayes et nombreux villages typiques. Les écluses au nombre restreint sont ouvertes tous les jours. Vous vous amarrez où et quand vous voulez pour inventer vos loisirs: équitation, pêche, vélo, baignade . . .

Exercise 3

Below is a list of reflexive verbs in the infinitive form. Make up sentences to give an account of your daily routine, choosing times from the box below, or using the times which fit in with your own routine. Look back at the example of 'se lever' in the *explanations* to remind yourself how the infinitive changes when you are using the 'je' form of the verb.

Example: Je me lève à sept heures.

(a) se réveiller	(to wake up)
(b) se lever	(to get up)
(c) se laver	(to wash oneself)
(d) se préparer pour sortir	(to get ready to go out)
(e) se promener en ville	(to take a walk in town)
(f) se reposer	(to take a rest)
(g) se coucher	(to go to bed)

> à midi   à huit heures du soir   à neuf heures du matin
> à sept heures   à dix heures du matin   à dix heures du soir
> à sept heures et demie   à huit heures

Exercise 4

Using the verbs in Exercise 3, form questions that you could put to another person. Questions can be formed using either 'à quelle heure?' or 'quand?'.

Examples: À quelle heure est-ce que vous vous levez le matin?
Quand est-ce que vous vous levez le matin?

Exercise 5

Practise using prepositions in the following groups of sentences:

(a) Use of 'à' and 'en'. Write answers to the question 'Où allez-vous?' using the destinations in the box below.

Example: Je vais au château.

> l'église   le Jardin des Plantes   le port
> Caen   le syndicat d'initiative   la mer   le château
> France   Normandie   Bretagne   Angleterre

(b) Use of 'de'. Now write sentences to answer the question 'Vous venez d'où?' using the destinations in the box on p.84.

Example: Je viens du port.
Je viens d'Angleterre.

France	le château	l'Hôtel de Ville
le port		la plage
Normandie	l'école	Angleterre

Écoutez
(Listening exercise)

 ### Exercise 6 Spontaneous dialogue Meeting and getting to know a new arrival

Anne meets two of her friends, Alain and Cédric, in the street and introduces them to her cousin Juliette from England. The problem here is listening to a whole lot of voices talking together and *still* being able to pick out certain key items. The exercises will help you to focus your listening and to disregard, at this stage, parts of the conversation which do not affect your answer.

(a) What expression does Anne use to introduce Juliette to her friends? She begins: 'Je vous...'

(b) What is the first question the boys ask Juliette?

Où est-ce que tu habites? ☐
Tu habites par ici? ☐
Tu habites où? ☐
Où habites-tu? ☐

(c) What three facts do you learn about Juliette from her first reply?

About her father?
About her mother?
About the country where she lives? (France ou Angleterre??)

(d) From where has Alain just returned?

(e) Cédric asks what Juliette does, and if she is a student (étudiante). How does he phrase these questions?

(f) What is Juliette studying? Tick the box to indicate what she says:

Je fais des études de langues. ☐ (languages)
Je fais des études de droit. ☐ (law)
Je fais des études de médecine. ☐ (medicine)
Je fais des études de philo. ☐ (philosophy)

(g) Why does Cédric say that Juliette is lucky? His words are:

Par contre,toi, tu es bilingue.

(h) Anne asks them a question:

Alors, les garçons, qu'est-ce que vous faites par ici?

What do they say they are planning to do?

Nous, on va aller en ville cet après-midi. ☐
Nous, on va aller à la plage cet après-midi. ☐
Nous, on va aller au cinéma cet après-midi. ☐
Nous, on va aller en disco cet après-midi. ☐

(i) They all agree to meet up after the girls have done their shopping. When do they decide to meet?

dans une heure ☐
dans vingt minutes ☐
dans quelques minutes ☐
dans une demi-heure ☐

Est-ce possible?
Arranging what you need

Dialogues

 ### Dialogue 1 Au téléphone On the telephone

Having decided to take a break for a few days at a camping site on the coast, John Smith rings up the proprietor to see if it is possible to hire equipment.

Propriétaire: Allô, Camping de la Plage, j'écoute.

John: Bonjour, monsieur. Je voudrais venir passer deux ou trois jours sur la côte avec ma famille, mais nous n'avons pas de matériel de camping. Est-ce qu'il est possible de louer une tente, et tout ce qu'il faut?

Propriétaire: Oui, monsieur, nous louons ici des tentes tout équipées. Qu'est-ce qu'il vous faut exactement? Une tente pour combien de personnes?

John: Nous sommes quatre personnes, deux adultes et deux enfants. Est-ce qu'on trouve dans la tente tout le nécessaire pour faire la cuisine?

Propriétaire: Mais oui, il y a des casseroles, des couteaux, des fourchettes, des cuillères, enfin, tout le nécessaire pour faire la cuisine. Mais nous n'avons pas de sacs de couchage à louer.

John: Ça ne fait rien. Nous avons nos propres sacs de couchage. Qu'est-ce qu'il y a aussi comme facilités dans le camping?

Propriétaire: C'est un camping cinq étoiles, monsieur, alors, bien sûr il y a tout – une épicerie, une salle de télévision, une salle de jeux, une buanderie, des douches et des salles de bains – enfin tout, vous voyez.

John: C'est parfait. Et vous êtes près de la mer?

Propriétaire: La plage est à deux minutes. Il y a un escalier qui descend des falaises.

John: Très bien, monsieur. Alors, j'aimerais réserver une tente avec tout l'équipement nécessaire pour trois jours, à partir de demain.

Propriétaire: Bien, monsieur. C'est d'accord. C'est à quel nom, s'il vous plaît?

John: John Smith.

Propriétaire: Comment est-ce que vous écrivez ça, monsieur?

John: S-M-I-T-H.

Propriétaire: Alors, à demain, monsieur.

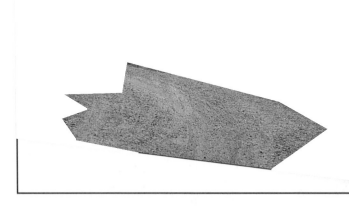

 ### Dialogue 2   À l'épicerie   At the grocer's

They arrive safely and find their tent erected. The next day, while the children go to play in the 'salle de jeux', Mary and John go to stock up at the grocer's.

Vendeuse: Bonjour, madame, bonjour, monsieur. Vous désirez?

Mary: Bonjour, madame. Je voudrais du lait et du pain, s'il vous plaît.

Vendeuse: Oui, madame. Un litre de lait? entier? écrémé?

Mary: Un litre de lait entier, s'il vous plaît.

Vendeuse: Et quelle sorte de pain?

Mary: Deux baguettes, s'il vous plaît.

Vendeuse: Voilà madame, un litre de lait et deux baguettes. C'est tout?

Mary: Non, je voudrais aussi du fromage, une livre de beurre et des pommes de terre.

Vendeuse: Voilà le beurre. Quel fromage voulez-vous?

John: Dans cette région, un camembert, bien sûr.

Vendeuse: Les camemberts sont là. Vous pouvez choisir. Et combien de pommes de terre?

Mary: Un kilo, s'il vous plaît. Comme charcuterie, qu'est-ce que vous avez?

Vendeuse: Il y a du jambon, du saucisson.

Mary: Je voudrais quatre tranches de jambon.

John: Et qu'est-ce que nous allons boire? Vous avez de la bière?

Vendeuse: Oui, monsieur, il y a de la bière, et il y a aussi du cidre de la région.

John: Alors, une bouteille de cidre. Et une bouteille de limonade pour les enfants.

Vendeuse: Voilà, monsieur.

Mary: Bon, alors c'est tout, je crois. Ça fait combien?

Vendeuse: Ça fait soixante-seize francs trente (76F 30) en tout, madame. Merci. Voilà votre monnaie.

Mary: Merci bien. Au revoir, madame.

Vendeuse: Au revoir, madame, au revoir, monsieur.

Vocabulary

Dialogue 1

(i) Useful expressions

tout ce qu'il faut tout le nécessaire	everything necessary
tout équipé(e)	fully equipped
qu'est-ce qu'il vous faut?	what do you need?
bien sûr	of course
la plage est à deux minutes	the beach is two minutes away
(c'est) d'accord	OK; that's agreed; all right
c'est à quel nom?	what name shall I put?
à demain	see you tomorrow

(ii) Nouns – masc.

le matériel: equipment
le couteau: knife
le sac (de couchage): (sleeping) bag
le jeu: game
un escalier: staircase; steps

Nouns – fem.

la côte: coast
la tente: tent
la personne: person
la cuisine: kitchen; cooking
la casserole: saucepan
la fourchette: fork
la cuillère: spoon
la facilité: facility
une étoile: star
une épicerie: grocer's
la salle: room
la télévision: television
la buanderie: laundry
la douche: shower
la salle de bain: bathroom
la falaise: cliff

(iii) Other words

écouter: to listen (to)
louer: to hire; to let
exactement: exactly
faire la cuisine: to cook
propre: own

descendre: to go down
réserver: to reserve
à partir de: as from; with effect from
écrire: to write
demain: tomorrow

88   MASTERING FRENCH

Dialogue 2

(i) Useful expressions

ça ira	that will be fine
quelle sorte de...?	what sort of...?

(ii) Nouns – masc.

Nouns – fem.

le lait: milk

la vendeuse: sales assistant

le lait entier: full-cream milk

la sorte: sort; kind

le lait écrémé: skimmed milk

la baguette: long, French loaf

le pain: bread

la livre: pound (= 500g)

le litre: litre

la pomme: apple

le beurre: butter

la pomme de terre: potato

le kilo: kilo

la tranche: slice

le jambon: ham

la bière: beer

le saucisson: salami-type sausage

la limonade: lemonade

le cidre: cider

Explanations

(a) *Partitive article (du, de la, de l', des) (grammar ref. 1.3)*

Je voudrais	**du** lait.	I would like	(some) milk.
	du pain.		(some) bread.
	du fromage.		(some) cheese.
Il y a	**de la** bière.	There is	(some) beer.
Il y a	**des** couteaux.	There are	(some) knives.
	des fourchettes.		(some) forks.
Avez-vous	**des** cuillères?	Have you got	any spoons?

It is very unusual for a French noun to stand alone. There is usually an article of some kind in front of the noun. You have already met the definite article (le, la, les) and the indefinite article (un, une). In the table above you see the *partitive article*. Sometimes this can be translated into English by the words 'some' or 'any', but very often it is possible for the noun to stand alone in English. As you would expect, the partitive article very often crops up when you are shopping.

(b) *Partitive article 'de'*

There are two cases where the partitive article is a simple 'de':

After a negative *use* **de** *only*	
Je n'ai pas **de** pain.	I haven't any bread.
Il n'y a pas **de** fromage.	There isn't any cheese.
Nous n'avons pas **de** bière.	We haven't any beer.

After a container *or* expressions of quantity, *use* **de** *only*	
une livre **de** beurre	a pound of butter
un litre **de** lait	a litre of milk
une bouteille **de** cidre	a bottle of cider

(c) *How much? / How many?* '*Combien (de)?*'

Combien de pommes de terre?	How many potatoes?
Combien de beurre?	How much butter?
Combien est-ce que ça coûte?	How much does that cost?
Ça fait **combien**?	How much does that come to?
Combien sont les pommes de terre?	How much are the potatoes?

(d) *Irregular plurals (grammar ref. 2.2)*

All nouns ending in '-eau', '-eu' and '-au' form the plural by adding '-x':

un couteau	a knife	$\rightarrow$	des couteaux	(some) knives
un jeu	a game	$\rightarrow$	des jeux	(some) games

Exercises

● *The key to these exercises begins on p.220.*

Parlez
(Speaking exercises)

Exercise 1   Shopping for food

Now it's your turn to play the part of a female customer in a shop. Look at the dialogue below and use the English prompts to help you prepare your role. Then turn on the recording and practise playing the part.

Vendeuse: Bonjour, madame. Vous désirez?
Customer: *(Say you'd like a pound of butter, a kilo of potatoes and some bread.)*
Vendeuse: Oui, madame. Combien de baguettes?
Customer: *(Say two baguettes. Say you'd also like two bottles of milk and ask what sort of cold meats there are.)*
Vendeuse: Voilà le lait, madame. Nous avons du jambon et du saucisson.
Customer: *(Say you'd like five slices of ham. Ask her if she has any cider.)*
Vendeuse: Je suis désolée, madame. Nous avons de la bière, mais nous n'avons pas de cidre.
Customer: *(No, you don't want beer. Say you'll take a bottle of lemonade for the children and ask how much it comes to.)*

Exercise 2

Here is a list of items you might want to shop for. Practise making up a shopping list and then short conversations to get what you want. Use 'Je voudrais...s'il vous plaît'. In some cases you may want to include a container or quantity (e.g. 'Je voudrais une boîte de...'). In other cases you will just ask for the item with no mention of a container or quantity (e.g. 'Je voudrais du...'; 'Je voudrais de la...'; 'Je voudrais des...').

Masculine	
du vin rouge	des fruits
du vin blanc	des légumes
du café	des œufs
du chocolat	des croissants
du thé	

Feminine
de la farine
de la viande
des cigarettes
des allumettes
des aspirines

Containers/quantities	
une boîte de	a box/tin of
une bouteille de	a bottle of
un paquet de	a packet of
un kilo de	a kilo of
une livre de	a pound of
beaucoup de	a lot of
un peu de	a little of

Lisez et écrivez
(Reading and writing exercises)

Exercise 3

At the top of p.92 are three boxes. Box 1 contains phrases that are always followed by the infinitive form of the verb. Box 2 contains infinitives. Box 3 contains a variety of words and phrases which can link up with an appropriate infinitive. Write sentences which take an item from each box. See how many sentences you can form on the same pattern as the examples.

Examples: C'est difficile de faire la cuisine.
Je veux écouter la radio.

Box 1	Box 2	Box 3
C'est difficile de...	acheter	la ville
C'est possible de...	aimer	à huit heures
Il faut...	aller	les enfants
Je vais...	arriver	l'escalier
Nous allons...	boire	au château
Je veux...	chercher	la radio
Nous voulons...	descendre	du jambon
Je peux...	écouter	un apéritif
Nous pouvons...	faire	de la bière
	louer	six jours
	prendre	l'église
	rester	à la côte
	venir	la cuisine
	visiter	une tente

Exercise 4

(a) Read the recipe and find the French words or phrases for the following:

   a pinch of
   melt
   grated cheese
   cover with the sauce

(b) What do you think the following words might mean?

   cuisson
   légumes
   le four
   servez dès la sortie du four

GRATIN DE LÉGUMES

Avec un reste
de légumes, du bouillon de poule

 PRÉPARATION: 15 mn

 CUISSON: 15 mn

 POUR 4 PERSONNES

Reste de légumes cuits (céleri, carottes, poireaux, oignon), 50 g de beurre, 2 cuillerées à soupe de farine, 4 dl de lait, 100 g de gruyère râpé, 1 pincée de noix de muscade râpée, sel et poivre, et crème.
1 Égoutez les légumes; coupez les carrottes en rondelles, les poireaux et le céleri en morceaux; préchauffez le four (200°).
2 Préparez une béchamel: faites fondre le beurre dans une casserole; ajoutez-y la farine; laissez cuire pendant 1 minute; mouillez petit à petit avec le lait; salez et poivrez; laissez bouillir 2 minutes sans cesser de remuer, puis retirez du feu; ajoutez 80 grammes de gruyère râpé et la noix de muscade, la crème.
3 Disposez les légumes dans un plat à gratin; nappez avec la sauce; saupoudrez avec le reste du gruyère; glissez le plat au four et faites cuire pendant 15 minutes.
4 Servez dès la sortie du four.

Écoutez

(Listening exercise)

 Exercise 5   Spontaneous dialogue   Planning a barbecue

Anne, Juliette, Alain and Cédric decide to plan a barbecue on the beach. They have to decide first if they have all they need. You might have to look up some words but the exercises will help you focus on key items, and you can try guessing the sort of things you might want for a picnic or barbecue.

(a) They decide to start making a list of what they have *not* got. (On peut commencer à voir ce qu'on n'a pas.) What is the first, essential item they have not got? Cédric proposes to solve this problem by using these items he has got at home. What do you think these items might be?

    une grille
    quelques briques
    un peu de bois

(b) Anne says she has got all the equipment for a picnic. Can you fill in the gaps in the items below?

    Assiettes et .... en carton; des .... et des fourchettes en ....;
    des .... en papier.

(c) Juliette says that she will get the drink. (Moi, je vais acheter la boisson.) What three drinks do they decide to buy? Choose from the following list.

    du vin   ☐
    du cidre   ☐
    du jus de fruit   ☐
    de la bière   ☐
    de la limonade   ☐
    du coca cola   ☐

(d) Cédric says he will deal with the food. (Je m'occupe de la nourriture.) What three items of meat do they decide they should get? Choose items from the list below. Look up any words you don't know.

    du bœuf   ☐
    des hamburgers   ☐
    du poulet   ☐
    du poisson   ☐
    des saucisses   ☐

(e) Which fruit do they decide to cook for a dessert? Something cooked.

    des .... cuites

(f) Where and at what time do they decide to meet up?

Qu'est-ce que vous allez voir? Planning a journey

Dialogue

 Des projets de voyage   Plans for a journey

Michel: Vous connaissez déjà bien Paris, mon cher John.

John: C'est vrai, mais c'est toujours un plaisir d'y retourner.

Nicole: Qu'est-ce que vous allez voir? Un jour, ce n'est pas long pour visiter Paris.

John: On va y aller par le train. C'est plus rapide que l'auto et nous n'aurons pas de problèmes pour garer la voiture. Le train arrive à Paris à neuf heures trente-trois (9h 33). Ça fera quand même une bonne journée.

Mary: Les enfants seront sûrement bien fatigués le soir, mais ça vaut la peine, je crois.

John: Évidemment, on ne va pas visiter tous les musées et toutes les galeries. Mais le Sacré Cœur et l'Arc de Triomphe les intéresseront, j'espère. Il y aura beaucoup de choses à voir.

Nicole: J'y pense, il y aura aussi le Centre Pompidou. Vous le connaissez déjà, peut-être?

John: Non, pas encore, mais je vais y aller. Ça m'intéresse beaucoup de le voir.

Michel: Et dans la cour devant le Centre vous verrez toutes sortes d'activités, des mimes, des jongleurs. Les enfants vont certainement trouver ça très amusant.

Mary: Et puis, il y a la Tour Eiffel. Les enfants veulent la voir de près, bien sûr!

Michel: Est-ce que vous aurez le temps de faire une excursion en bateau-mouche sur la Seine?

John: J'espère bien. Nous aurons peut-être assez de temps l'après-midi. Mais ça sera bien assez pour la journée. Ça donnera une première impression aux enfants, et ils reviendront sans doute quand ils seront plus âgés.

Michel: La meilleure façon de découvrir Paris, c'est de marcher, de flâner dans les rues.

Champs-Élysées, Paris

John: Oui, vous avez raison, c'est à pied qu'on voit bien Paris, mais aussi en autobus. J'aime bien les autobus parisiens. C'est aussi une bonne façon de voir la ville.

Nicole: Le métro est parfois plus rapide.

John: C'est sans doute vrai, mais je ne l'aime pas. On ne voit rien, et il y a toujours beaucoup de monde.

Michel: Et vers quelle heure est-ce que vous rentrerez le soir?
John: Les trains sont fréquents. On prendra le train de dix-
huit heures vingt-trois (18h 23), je crois, et on sera de retour à Caen à vingt
heures vingt-trois (20h 23).
Michel: Je viendrai vous chercher à la gare, si vous voulez.
Mary: C'est vraiment gentil. Ça ne vous dérange pas? Vous êtes sûr?
Michel: Non, ça ne me dérange pas du tout. Je serai à la gare à 20h 23 alors.
John: Bon, et maintenant, au lit. Demain matin il va falloir partir de bonne
heure.
Michel: Eh bien, au revoir, alors. Et bonne journée à Paris.

Readings

The following are edited extracts from John Smith's guide to Paris. Using the vocabulary on p. 98, see how much you can understand. A full translation will be found on p. 222.

L'Avenue des Champs-Élysées

De la Concorde au Rond-Point
Remonter vers l'Étoile par les allées de marronniers bordant l'avenue. C'est la partie la plus fréquentée de la promenade. Les enfants y sont nombreux, attirés par les petites boutiques, les balançoires.

Du Rond-Point à l'Étoile
Remonter l'avenue en flânant. On marchera sur le côté droit, le plus animé et le plus typique. Une rue, un café, un cinéma portent le nom de Colisée. On arrive place de l'Étoile au pied de l'Arc grandiose.

La Tour Eiffel

C'est le monument parisien le plus universellement connu. Ascension: tous les jours de 10h 45 à 18h (de 9h 30 à 18h en juillet et août). La vue pour le visiteur qui monte au sommet peut porter jusqu'à soixante-sept kilomètres.

La Basilique du Sacré Cœur

La haute silhouette blanche fait maintenant partie du paysage parisien. La montée au dôme (de 10h à 13h, et de 14h à 17h) fournit un panorama magnifique.

Paris, vu de son fleuve

Il y a des services réguliers de bateaux-mouches tous les jours du premier avril au cinq octobre. En hiver, un service par jour, à 15h 15. Embarcadère: pont de Solférino.

Vocabulary

Dialogue

(i) Useful expressions

quand même	all the same
ça vaut la peine	it's worth it
ça m'intéresse beaucoup	it interests me a good deal
ils veulent la voir de près	they want to see it from close up
j'espère bien	I hope so
ce sera bien assez	that will be quite enough
tellement de monde	so many people
on sera de retour	we shall get back
je viendrai vous chercher à la gare	I'll come to meet you at the station
ça ne vous dérange pas?	it's no trouble for you?
il va falloir...	we shall have to...
de bonne heure	early

(ii) Nouns – masc.

le train: train
le cœur: heart
l'arc: arch
le triomphe: triumph
le centre: centre
le mime: mime
le jongleur: juggler
le bateau: boat
le bateau-mouche: pleasure steamer
le doute: doubt
le métro: underground train
le retour: return

Nouns – fem.

une auto: car
la peine: trouble; worry
la galerie: gallery
la cour: courtyard
une activité: activity
la tour: tower
la façon: method; way
la gare: railway station

(iii) Other words

cher (chère): dear
retourner: to return
long (longue): long
rapide: fast
garer: to park
fatigué(e): tired
évidemment: evidently
sacré(e): holy
intéresser: to interest
espérer: to hope
amusant: fun
puis: then

donner: to give
revenir: to come back
âgé(e): old
parisien(ne): Parisian
marcher: to walk
flâner: to stroll
parfois: sometimes
sans doute: probably
vers: about
fréquent(e): frequent
falloir: to be necessary
partir: to leave

Readings

(i) Nouns – masc.

le rond-point: roundabout
le marronnier: horse chestnut
le côté: side
le cinéma: cinema
le sommet: top; summit
le kilomètre: kilometre
le paysage: landscape
le dôme: dome
le panorama: panorama
le fleuve: river
le pont: bridge
un embarcadère: landing-stage

Nouns – fem.

une allée: avenue; drive (usually lined
    with trees)
la partie: part
la promenade: walk
la boutique: small shop
la balançoire: swing
une ascension: climb; ascent
la vue: view
la silhouette: silhouette
la montée: climb

(ii) Other words

remonter: to go up; to walk up
bordant: bordering; lining
fréquenter: to frequent
nombreux (nombreuse): numerous
attirer: to attract
animé(e): animated
typique: typical
grandiose: grand; grandiose
universellement: universally
juillet: July
août: August

monter: to climb
haut(e): high
blanc (blanche): white
faire partie de: to be part of
fournir: to offer; to provide
magnifique: magnificent
vu de: seen from
régulier (régulière): regular
avril: April
octobre: October

● *Note that all the months and seasons are to be found in grammar ref. 9.2.*

Explanations

(a) *Future tense of regular verbs (grammar ref. 5.2 (c))*

To form the future tense of regular verbs, take the infinitive and add to it the endings of the present tense of 'avoir', as in the following examples:

arriver	*to arrive*
j'arriver**ai**	I shall arrive
tu arriver**as**	you will arrive
il arriver**a**	he will arrive
elle arriver**a**	she will arrive
nous arriver**ons**	we shall arrive
vous arriver**ez**	you will arrive
ils arriver**ont**	they will arrive

choisir	*to choose*
je choisir**ai**	I shall choose
tu choisir**as**	you will choose
il choisir**a**	he will choose
elle choisir**a**	she will choose
nous choisir**ons**	we shall choose
vous choisir**ez**	you will choose
ils choisir**ont**	they will choose

Regular verbs with an infinitive ending in '-re', such as 'prendre', 'attendre', drop the final '-e' before adding the endings, for example:

je prend**rai**   I shall take
il attend**ra**   he will wait

(b) *Future tense of irregular verbs*

Some of the most common verbs form an irregular future:

être	(to be)	→	je se**rai**	(I shall be)
avoir	(to have)	→	j'au**rai**	(I shall have)
faire	(to do)	→	je fe**rai**	(I shall do)
voir	(to see)	→	je ver**rai**	(I shall see)
venir	(to come)	→	je vien**drai**	(I shall come)

Note that the *endings* are the same for all verbs, even if the stem of the verb is irregular.

(c) *Future with 'aller'*

You have already met the form of the future tense using the verb 'aller':

Nous allons visiter le château. { We are going to visit the castle. / We shall visit the castle. }

Je vais visiter le musée. { I am going to visit the museum. / I shall visit the museum. }

Very often French speakers use this way to express the future, especially if they are talking about something which will happen in the near future.

(d) *Object pronouns (grammar ref. 4.1 (a) (c))*

Compare the following sentences from the chapter with their English equivalents. The pronouns are shown in **bold**:

Ça **m'**intéresse.
That interests **me**.

Vous **le** connaissez déjà?
Do you know **it** already?

In these phrases, 'me' and 'it' are pronouns, and each is the direct object of a verb. You will see that direct object pronouns come *after* the verb in English and *before* the verb in French. Here are more examples, showing all the object pronouns used with the verb 'connaître' (to know):

il **me** connaît	he knows **me**
il **te** connaît	he knows **you**
il **le** connaît	he knows **him**
il **la** connaît	he knows **her**
il **nous** connaît	he knows **us**
il **vous** connaît	he knows **you**
il **les** connaît	he knows **them**

When the verb is in the negative, the pronoun still comes immediately in front of the verb, for example:

Je ne **le** connais pas.	I don't know **him**.
Je ne **l'**aime pas.	I don't like **him/her/it**.
Ça ne **m'**intéresse pas.	That doesn't interest **me**.

Note the way pronouns are used when an infinitive follows a verb:

Je viendrai **vous** chercher.	I shall come to fetch **you**.

The pronoun belongs to the idea of 'fetching' and so comes in front of the infinitive 'chercher', which here means 'to fetch'.

(e) *Connaître/Savoir*

Note the following examples:

savoir

Je ne **sais** pas.	I don't know.
Je **sais** que Paris est la capitale de la France.	I know that Paris is the capital of France.
Savez-vous où est le port de Caen?	Do you know where the port of Caen is?

connaître

Vous **connaissez** déjà Paris?	Do you know Paris already?
Vous **connaissez** ma femme?	Do you know my wife?
Je ne **connais** pas le port.	I don't know the port.

You will see from the examples that 'savoir' is used for knowing a fact or *knowing about* something; 'connaître' means *being acquainted with* a person or place.

(f) *Word order*

Un jour, ce n'est pas long.
Un voyage à Paris, ça vaut la peine.
Le train, c'est la meilleure façon d'aller à Paris.

You will find that this is a very characteristic French way of making a statement. There is a slight pause after the subject of the sentence and then 'ce' or 'ça' is used to repeat the idea of the subject. The English versions of the above sentences are:

> One day isn't very long.
> It's worth taking a trip to Paris.
> The train is the best way of going to Paris.

(g) Using 'bien' for emphasis

J'aime **bien**...	I'm **very** fond of...
Ça sera **bien** assez.	That will **certainly** be enough.
J'espère **bien**.	I **certainly** / **very much** hope so.

As you see, 'bien' has the effect of adding emphasis to the statement.

Exercises

● *The key to these exercises begins on p.221.*

Parlez
(Speaking exercise)

Exercise 1   A visit to Paris

Now speak to a friend about your plans to visit Paris. Look at the dialogue and use the English prompts to help you prepare your role. Then turn on the recording and practise playing your part.

Ami: Alors, demain c'est la visite à Paris. Qu'est-ce que vous allez faire?
You: *(Say that you will certainly see Notre-Dame and visit the Louvre.)*
Ami: Vous partez avec les enfants?
You: *(Say yes, so you'll certainly take an excursion on a bateau-mouche.)*
Ami: Et ils voudront voir la Tour Eiffel?
You: *(Say yes, you'll see the Eiffel Tower and also the Arc de Triomphe.)*
Ami: Il y a beaucoup de choses à faire et vous avez peu de temps. Où est-ce que vous déjeunerez?
You: *(Say that there will not be time to eat in a good restaurant, so you'll probably take some sandwiches (des sandwichs).)*
Ami: Alors, passez une bonne journée.
You: *(Thank him and say you hope the weather will be fine.)*

Lisez et écrivez
(Reading and writing exercises)

Exercise 2

Read the horoscope and see if you can answer the following questions:

(a) What will be your main problem today if you were born between 21 March and 19 April?
(b) If you were born between 21 May and 20 June, what will you do to help someone?
(c) If you were born between 23 August and 22 September, your career should improve. What will be the two causes of this improvement?
(d) For those born between 23 September and 22 October, what is likely to happen if they are unmarried?
(e) If you were born between 20 January and 18 February, when should you be careful not to spend too much money?

l'horoscope

Jeudi 21 février

BELIER
21 mars au 19 avril

Vous aurez peut-être aujourd'hui quelque ennui d'argent. Mais quelque chose d'agréable vous attend ce soir. Vous devriez sortir et dire ce que vous pensez!

TAUREAU
20 avril au 20 mai

On va rechercher votre compagnie et vous serez l'étoile d'une soirée. Les bonnes nouvelles d'aujourd'hui affecteront le cercle de famille.

GEMEAUX
21 mai au 20 juin

Aujourd'hui une relation sociale se révélera utile à vos affaires. Vous aurez la capacité de donner un bon conseil à quelqu'un. Ce soir, vous serez l'âme d'une réception, et brillerez par votre optimisme!

CANCER
21 juin au 22 juillet

Des nouvelles venues du lointain vous réchaufferont le cœur. Prenez garde de ne pas égarer un objet de valeur. Ce soir, les développements de vos finances seront positifs.

LION
23 juillet au 22 août

Montrez-vous aujourd'hui un bon auditeur. Votre vie sociale aura de l'influence sur vos affaires. Les partenaires partageront leurs tâches. Heureux moments ce soir en société.

VIERGE
23 août au 22 septembre

Chance et auto-discipline s'allieront aujourd'hui pour faire avancer votre carrière. Essayez de ne pas faire trop de bruit pour pas grand'chose. Renforcement des liens affectifs.

BALANCE
23 septembre au 22 octobre

Essayez aujourd'hui de ne pas être trop critique. Les célibataires pourraient rencontrer l'amour dans leur travail. Une possibilité de voyage va se présenter.

SCORPION
23 octobre au 21 novembre

En début de journée, ne vous laissez pas envahir par les détails. Une possibilité de briller va se présenter et les liens affectifs seront remis en valeur. Restez chez vous ce soir.

SAGITTAIRE
22 novembre au 21 décembre

Travaillez en profondeur si vous voulez réussir. Vous apprécierez la compagnie de vos collègues et, dans la soirée, on se sentira en accord profond.

CAPRICORNE
22 décembre au 19 janvier

C'est une bonne journée pour montrer aux autres combien vous les appréciez. Dans votre travail, votre compétence vous apportera la réussite. Opportunités évidentes pour gagner de l'argent.

VERSEAU
20 janvier au 18 février

Les achats pour la maison seront un « plus ». La soirée placera un accent tout particulier sur les amusements mais attention: pas de dépenses excessives!

POISSONS
19 février au 20 mars

Vous risquez de vous méprendre sur les intentions de quelqu'un. Les sorties dans les environs vous plairont beaucoup et, ce soir, vous penserez famille avant tout.

Exercise 3

Respond to the following questions by using the cues to write sentences which include an object pronoun. To reply to the questions with 'vous', answer as if for your whole family (using 'nous' or 'on').

Example: Vous connaissez déjà Madame Dupont?
(Say no, you don't know her yet.)
Non, nous ne la connaissons pas encore.

(a) Les enfants connaissent déjà Paris? *(No, they don't know it yet.)*
(b) Vous prendrez le train? *(Yes, you'll catch it at 7 am.)*
(c) Vous aimez les jongleurs? *(Yes, you like them very much.)*
(d) Vous ferez une excursion en bateau-mouche? *(Yes, you will do it in the afternoon.)*
(e) Vous aimez le métro? *(No, you don't like it at all.)*

Écoutez
(Listening exercise)

 Exercise 4   Spontaneous dialogue   Returning to England

Bruce and Mary discuss their homeward journey with their French friends Pierre and Odile. They talk about what they will do on the way, and when they will return. The exercises will help you to focus on the bits that are difficult. Try to listen to the key words and not be too put off by the sort of conversational exchanges which are a normal part of socialising.

(a) When does Mary think they will set off home? Choose the phrase you hear her use on the tape.

On pense partir mercredi. ☐
On pense partir vendredi. ☐
On pense partir samedi. ☐
On pense partir jeudi. ☐

(b) Where do they decide to stop for lunch (déjeuner)?

Honfleur ☐
Barfleur ☐
Harfleur ☐
Rouen ☐

(c) How long does it take to get to Boulogne (according to Mary – there seems to be some difference of opinion!)?

Il faut compter treize heures de route. ☐
Il faut compter quatre heures de route. ☐
Il faut compter six heures de route. ☐
Il faut compter trois heures de route. ☐

(d) What will they do in Boulogne on the Saturday morning?

> Vous pourriez aller au ………. de Boulogne le samedi matin. C'est tellement animé.

(e) They are asked: 'Vous allez prendre le tunnel?' Here is the reply. Can you work out what it means? The key words (you might want to look them up) are 'pressé', and 'on peut prendre notre temps'.

> On prendra le tunnel quand on sera vraiment pressé. Comme ce n'est pas le cas et que samedi prochain on est encore en vacances, alors, on peut prendre tout notre temps.

(f) Why is Mary so certain that she will be back before the following summer? Fill in the gaps in the following statement with the words in the box below the extract:

> Il faut que j'organise un ………. à Boulogne pour mes ……….
> en avril ………. . Donc on ………. sûrement vous ………. bonjour.

> élèves = pupils
> voyage = journey
> dire = to say
> passera = (we) shall call in
> prochain = next

(g) The following sentence has been jumbled. Can you reorganise the words to make a correct sentence meaning: 'Have a good journey home'?

> de bon voyage retour souhaite vous je un

Un aller-retour pour Paris
A day's sightseeing

Dialogues

 Dialogue 1   À la gare   At the station

John buys the tickets for the trip to Paris.

John: Deux adultes et deux enfants, aller-retour pour Paris, s'il vous plaît.
Compartiment non-fumeur si possible.
Homme au guichet: Deux aller-retour et deux demi-tarif. Ça fait mille
quatre-vingts francs (1080F), s'il vous plaît, monsieur.
John: Merci. Il part de quelle voie, le train pour Paris, s'il vous plaît?
Homme: Voie numéro trois, à sept heures trente-quatre (7h 34).

 Dialogue 2   Dans le train   On the train

The train is already filling up fast and the Smith family have difficulty finding
four seats together in the compartment.

John: Excusez-moi, madame. Est-ce que ces places sont libres?
Dame: Mais oui, monsieur. Il n'y a personne là.
John: Et à côté de vous, c'est libre aussi?
Dame: Mais oui, monsieur.
Mary: Bien, je m'assieds à côté de vous. Vous permettez? Et les enfants en
face de moi.
John: Et moi, je vais m'asseoir ici, tout près. Vous permettez, monsieur?
Monsieur: Certainement, monsieur.
John: On est bien ici.
Monsieur: Oui, ce train est très confortable. Et le voyage à Paris est très
rapide. Bien sûr, ce n'est pas aussi rapide qu'avec le TGV. Mais quand
même on n'a pas le temps de s'ennuyer.
Dame: On va bientôt partir, sans doute. Vous avez l'heure, madame?
Mary: Oui, il est sept heures et demie.

Dame: Encore quatre minutes, alors. Vous faites souvent le voyage à Paris, madame?

Mary: Oh, non! Nous sommes anglais, et c'est notre première visite à Caen, alors c'est aussi la première fois que nous faisons ce voyage. Mais nous connaissons déjà Paris.

Dame: Vous parlez bien français. Est-ce que les enfants le parlent aussi?

Mary: Un peu, seulement. Mais ils vont l'apprendre à l'école, et nous viendrons probablement chaque année en France.

Dame: C'est très bien. Ah, nous partons! Qu'est-ce que vous allez voir à Paris?

Mary: On ira sans doute à la Tour Eiffel, au Sacré Cœur, etc. C'est surtout pour les enfants, cette visite. On ne va pas avoir le temps de tout voir, bien sûr, mais ça sera un début.

Dame: Bien sûr!

A river trip on the Seine passing Notre-Dame, Paris

 ### Dialogue 3 *À Paris In Paris*

Among the various activities of the day the family manage to take a trip on the river. They are given a commentary over the loudspeaker.

Guide: Alors, mesdames, messieurs, sur votre gauche vous voyez les Jardins des Tuileries. Un peu plus loin, ce grand bâtiment, c'est le Palais du Louvre. Maintenant, vous voyez devant vous le pont Neuf et les tours de la cathédrale Notre-Dame. Notre-Dame est située sur l'Île de la Cité. Sur cette île se situent les origines de la ville de Paris. Ce bâtiment sur votre gauche, et en face de Notre-Dame, est la Préfecture de Police. Sur la droite, maintenant, le quai Saint-Michel, avec ses bouquinistes célèbres, et ce boulevard-là s'appelle le boulevard Saint-Michel, célèbre pour ses cafés et pour ses étudiants, parce que c'est dans ce quartier de Paris que se trouve la Sorbonne, l'université ancienne de Paris. Cette deuxième île sur la gauche s'appelle l'Île Saint-Louis. Nous passons maintenant sous le pont Sully, et à gauche, le boulevard Henri Quatre mène à la place de la Bastille. Un peu plus loin, à droite, ces arbres et ces espaces verts, c'est le Jardin des Plantes ...

Dialogue 4   *Au café   At the café*

They take a break for refreshment. The cafés seem crowded, but the Smiths find a table on the 'terrasse', where one person is sitting alone.

John: Excusez-moi, monsieur. Ces chaises ne sont pas prises?

Monsieur: Non, monsieur. Il n'y a personne.

John: Alors, vous permettez?

Monsieur: Je vous en prie.

John: Il y a tellement de monde, aujourd'hui.

Monsieur: À Paris, en été, c'est toujours comme ça. Il y a tellement de touristes.

John: Oui, tout le monde veut voir Paris. Mais ici, on est bien.

Monsieur: Ce n'est pas mal. On a une belle vue sur la Seine et sur les jardins. Vous êtes ici pour longtemps?

John: Oh, non! Aujourd'hui, seulement. Nous passons un jour seulement à Paris.

Serveuse: Bonjour, monsieur; bonjour, madame. Qu'est-ce que vous prenez?

John: Une bière, un citron pressé et deux limonades, s'il vous plaît.

Serveuse: Bien, monsieur.

Monsieur: Vous avez une journée bien chargée, alors.

John: On ne peut pas tout voir, évidemment. Nous reviendrons, et la prochaine fois nous resterons plus longtemps, j'espère.

Vocabulary

Dialogue 1

Nouns – masc.

un aller-retour: return ticket
le compartiment non-fumeur:
    non-smoking compartment
le guichet: ticket window
le demi-tarif: half-price ticket

Nouns – fem.

la voie: (railway) track

Dialogue 2

(i) Useful expressions

vous permettez?	may I?; may we?
tout près	close by
on est bien ici	this suits us fine
vous avez l'heure?	have you got the time?

(ii) Nouns – masc.

le TGV (le Train à Grande Vitesse):
　French high-speed train

(iii) Other words

personne: nobody
à côté de: beside; next to
je m'assieds (s'asseoir): I sit down
en face de: opposite
confortable: comfortable

s'ennuyer: to get bored
apprendre: to learn
probablement: probably
le début: beginning

Dialogue 3

(i) Nouns – masc.

le guide: guide
le bâtiment: building
le palais: palace
le bouquiniste: bookseller
le boulevard: boulevard
un étudiant: student
un arbre: tree
un espace: space

Nouns – fem.

la cathédrale: cathedral
une île: island
la cité: city
une origine: origin
la préfecture: police HQ
une université: university

(ii) Other words

neuf (neuve): (brand) new
situé(e): situated
se situer: to be situated
célèbre: famous
se trouver: to be situated

ancien (ancienne): ancient; old
deuxième: second
sous: under
mener: to lead

Dialogue 4

(i) Nouns – masc.

le touriste: tourist
le citron: lemon

Nouns – fem.

la chaise: chair

(ii) Other words

pris(e): taken; occupied
tellement: so many
mal: bad
longtemps: a long time

pressé(e): squeezed (as in the drink
　'citron pressé')
chargé(e): loaded; full
prochain(e): next

Explanations

(a) *This, that 'Ce', 'cet', 'cette', 'ces' (grammar ref. 3.6)*

Masculine			
ce bâtiment	this building	**ce** bâtiment-**là**	that building
ce train	this train	**ce** train-**là**	that train
cet agent	this policeman	**cet** agent-**là**	that policeman

Feminine			
cette visite	this visit	**cette** visite-**là**	that visit
cette île	this island	**cette** île-**là**	that island

Masculine plural and feminine plural			
ces bâtiments	these buildings	**ces** bâtiments-**là**	those buildings
ces trains	these trains	**ces** trains-**là**	those trains
ces agents	these policemen	**ces** agents-**là**	those policemen
ces visites	these visits	**ces** visites-**là**	those visits
ces îles	these islands	**ces** îles-**là**	those islands

(b) *Numbers (grammar ref. 9.1, 9.2)*

Cardinal numbers		*Ordinal numbers*	
1	un/une	**premier/première**	first
2	deux	deux**ième**	second
3	trois	trois**ième**	third
4	quatre	quatr**ième**	fourth
5	cinq	cinqu**ième**	fifth
6	six	six**ième**	sixth
7	sept	sept**ième**	seventh
8	huit	huit**ième**	eighth
9	neuf	neuv**ième**	ninth
10	dix	dix**ième**	tenth

As you see from the examples, all the ordinal numbers in French are formed on the same pattern except for 'premier'. Ordinal numbers are used as in English, with two main exceptions:

(i) With dates

Examples:

le 2 avril   = le **deux** avril   April 2nd
le 9 mai   = le **neuf** mai   May 9th
le 19 juin   = le **dix-neuf** juin   June 19th

But note:

le 1er mars = le **premier** mars March 1st
le 1er mai = le **premier** mai   May 1st

You will remember that in Chapter 10, the extract from the guide-book giving details about 'bateaux-mouches' said:

Services réguliers tous les jours du **premier** avril au **cinq** octobre.

(ii) With names of kings and queens

Examples:
le boulevard Henri **Quatre**
la reine Elizabeth **deux**

But note:

Charles **premier**
Elizabeth **première**

(c) *Duration of time: 'depuis', 'pour'*

(i) 'Depuis'

Nous	sommes	ici	depuis	quatre jours.
We	have been	here	for	four days.
Elle	est	à Caen	depuis	quelques jours.
She	has been	in Caen	for	a few days.

In sentences of this type, French uses the *present tense* of the verb to show that, although the action described started sometime in the past, it is still going on in the present. For example, the first sentence above means 'We came here four days ago *and we are still here*'. The present tense seems more logical.

(ii) 'Pour'

| Je | vais | à Paris | pour | trois semaines. |
| I | am going | to Paris | for | three weeks. |

In this case, 'pour' is used to refer to a period of time looking to the future.

(d) 'Se trouver'

Dans ce quartier **se trouve** la Sorbonne. The Sorbonne **is** in this district.
Où **se trouve** votre hôtel? Where **is** your hotel?

'Se trouver' is used with the sense of 'to be situated', or 'to be located'. English often uses only the verb 'to be', as in the examples above.

(e) *Nobody* *'Ne... personne'*

Il **n'**y a **personne** là. There is nobody there.
Je **ne** connais **personne** ici. I know nobody here.

Exercises

● *The key to these exercises begins on p.222.*

Parlez
(Speaking exercises)

Exercise 1 Passing the time

While on a visit to Paris with your family, you decide to have coffee on the 'terrasse' of a café, and you get involved in conversation with another customer (a man). Look at the dialogue below and use the English prompts to help you prepare your part of the conversation (you are playing the part of a man). Then turn on the recording and practise playing your part.

You: *(Ask the person at the table if these seats are free.)*
Client: Mais oui, monsieur, il n'y a personne.
You: *(Ask if you and your family can sit here.)*
Client: Je vous en prie, monsieur.
You: *(Say that there are so many people in town today.)*
Client: En été, c'est toujours comme ça. Vous êtes là pour longtemps?
You: *(Say no, you are spending a day in Paris with your family.)*
Client: Une journée, c'est très peu. Qu'est-ce que vous allez voir pendant votre visite?
You: *(Tell him a few of the places you hope to visit.)*
Client: Alors, bonne journée, monsieur.

Exercise 2

You've jotted down the following notes to remind yourself of the details for the train tickets you are going to buy, and also the information that you need. Make up the sentences that you would need to say to get what you want.

quatre adultes	combien?
aller-retour	départ quelle heure?
Paris	départ quelle voie?
	arrivée quelle heure?

Lisez et écrivez

(Reading and writing exercises)

Exercise 3

Here is a page of the SNCF leaflet for the TGV Sud-Est. Can you understand how to find the train you need? Answer the questions at the top of p.114.

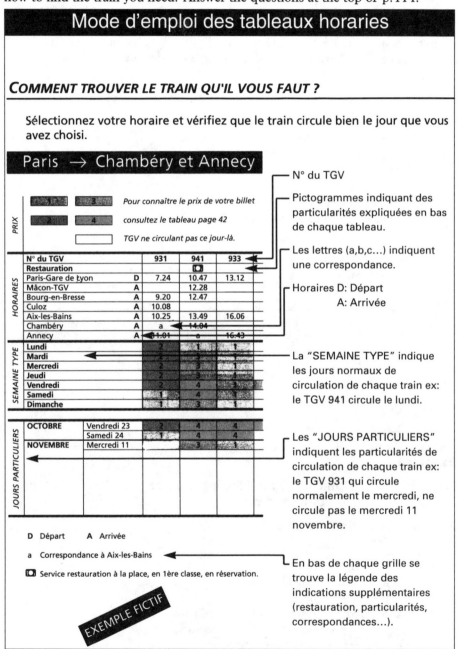

Mode d'emploi des tableaux horaires

COMMENT TROUVER LE TRAIN QU'IL VOUS FAUT ?

Sélectionnez votre horaire et vérifiez que le train circule bien le jour que vous avez choisi.

Paris → Chambéry et Annecy

Pour connaître le prix de votre billet consultez le tableau page 42

TGV ne circulant pas ce jour-là.

— N° du TGV

— Pictogrammes indiquant des particularités expliquées en bas de chaque tableau.

— Les lettres (a,b,c...) indiquent une correspondance.

N° du TGV		931	941	933
Restauration			🍽	
Paris-Gare de Lyon	D	7.24	10.47	13.12
Mâcon-TGV	A		12.28	
Bourg-en-Bresse	A	9.20	12.47	
Culoz	A	10.08		
Aix-les-Bains	A	10.25	13.49	16.06
Chambéry	A	a	14.04	
Annecy	A	11.01	a	16.43

— Horaires D: Départ
   A: Arrivée

SEMAINE TYPE			
Lundi	2	1	1
Mardi	2	2	1
Mercredi	2	3	1
Jeudi	2	3	1
Vendredi	2	4	1
Samedi	1	4	1
Dimanche	1	3	1

— La "SEMAINE TYPE" indique les jours normaux de circulation de chaque train ex: le TGV 941 circule le lundi.

JOURS PARTICULIERS				
OCTOBRE	Vendredi 23	2	4	4
	Samedi 24	1	4	4
NOVEMBRE	Mercredi 11		3	1

— Les "JOURS PARTICULIERS" indiquent les particularités de circulation de chaque train ex: le TGV 931 qui circule normalement le mercredi, ne circule pas le mercredi 11 novembre.

D Départ   **A** Arrivée

a Correspondance à Aix-les-Bains

🍽 Service restauration à la place, en 1ère classe, en réservation.

— En bas de chaque grille se trouve la légende des indications supplémentaires (restauration, particularités, correspondances...).

EXEMPLE FICTIF

(a) What is the number of the TGV which leaves Paris at 10.47?

(b) What time does the TGV No. 941 arrive in Chambéry?

(c) How long does it take the TGV No. 931 to get from Paris to Aix-les-Bains?

(d) What kind of service do you find on TGV No. 941? Can anyone get this service?

 Exercise 4

From the plan of the Île de la Cité on p. 117, describe what you see using the verbs 'se trouver' or 'être situé', and choosing a suitable preposition from the ones given below.

Example: La Préfecture de Police se trouve en face de la cathédrale de Notre-Dame.

(a) La Préfecture de Police

(b) La cathédrale de Notre-Dame

(c) Le Palais de Justice

(d) La rue de la Cité

(e) Le Marché aux Fleurs

(f) La place du Parvis Notre-Dame

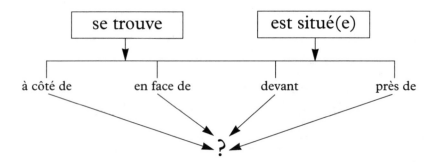

 Exercise 5

Replace 'le', 'la', 'l'' and 'les' in the following sentences with the correct forms of 'ce', 'cette', 'ces' (= 'this' or 'these').

Example: **Les** places sont libres.
Answer: **Ces** places sont libres.

(a) **Le** train est très confortable.

(b) C'est pour les enfants, **la** visite.

(c) **Le** grand bâtiment est le Louvre.

(d) **La** deuxième île s'appelle l'Île Saint-Louis.

(e) **L'**agent de police est devant la Préfecture.

(f) **Les** touristes aiment visiter Paris.

Écoutez
(Listening exercise)

 Exercise 6 Spontaneous dialogue Cycling in France

An English couple are on a cycling holiday in the north of France. You will hear them refer to the Côte d'Opal, on the Channel coast. They stop at a café and chat to a couple of locals. They get directions, using a map of the area. See how much of the conversation you can understand, using the exercises to help you.

(a) Here is the answer to the opening question. What was the question?

> Eh bien, on est là pour une semaine.

(b) The woman cyclist wants advice (conseil) about the best route to follow. Here is what she says:

> Quelle est la route que vous nous conseillez de suivre, via la route la plus agréable et la plus jolie?

How would you say in English the last part of this sentence (la route la plus agréable et la plus jolie)?

(c) The local person gives explanations with the aid of a map (une carte). Fill in the gaps in the explanation below, choosing words from the list given after the extract:

> Vous prenez la .... petite route à .... Sur la gauche il y a un .... pour piétons et .... Ce chemin va .... cette rivière. C'est vraiment très très .... D'abord c'est .... À bicyclette c'est ....

Fill in the gaps by choosing words from this box:

> droite = right   vélos = bikes   première = first
> le long de = along   plat = flat   chemin = path
> agréable = pleasant   parfait = perfect

(d) What will they ride through on their way to the airport of Le Touquet?

> une forêt ☐
> une plage ☐
> une rivière ☐
> un aéroport ☐

(e) The French word 'une randonnée' is used to mean 'a ride', 'a walk', 'a ramble'. (For example, the long-range French walking paths are called 'chemins de grande randonnée'.) The locals wish the cyclists a good trip using this word. What do they say?

12 Vous avez passé une journée agréable?
Talking about the day's events

Dialogues

Dialogue 1

When the Smiths' train arrives back in Caen that evening, Michel Lebrun is waiting for them.

John: Ah, Michel. C'est vraiment très gentil de venir nous chercher.

Michel: Mais je vous en prie. Ça me fait plaisir de vous rendre service. Vous avez passé une journée agréable?

Mary: Oui, vraiment formidable. On a eu de la chance avec le temps. Les enfants ont beaucoup aimé, mais ils sont épuisés maintenant. Nous avons tellement marché, mais nous avons vu plein de choses.

Michel: Ah, c'est fatigant, Paris. Mais quelle belle ville! Ma voiture est garée là, juste en face. Vous n'avez pas de bagages?

John: Non, seulement un petit sac. Nous avons pris des croque-monsieur et des hot dogs à la terrasse d'une brasserie.

Michel: Moi aussi, j'adore ça! Être assis à la terrasse d'un café et regarder les gens passer.

John: Oui, et on a mangé rapidement. Comme ça on a eu plus de temps pour visiter. Mais nous avons mangé dans le train pendant le voyage de retour.

Dialogue 2 (suite) (continued)

Michel: Alors, qu'est-ce que vous avez vu?

Mary: D'abord, on a pris l'autobus de la Gare Saint-Lazare à la place de la Concorde. On a remonté les Champs-Élysées jusqu'à l'Arc de Triomphe.

Michel: Mais dites donc! C'est assez loin, ça!

John: Oui, mais ça vaut la peine. Ça donne une impression générale de la ville.

Mary: Ensuite, on a pris un bus pour aller à la Tour Eiffel. Mais nous n'avons pas eu le temps d'y monter.

John: Non, pour ça il faut vraiment plus de temps.

Michel: Oui, sûrement. Ah, nous y voilà déjà.

John: Vous voulez bien entrer prendre quelque chose avec nous?

Michel: Avec plaisir, si ça ne vous dérange pas.

John: Mais non, au contraire.

Dialogue 3 (suite) (continued)

Mary: Je vais coucher les enfants. Je vous rejoins dans un quart d'heure.

Michel: Bien. Alors, bonne nuit, les enfants. Dormez bien ... Et après la Tour Eiffel alors, qu'est-ce que vous avez fait?

John: Nous avons mangé un snack tout près de la Tour Eiffel, nous avons marché encore un peu, et puis on a pris un bateau-mouche pour se reposer un peu, et pour voir la ville sous un autre angle. Nous avons vu l'Île de la Cité, et puis, après le bateau-mouche, on a pris quelque chose dans un café, et on a repris l'autobus pour aller vers Montmartre regarder l'église du Sacré Cœur.

Michel: Est-ce que vous avez eu le temps de faire un peu les magasins?

John: Oui, vers la fin de l'après-midi nous avons passé presque une heure dans les magasins de la rue de Rivoli. Moi, je n'ai rien acheté, mais Mary a trouvé un chemisier et une jolie robe. Elle n'a pas pu résister. Les enfants, eux, ont acheté quelques souvenirs.

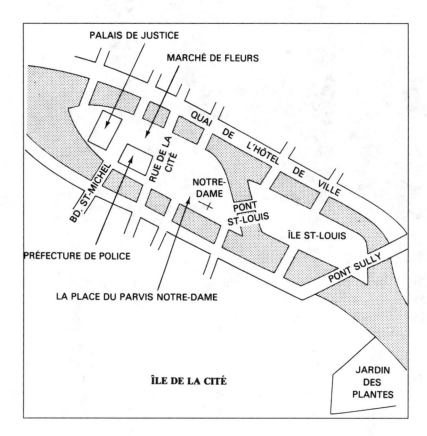

A bookseller's stand on the rive gauche of the Sein, Paris

Dialogue 4 (suite)

John: Voilà enfin Mary. Alors Michel, qu'est-ce que vous prenez?

Michel: Je prendrai bien un petit cognac, s'il vous plaît.

John: Moi aussi, je crois, et toi, Mary?

Mary: Moi, j'aimerais bien un Grand Marnier ce soir.

John: Monsieur, deux cognacs et un Grand Marnier, s'il vous plaît.

Garçon: Bien, monsieur.

Michel: Alors, les enfants sont au lit. Ils sont fatigués, sans doute.

Mary: Oui, c'est vrai, mais ils ont été ravis de cette journée. Demain matin, ils pourront faire la grasse matinée. On n'a rien prévu pour demain.

Michel: Vous avez acheté des souvenirs de Paris?

Mary: Pas grand-chose. Les enfants ont acheté des cartes postales et quelques petits trucs. Moi j'ai acheté une robe et un chemisier. John n'a rien acheté.

John: Malheureusement, Mary et moi n'avons pas eu le temps d'aller chercher des livres chez les bouquinistes. Pour ça, il nous faut une journée à Paris sans les enfants.

Michel: C'est vrai. Bien, il est déjà dix heures passées. Il faut que je m'en aille maintenant.

John: Oui. Alors, merci encore, hein? C'était gentil de venir nous chercher.

Michel: Il n'y a vraiment pas de quoi. Reposez-vous bien. Au revoir.

Vocabulary

Dialogue 1

(i) Useful expressions

c'est vraiment très gentil	it's really nice of you
ça me fait plaisir de	it's a pleasure to
plein de choses	lots of things

(ii) Nouns – masc. **Noun – fem.**

les bagages: luggage   la brasserie: café-bar
le croque-monsieur: cheese on toast
le hot-dog: hot dog
le voyage: journey

(iii) Other words

rendre service: to do a favour	épuisé(e): exhausted
agréable: pleasant; nice	fatigant(e): tiring
formidable: terrific	

Dialogue 2

(i) Useful expressions

dites donc!	An expression with a variety of meanings. Here it is an expression of surprise, for instance 'good heavens!'. But it is also used at the beginning of a statement to mean 'I say ...' or 'Tell me ...'
au contraire	on the contrary

(ii) Nouns – masc.

le bus: bus (same as 'autobus')
le contraire: opposite

(iii) Other words

d'abord: first of all

entrer: to come in; to go in; to enter

Dialogue 3

(i) Useful expressions

sous un autre angle — from another point of view
faire les magasins — to 'do' the shops

(ii) Nouns – masc.

Nouns – fem.

le snack: snack
un angle: angle
le magasin: shop
le chemisier: shirt-blouse
le souvenir: souvenir

la nuit: night
la fin: end
la robe: dress

(iii) Other words

coucher: to put to bed
je rejoins (rejoindre): I rejoin
dormir: to sleep
puis: then

autre: other
reprendre: to take again
presque: almost
résister: to resist

Dialogue 4

(i) Useful expressions

faire la grasse matinée — to have a long lie-in
on n'a rien prévu — we have nothing in mind; we have no plans

il nous faut ... — we need ...
dix heures passées — past ten o'clock
il faut que je m'en aille — I must be going
c'était gentil — it was kind
il n'y a vraiment pas de quoi — you really don't need to thank me

(ii) Nouns – masc.

Nouns – fem.

le cognac: brandy
le truc: thing
le livre: book
le bouquiniste: bookseller

la matinée: the morning *(grammar ref. 9.2 (f))*
la carte postale: postcard

(iii) Other words

prévu(e): planned
gras(se): fat
grand-chose: a lot

sans: without
hein? (See Chapter 13, *explanations (h)*)

Explanations

(a) *The perfect tense (grammar ref. 5.2 (f))*

acheter	to buy
J'ai **acheté** une robe.	I **have bought** OR I **bought** a dress.
Tu **as acheté** une robe.	You **have bought** OR You **bought** a dress.
Il **a acheté** une robe.	He **has bought** OR He **bought** a dress.
Elle **a acheté** une robe.	She **has bought** OR She **bought** a dress.
Nous **avons acheté** une robe.	We **have bought** OR We **bought** a dress.
Vous **avez acheté** une robe.	You **have bought** OR You **bought** a dress.
Ils **ont acheté** une robe. Elles **ont acheté** une robe.	They **have bought** OR They **bought** a dress.

The perfect tense is formed in French in the same way as in English, by combining the verb 'to have' (called the auxiliary verb) with the past participle. For example:

il	a	acheté
he	has	bought
vous	avez	parlé
you	have	spoken

The main difference to note is that, in French, this tense has two jobs to do. You can see from the table above that 'j'ai acheté' means both 'I bought' and 'I have bought'. In the same way, 'vous avez parlé' means both 'you spoke' and 'you have spoken'. Look at these further examples from the chapter:

Nous	**avons vu**	plein de choses.
We	**saw**	a lot of things
We	**have seen**	a lot of things.
Nous	**avons mangé**	un snack.
We	**ate**	a snack.
We	**have eaten**	a snack.

You always use the same tense in French, but you choose the English tense which best fits the circumstances.

(b) *Putting questions in the perfect tense*

Here again, English has two possibilities and French only one, as you see in the following examples:

Vous avez passé une journée agréable?	{ Have you had a nice day? { Did you have a nice day?
Vous avez mangé un snack?	{ Have you eaten a snack? { Did you eat a snack?
Qu'est-ce que vous avez vu?	{ What did you see? { What have you seen?

This is an example of where English is more complicated than French!

(c) *Perfect tense of regular verbs ending in '-ir' and '-re'*

The perfect tense of the regular '-er' verb 'acheter' is given above in section (a). As you see, the past participle of an '-er' verb ends in '-é': 'ache**ter**' → 'ache**té**'. The pattern for other regular verbs is as follows:

chois**ir** → chois**i**	attend**re** → attend**u**

Nous **avons attendu** un autobus.   We waited for a bus.
Vous **avez** déjà **choisi**?   Have you already chosen?

(d) *Perfect tense of irregular verbs*

A number of verbs have an irregular past participle, for example:

prendre	*to take*	*voir*	*to see*	*avoir*	*to have*
j'ai **pris**	I took	j'ai **vu**	I saw	j'ai **eu**	I had
être	*to be*	*faire*	*to do*	*pouvoir*	*to be able*
j'ai **été**	I was	j'ai **fait**	I did	j'ai **pu**	I was able

Nous **avons vu** plein de choses.   We saw a lot of things.
On **a pris** seulement un petit sac.   We only took a little bag.
Nous **avons pu** dîner dans le train.   We were able to have dinner on the
                                                                    train.

(e) *Negatives in the perfect tense (grammar ref. 5.10 (a))*

Nous **n'**avons **pas** eu le temps d'y monter.	We didn't have time to go up it.
Moi, je **n'**ai **rien** acheté.	I didn't buy anything.

As you see, the two parts of the negative (ne...pas / ne...rien / ne...personne) come either side of the *auxiliary verb*.

(f) Pour aller à... (grammar ref. 5.7 (d))

Nous avons pris un bus **pour aller** à la Tour Eiffel.

We took a bus (**in order**) **to go** to the Eiffel Tower.

When 'pour' is followed by the infinitive, it has the force of 'in order to...' do something.

Exercises

● *The key to these exercises begins on p.223.*

Parlez
(Speaking exercises)

Exercise 1   Did you have a good time?

Now it's your turn to talk with a friend about a day's visit to Paris. Look at the dialogue below and use the English prompts to help you prepare your role. Then turn on the recording and practise playing your part.

Amie: Alors, vous avez passé une bonne journée avec la famille?
You: *(Say that you had a good day. You walked a lot.)*
Amie: Qu'est-ce que vous avez fait tout d'abord?
You: *(Say that first of all you took the métro to the Île de la Cité and visited Notre-Dame. Then you had coffee, and afterwards went to the Louvre.)*
Amie: Alors, c'était une matinée très chargée. Vous avez déjeuné au restaurant?
You: *(Say no, there wasn't enough time. You ate sandwiches.)*
Amie: Vous avez eu le temps de faire des courses?
You: *(Not much. The children had just enough time to buy souvenirs.)*
Amie: Et il a fait beau temps pendant la visite?
You: *(Yes, you were lucky. It was fine all day.)*

Exercise 2

Now think of somewhere you have visited recently which you could talk about to a French friend. Think of how you would talk about what you did and what you saw, using phrases from the texts of this chapter.

Lisez et écrivez
(Reading and writing exercises)

Exercise 3

Imagine you are travelling in France and you come across the following short article about the Île d'Aix, offshore from La Rochelle. How much can you find out about the island? See if you can get enough information to answer the

CAP SUR L'ÎLE D'AIX

Tout d'abord, sur la carte de la France, on ne la voit pas. Et pourtant ce tout petit point, situé au large de La Rochelle, c'est bien elle, c'est l'île d'Aix. L'île à la forme d'un croissant qui doit mesurer approximativement 3 km de long et juste 700 m dans sa plus grande largeur.

Pour y aller, pas d'autre solution que le bateau. La traversée dure à peine une vingtaine de minutes. Très vite, les contours de l'île se précisent. Au sud, un vieux sémaphore domine un village fortifié. Ici, le visiteur pénètre dans un autre monde, silencieux, tranquille.

Le village, entouré de remparts, est constitué de petites maisons, sans étages, blanchies à la chaux et équipées de volets bleus. Pas de poteaux ni de fils électriques, ceux-ci ont été enterrés pour respecter la beauté des lieux. Pas de véhicules, ou si peu, l'île est beaucoup trop petite et l'on préfère tellement circuler à vélo ou en calèche. Pas de problème de surpopulation. Aix ne compte que 200 habitants. En d'autres termes, un petit paradis.

questions. Try to guess the meaning of words from the context, but look them up in a dictionary if you need further help.

(a) How do you learn from the opening sentence that the island is very tiny?
(b) What is the shape of the island compared to?
(c) How many ways are there of getting to the island?
(d) How long does the crossing last?
(e) What is striking for the visitor to the fortified village?
(f) Can you describe anything about the houses?
(g) Is there any traffic?
(h) How can the visitor get around?
(i) Is there a population problem?

Exercise 4

Below are three boxes. Box 1 contains various subjects. Box 2 contains the perfect tense of some irregular verbs. Box 3 contains the final parts of sentences. Write out as many full sentences as you can. Each sentence should contain an item from each box. (The *key* will give you seven examples of possible sentences but you may be able to find more than seven.)

Example: Ma femme a eu le temps de se reposer.

Box 1	Box 2	Box 3
J'	a eu	la Tour Eiffel
Ma femme	a vu	le temps de se reposer
Mon ami Michel	ai pris	souvent à Paris
Nous	a fait	voir la cathédrale
Vous	avons eu	le bus
Mes enfants	avez été	le train
Les Lebrun	ont pu	un choc
	ont repris	une visite à Paris

Écoutez

(Listening exercise)

 ### Exercise 5 Spontaneous dialogue Where did you go on holiday?

Luc and Brigitte get back from holiday and dine with their friends Monsieur and Madame Lefèvre. They tell about their holidays, and how they took plenty of time to get down to Provence.

(a) Below is a transcription of the opening statement by Brigitte. Listen to the tape and follow this text. When you feel that you have fully understood, cover the text and try to write out this paragraph as you listen to the tape.

Eh bien, vous savez qu'on voulait retrouver la Provence, et qu'on aime bien y aller tous les ans et surtout en mai quand il ne fait pas trop chaud, qu'il n'y a pas trop de touristes. Eh bien, sur la route on a découvert des endroits tellement jolis, qu'on a pris notre temps et finalement on a pris plus de dix jours avant d'arriver en Provence.

(b) In which region were they first of all?

en Suisse	☐
en Suisse Normande	☐
en Suisse Romande	☐
à Sisteron	☐

(c) What is the best way to discover this region (le moyen de découvrir la région)?

en vélo	☐
à pied	☐
en voiture	☐
en train	☐

(d) What region did they visit next?

Boulogne	☐
Bastogne	☐
Valognes	☐
Bourgogne	☐

(e) Name two towns visited during this part of their journey. Choose from the following list:

Bastogne
Barfleur
Beaune
Briançon
Deauville
Dijon
Dunkerque
Domrémy

(f) Luc is asked the question:

Vous avez goûté la cuisine de la région... est-ce que vous avez goûté des spécialités régionales?

He replies that they have never eaten so well in their lives. Can you write down the French reply?

(g) Brigitte thinks that a likely result of eating so well is that they have put on weight. How much? (She says, 'We must both have put on at least...'.)

On a dû prendre tous les deux au moins dix kilos. ☐
On a dû prendre tous les deux au moins un kilo. ☐
On a dû prendre tous les deux au moins deux kilos. ☐
On a dû prendre tous les deux au moins trois kilos. ☐

(h) Eventually they arrive at Aix-en-Provence. Fill in the gaps in the following passage explaining what they did at Aix.

On a .... la ville, les .... On a surtout passé notre temps à .... , à boire des cafés en ...., sous les platanes.

(i) Monsieur Lefèvre says that the conversation makes him want to set off too. He says:

Ça me donne bien envie de partir quand j'entends tout ça.

What would be the best way of saying this in English?

13 Vous l'avez vu? Witnessing an accident

Dialogues

Dialogue 1

Mary and the children get up late and have a leisurely breakfast. John went out a little earlier for a walk, but Mary grows rather anxious when he fails to return. She asks the hotelier if he has seen her husband.

Mary: Excusez-moi, monsieur. Est-ce que vous avez vu mon mari? Il est sorti il y a une heure pour acheter un journal et pour se promener. Il n'est pas encore rentré, et ça m'étonne.

Hôtelier: Je l'ai vu sortir, madame. Mais il n'est pas rentré, j'en suis sûr.

Mary: Je suis inquiète pour lui. Qu'est-ce qui a pu arriver?

Hôtelier: Ne vous inquiétez pas, madame. Il fait beau ce matin, et il est allé se promener, sans doute.

Mary: Vous croyez? J'espère que vous avez raison, mais je suis inquiète quand même.

Dialogue 2

John's delay is caused by the fact that he has witnessed an accident, and the police are questioning passers-by.

Agent: Excusez-moi, monsieur. Vous voulez bien répondre à quelques questions? Vous avez été témoin de l'accident, non?

John: Oui, j'ai vu l'accident.

Agent: Comment vous appelez-vous, monsieur?

John: John Smith. Je suis anglais.

Agent: Quelle est votre adresse à Caen?

John: Hôtel Beau Rivage.

Agent: Bien alors, qu'est-ce qui s'est passé exactement?

John: Eh bien, quand je suis arrivé ici au passage clouté, j'ai attendu pour traverser. Tout d'un coup, j'ai entendu un choc violent. Une voiture a brûlé le feu rouge et est rentrée dans une voiture qui arrivait en sens inverse.

Agent: Selon vous, c'était bien le chauffeur de la voiture rouge, la Citroën, qui était en tort?

John: À mon avis, oui.

Agent: Eh bien, merci, monsieur. On aura peut-être besoin de vous contacter pendant votre séjour ici, s'il faut vérifier les faits. Quel est votre numéro de téléphone à l'hôtel?

John: Alors, voilà la carte de l'hôtel. C'est le trente et un, soixante-quinze, quatre-vingt-douze, soixante-dix-neuf (31 75 92 79).

Agent: Merci, monsieur.

 ### *Dialogue 3*

John returns late to his hotel.

Hôtelier: Ah! Monsieur Smith, vous voilà enfin. Votre femme est très inquiète pour vous.

John: Oui, je suis en retard. C'est à cause d'un accident de la circulation. La police a voulu me poser des questions.

Hôtelier: Vous avez eu un accident?

John: Pas personnellement, mais j'ai été témoin d'un accident.

Hôtelier: Ah! Heureusement, monsieur. Je téléphone tout de suite à votre chambre pour prévenir votre femme ... Allô, Madame Smith ... oui, il est là. Il vient d'arriver ... Elle descend immédiatement, monsieur, avec les enfants. Alors, vous avez été témoin d'un accident?

John: Oui, quelqu'un ne s'est pas arrêté au feu rouge. Ça s'est passé à un carrefour.

Hôtelier: C'est incroyable, ça: brûler un feu rouge. Et ça arrive encore assez souvent, pourtant! Mais voilà votre femme.

Vocabulary

Dialogue 1

(i) Useful expressions

j'en suis sûr	I'm sure (of it)
je suis inquiète pour lui	I'm worried about him
qu'est-ce qui a pu arriver?	what can have happened?
vous avez raison	you're right

(ii) Nouns – masc.   Noun – fem.

le mari: husband	la raison: reason
le journal: newspaper	

(iii) Other words

sortir: to go out; to leave	arriver: to happen; to arrive
il y a: ago	avoir raison: to be right
étonner: to astonish	

Dialogue 2

(i) Useful expressions

tout d'un coup	all of a sudden
en sens inverse	in the opposite direction
à mon avis	in my opinion

(ii) Nouns – masc.   Noun – fem.

le témoin: witness	une adresse: address
un accident: accident	
le rivage: bank (of river)	
le passage clouté: pedestrian crossing	
le choc: collision; shock	
le sens: direction	
le tort: wrong; fault	
un avis: opinion	
le besoin: need	
le fait: fact	

(iii) Other words

se passer: to happen
inverse: opposite
brûler: to burn
brûler le feu rouge: to jump the lights
selon vous: according to you; in your
    opinion
être en tort: to be at fault; to be in the
    wrong

rentrer dans: to collide with; to crash
    into
violent(e): violent
avoir besoin de: to need
contacter: to contact
vérifier: to check

Dialogue 3

(i) Useful expressions

je suis en retard
tout de suite
et ça arrive encore assez souvent
    pourtant

I am late
immediately
and yet that happens quite often

(ii) Nouns – masc.

le retard: delay
le feu: traffic light (also 'fire')
le carrefour: crossroads

Noun – fem.

la circulation: traffic

(iii) Other words

à cause de: because of
poser (une question): to put/ask
    (a question)
personnellement: personally
prévenir: to warn

descendre: to go down
immédiatement: immediately
s'arrêter: to stop
incroyable: incredible

Explanations

(a) *More about the perfect tense*

Il **est** sorti.	He has gone out.
Il n'**est** pas encore rentré.	He hasn't come back yet.
Je **suis** arrivé.	I have arrived.

These examples show you that there are a number of verbs which form the
perfect tense with 'être' as the auxiliary verb instead of 'avoir'. There are two
main groups of verbs of this kind.

(i) Verbs of motion, for example: 'aller', 'arriver', 'monter'.

    Il **est allé** à Paris.   He went to Paris.
    Elle n'**est** pas encore **arrivée**.   She hasn't arrived yet.
    Nous **sommes montés** dans le train.   We got on the train.

(ii) Reflexive verbs, for example: 'se passer', 's'arrêter'.

Qu'est-ce qui **s'est passé**? What has happened?

Il ne **s'est** pas **arrêté**. He didn't stop.

(b) *Agreement of the past participle*

Study the following examples of verbs of motion:

John Smith n'est pas rentré.	John Smith hasn't returned.
Madame Smith n'est pas rentrée.	Mrs Smith hasn't returned.
Les enfants ne sont pas rentrés.	The children haven't returned.
Les femmes ne sont pas rentrées.	The women haven't returned.

Il est allé se promener.	He has gone for a walk.
Elle est allée se promener.	She has gone for a walk.
Ils sont allés se promener.	They have gone for a walk.
Elles sont allées se promener.	They (female) have gone for a walk.

You will see from these examples that when 'être' is used as the auxiliary verb for forming the perfect tense, the past participle agrees with the subject of the verb. As often happens with such agreements, they may make no difference to pronunciation, and are only important in correct written French. For example, in the two examples above, the verbs 'rentrer' and 'aller' each have four different forms, depending on whether the agreement is feminine or plural, but all four past participles in each case are pronounced exactly the same.

(c) *Perfect tense of reflexive verbs*

Note the pattern for the perfect tense from the following example:

se lever	
je me suis levé	nous nous sommes levés
tu t'es levé	vous vous êtes levé(s)
il s'est levé	ils se sont levés
elle s'est levée	elles se sont levées

(d) *Position of object pronoun*

In the perfect tense, the object pronouns (including reflexive pronouns), come immediately before the auxiliary verb, for example:

Je **l'ai** vu sortir. I saw **him** go out.

Qu'est-ce qui **s'est** passé? What has happened?

Il ne **s'est** pas arrêté. He didn't stop.

(e) *Verbs + direct infinitive*

Verbs of motion, such as 'aller', and a small number of other verbs such as 'voir', are followed by a direct infinitive:

Je l'ai **vu sortir**.	I saw him leaving.
Il est **allé se promener**.	He went for a walk.

(f) *'Avoir besoin de...' To need ... 'Avoir raison...' To be right...*

For example:

Vous avez raison.	You are right.
On aura besoin de vous.	We shall need you.

(g) *Because: Is it 'parce que...' OR 'à cause de...'?*

parce que = because

parce qu'ils sont fatigués **because** they are tired

à cause de = because of

à cause d'un accident **because of** an accident

(h) *Question tags 'non?' 'hein?'*

Vous avez été témoin de l'accident, **non?**	You were witness to the accident, **weren't you?**
Vous êtes anglais, **non?**	You're English, **aren't you?**
Qu'est-ce que tu feras, **hein?**	What will you do then, **eh?**
Ça suffit, **hein?**	That's enough, **isn't it?**

The meaning of this last example might depend on the tone of voice. It might be a shopkeeper measuring out something for you, or it might be an exasperated parent telling a child to behave: 'That's enough, OK?'. 'Hein?' is often used with a rising intonation at the end of a statement when it doesn't always have an English equivalent. For example, in Chapter 12 John said 'Alors, merci encore, hein?'.

(i) *Telephone numbers*

French telephone numbers consist of four groups of paired figures, and are expressed in the following way:

92 81 43 77 = quatre-vingt-douze; quatre-vingt-un; quarante-trois; soixante-dix-sept
54 32 26 66 = cinquante-quatre; trente-deux; vingt-six; soixante-six

(j) *Ago*

Note the use of 'il y a' to mean 'ago':

il y a une heure — an hour **ago**
il y a trois ans — three years **ago**

Exercises

● *The key to these exercises begins on p.224.*

Parlez

(Speaking exercises)

Exercise 1   Witness to an accident

You are asked to play the part of a woman being interviewed by the police about an accident witnessed earlier this morning. Look at the interview below and use the English prompts to help you prepare your role. You will also get some help from Dialogue 2 on p. 127. Then turn on the recording and practise playing the part of the interviewee.

Agent: Alors, madame, vous avez été témoin de cet accident sur la place du Théâtre ce matin, non?

Interviewee: *(Say yes, you saw the accident.)*

Agent: Bon, madame, alors si vous voulez bien me donner des détails. Vous êtes à l'Hôtel Bellevue, c'est ça? À quelle heure est-ce que vous êtes sortie de l'hôtel?

Interviewee: *(Say you came out of the hotel at about 9.05.)*

Agent: Et vous êtes allée à pied jusqu'à la place du Théâtre?

Interviewee: *(Say yes, you walked. Say you arrived at the square at about 9.15.)*

Agent: Oui, et qu'est-ce qui s'est passé?

Interviewee: *(Say that a car did not stop at the lights and that it hit another car that was passing.)*

Agent: Voulez-vous faire un petit dessin de l'accident s'il vous plaît? Et puis donner les détails sur cette fiche. Merci, madame.

Exercise 2

Now see if you can talk about everything you did yesterday. Here are a few ideas to start you off. Then, add in anything else which you have learned to say in the past tense.

Alors, hier je me suis levé à sept heures. J'ai déjeuné à huit heures et je suis sorti pour aller au travail. Puis ...

If you are female, the statements will *sound* the same, but the written version will have feminine agreements, for example:

Alors, hier je me suis levée à sept heures. J'ai déjeuné à huit heures et je suis sortie pour aller au travail. Puis ...

Lisez et écrivez

(Reading and writing exercises)

Exercise 3

Find a path through the 'flow chart' given below. Start with leaving the hotel, and then you can take any route as long as you follow an arrow. For each box, write a short sentence using the phrase given. You are talking about what happened in the *past*, so each of your sentences should be in the past tense. Some of the verbs take 'être' and some take 'avoir'. Start with, 'Je suis sorti(e) de l'hôtel.' Instead of just talking about yourself, try one of the columns as though talking about you and your family or friends (Nous sommes sortis de l'hôtel OR On est sorti de l'hôtel).

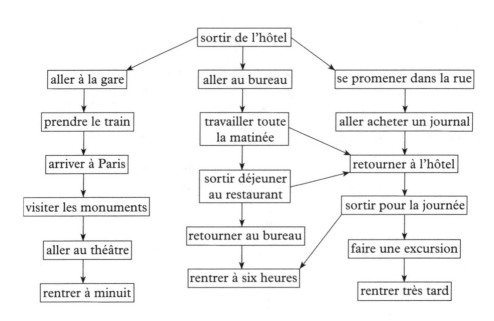

Exercise 4

You read the following short article in a local newspaper. You understand that there has been a tremendous storm (un orage spectaculaire) and absolutely torrential rain (des pluies diluviennes). Read the following questions and then see if you can find the information in the article. You might need to look one or two words up in a dictionary.

(a) Explain why Monsieur and Madame Delville were delayed on their way home on Saturday evening.
(b) What time did they finally arrive home?
(c) Why could Madame Delville not get off to sleep?
(d) What happened at about 3 or 4 am?
(e) How much can you describe of the scene that met them when they went downstairs?

NUIT D'ORAGE PRÈS D'AIX-EN-PROVENCE

Des pluies diluviennes se sont abattues sur la région d'Aix-en-Provence dans la soirée de samedi. Et vers 4 heures du matin un orage spectaculaire s'est déclaré. Madame Delville raconte à notre reporteur ce qui s'est passé.

"Mon mari et moi nous sommes rentrés assez tard d'une soirée passée avec des amis à Aix. Sur la route de retour nous nous sommes arrêtés plusieurs fois car la pluie tombait si fort qu'il était imposs-ible d'avancer. Nous sommes enfin arrivés chez nous vers deux heures du matin.

"Mon mari s'est couché tout de suite. Je ne pouvais pas m'endormir à cause du bruit que faisait la tempête. Je me suis demandée si le toit allait résister ou être arraché par la tempête.

"Tout à coup, il devait être 3 ou 4 heures du matin, il y a eu un effroyable coup de tonnerre et j'ai entendu en bas un bruit terrible. Je me suis levée, je me suis habillée rapidement. Mon mari s'est réveillé et, encore endormi, il répétait, 'Qu'est-ce qui s'est passé?' Je lui ai dit, 'Quelque chose est sûrement arrivé en bas à cause de l'orage. Il faut aller voir.' Il s'est vite habillé et nous sommes descendus.

"Quand nous sommes arrivés dans le salon je ne pouvais en croire mes yeux. Par la force de la tempête et de l'orage, la grande fenêtre donnant sur le jardin était grande ouverte et un très beau vase chinois ainsi que le grand miroir du salon étaient par terre, cassés en mille morceaux."

Exercise 5

Using the passage in Exercise 4, see if you can find the French equivalents for the following words and phrases:

(a) the return journey
(b) suddenly
(c) frightening
(d) downstairs
(e) I couldn't believe my eyes
(f) wide open

Écoutez

(Listening exercise)

Exercise 6   Spontaneous dialogue   How did it go?

A French teacher of English has returned home after taking a group of pupils to England. A colleague wants to find out how it went. They had a breakdown, had to get hold of another bus and arrived late at the boat. See how much of the conversation you can pick up, using the exercises to help focus your listening.

(a) Replace the verbs in the following gapped text, using the correct form of the perfect tense. The infinitive form of each verb, and its meaning, is given in the box below the extract.

> Nous .... très tôt le matin. On ....
> Cambridge, il était 6 heures et demie du matin. Et puis, on ....
> .... le bus jusqu'à Londres. On .... à Londres vers 9
> heures... Et puis à 4 heures on .... vers Douvres.

> | partir = to set off   quitter = to leave   prendre = to take |
> | :---: |
> | arriver = to arrive   partir = to set off |

(b) What problem did they have with their bus? What is the French for 'to break down'?

(c) The bus-driver made two phone calls to deal with the problem. Whom did he telephone?

(d) How much time did they lose because of this problem (on a perdu = we lost)?

une heure 45 minutes   ☐
une heure   ☐
plus d'une heure   ☐
45 minutes   ☐

(e) The colleague thinks his friend has been very lucky. He says:

> Vous avez eu une sacrée chance que l'autre chauffeur puisse venir comme ça, tout de suite.

Can you work out what this means?

(f) Arriving 10 minutes before departure is normally too late to get on the ferry. How did the group get onto the boat despite their late arrival? The teacher says:

> L'employé nous a aimablement laissés embarquer parce que je lui ai expliqué la situation.

What do you think this means? Choose from the following:

The employee was kind enough to let us embark because I
explained the situation to him. ☐

The employee was kind enough to let us embark because we had
plenty of time. ☐

The employee was kind enough to let us embark because he
thought there was no problem. ☐

The employee was kind enough to let us embark because he
realised we had broken down. ☐

(g) What was the reaction of the pupils on the trip?

Les enfants ont trouvé l'aventure..........

14 Vous avez des idées? Making more plans

Dialogues

Dialogue 1

The Smiths' friends from the South of France, Pierre and Anne-Marie Jacquier, are touring in Normandy, and have called in to see them. After a meal at the hotel they make plans for an excursion together.

Pierre: Alors, qu'est-ce que vous nous proposez pour cette excursion? Vous avez déjà des idées?

John: Pas vraiment. Il y a plusieurs possibilités, et c'est bien difficile de choisir. Mais nous n'avons pas encore visité Bayeux et on veut absolument voir la tapisserie.

Anne-Marie: Bonne idée. En plus, Bayeux n'est pas loin de la mer. Comme ça, on pourra s'arrêter en route et aller se baigner.

Mary: Oui, ça va faire plaisir aux enfants, et les plages de cette côte sont tellement belles.

Anne-Marie: Et à Bayeux on pourra aussi visiter la cathédrale. Vous n'y êtes pas encore allés?

John: Non, on a été jusqu'à Arromanches, mais on n'a pas eu le temps de visiter Bayeux ce jour-là.

Pierre: J'y suis allé il y a bien des années, mais j'y retournerai avec plaisir.

John: Alors, vous voulez aller directement à Bayeux? Ou est-ce qu'on va à la plage d'abord?

Anne-Marie: Je crois que ça va dépendre un peu du temps. Quelle est la météo pour demain?

Pierre: Regardons le journal. 'Temps ensoleillé sur les côtes du Calvados. Possibilité d'orages vers la fin de l'après-midi.' Alors, je crois qu'on commence par la plage.

John: Et puis, ensuite Bayeux. Et pour manger, qu'est-ce qu'on va faire?

Pierre: Il y a un petit restaurant à Bayeux qu'un ami m'a recommandé. Il paraît qu'il n'est pas cher du tout, et qu'on y mange bien.

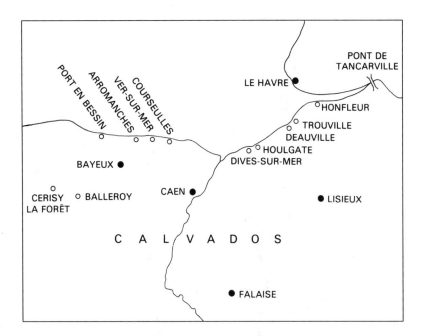

Mary: L'après-midi il faudra peut-être se détendre un peu et trouver un peu d'espace où les enfants pourront courir.

Pierre: Vers le sud de Bayeux il y a la forêt de Balleroy qui est très jolie, paraît-il. On pourra s'y arrêter pour jouer ou pour se promener, comme on voudra.

John: C'est une bonne idée. Et il y a aussi le château de Balleroy qui mérite une visite, paraît-il. Écoutez, j'ai ici le guide de la région, je vais vous lire un petit extrait: 'Le château de Balleroy, construit de seize cent vingt-six (1626) à seize cent trente-six (1636) par François Mansart, appartient depuis trois siècles aux marquis de Balleroy ... Cette construction, d'une grande sobriété, s'élève majestueusement dans l'unique rue du village', etc.

Pierre: Bien, bien, John. On sait bien qu'il vous faut un château par jour pour vous satisfaire pendant les vacances!

Anne-Marie: De toute façon, il y a quelque chose pour tout le monde pendant cette journée. Je crois qu'on va bien s'amuser, hein?

 ## Dialogue 2

They decide to set out in two cars for their excursion.

John: Alors, tout est prêt pour le départ. On y va dans deux voitures, je suppose.

Pierre: Oui, je crois qu'on est trop nombreux pour une seule. Où est-ce qu'on se retrouve si on se perd en route? C'est bien la route de Courseulles qu'on prend, non?

John: Oui, et après il faut suivre la route de la côte. On se retrouvera à Ver-sur-Mer. Là on va pouvoir nager, et nous ne serons qu'à quelques kilomètres de Bayeux.

Pierre: Bien. Mais ne roulez pas trop vite. Notre voiture est assez vieille!

Bayeux Cathedral

 ### Dialogue 3

After a couple of hours on the beach they decide to move on.

Mary: Quel temps magnifique. On est si bien ici, mais il va falloir qu'on s'en aille bientôt, je crois. Autrement on n'aura pas le temps de déjeuner et de tout voir.

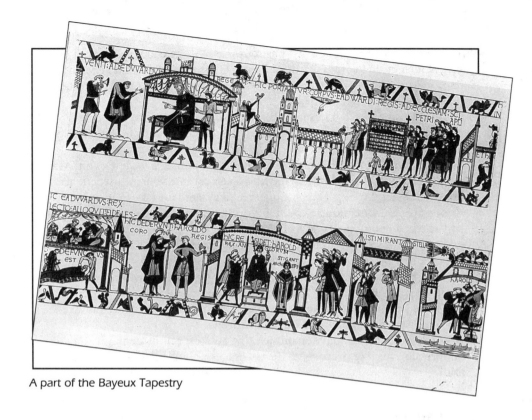

A part of the Bayeux Tapestry

Pierre: Que c'est bon, le soleil! Mais vous avez raison. Je vais dire aux enfants de s'habiller.

Anne-Marie: J'ai le temps d'écrire encore une carte postale?

Mary: Mais bien sûr. Moi aussi, j'ai des cartes à mettre à la poste.

John: On achètera des timbres à la poste de Bayeux.

* * *

Mary: Bonjour, madame. Je voudrais des timbres pour cartes postales. C'est pour l'Angleterre, mais c'est le même tarif dans tous les pays de l'Union Européenne, non?

Dame au guichet: Oui, pour une carte postale c'est le même tarif que pour une lettre. C'est 2F 50. Mais il y a le tarif lent à 2F 20, si vous voulez.

Mary: Bon, alors donnez-moi quatre timbres à 2F 50 et un timbre à 2F 20, s'il vous plaît.

Dialogue 4 Dans la forêt In the forest

After lunch in the restaurant, and a visit to the cathedral and tapestry, they drive out to the forest and relax.

John: C'est tellement varié, le paysage normand. Il y a la côte, la plaine autour de Caen, toute cette verdure des prés, des pommiers et des bois, et ici il y a la forêt.

Pierre: Oui, c'est vrai – et ce n'est pas tout. Le paysage change encore si on va vers Rouen et de l'autre côté de la Seine. C'est très différent de chez nous dans le Midi. Mais pour vous, ce paysage ressemble beaucoup à certaines parties de l'Angleterre, non?

Mary: C'est vrai que ces pâturages, ces vaches, ces pommiers, tout cela ressemble à certains paysages du sud de l'Angleterre; dans le Somerset ou dans le Devon, par exemple.

John: D'ailleurs, le département du Calvados est jumelé avec le Devon. Mais il ne faut pas oublier quand même que Caen est une ville industrielle très importante. Et il y a Le Havre, qui est le deuxième port de France, et Rouen avec sa zone industrielle. La Normandie n'est pas seulement un pays de vaches, de pommes et de fromages.

Anne-Marie: Vous avez raison, mais l'agriculture reste quand même très importante pour l'économie de la région.

John: Oui, c'est vrai. Il y a ce côté agricole et aussi le côté historique, comme la tapisserie de Bayeux, ces belles églises et ces châteaux.

Mary: Trois semaines de vacances, ce n'est certainement pas assez pour tout voir. Ce n'est qu'un début. Nous reviendrons.

John: Oui, c'est sûr. Et maintenant, je crois qu'il est temps de partir. J'ai l'impression qu'il se prépare un de ces orages prévus pour la fin de l'après-midi.

Vocabulary

Dialogue 1

(i) Useful expressions

bonne idée	good idea
en route	on the way
il y a bien des années	many years ago
pas cher du tout	not at all expensive
de toute façon	in any case

(ii) Nouns – masc.   **Nouns – fem.**

un orage: thunderstorm	une idée: idea
le sud: south	la possibilité: possibility
un extrait: extract	la route: road
le siècle: century	la tapisserie: tapestry
le marquis: marquis	la météo: weather forecast
le village: village	la forêt: forest
	la construction: building
	la sobriété: restraint; sobriety

(iii) Other words

proposer: to suggest
plusieurs: several
absolument: absolutely
faire plaisir à: to please
se baigner: to bathe; to swim
bien des: many; a lot of
directement: directly; straight
dépendre de: to depend on
ensoleillé(e): sunny
commencer par: to begin with
recommander: to recommend
il paraît: it seems
cher (chère): expensive

se détendre: to relax
courir: to run
jouer: to play
mériter: to deserve
lire: to read
construit(e): built
appartenir à: to belong to
s'élever: to rise
majestueusement: majestically
unique: only
satisfaire à: to satisfy
s'amuser: to enjoy oneself; to have a
  good time

Dialogue 2

(i) Other words

le départ: departure
supposer: to suppose
seul: single; one only
se retrouver: to meet up

suivre: to follow
nager: to swim
rouler: to drive; to travel (by car)

Dialogue 3

(i) Useful expressions

il va falloir qu'on s'en aille
que c'est bon, le soleil!
c'est le même tarif
quatre timbres à 2F 50

we'll have to go
isn't this sun marvellous!
it's the same rate
four stamps at 2F 50

(ii) Nouns – masc.

le soleil:sun
le timbre: stamp
le tarif: rate

Nouns – fem.

la poste: post office
la lettre: letter

(iii) Other words

autrement: otherwise
s'habiller: to get dressed
écrire: to write

mettre: to put
mettre à la poste: to post (a letter)

Dialogue 4

(i) Useful expressions

de l'autre côté de	on the other side of
ce n'est qu'un début	it's just a beginning
nous reviendrons	we'll come again
il se prépare un orage	a storm is brewing

(ii) Nouns – masc.

Nouns – fem.

le pré: meadow
le pommier: apple tree
les bois: woods
le Midi: South of France
le pâturage: pasture
un exemple: example
le département: department
le pays: country

la plaine: plain
la verdure: greenery
la vache: cow
la zone: zone
l'agriculture: farming; agriculture
l'économie: economy

(iii) Other words

varié(e): varied
autour de: around
changer: to change
différent (de): different (from)
ressembler à: to resemble

d'ailleurs: moreover
jumelé(e): twinned
industriel(le): industrial
agricole: agricultural
historique: historical

Explanations

(a) *Relative pronouns: who; which (grammar ref. 4.2)*

(i) 'Qui'

La forêt de Balleroy	**qui**	est très jolie.
Balleroy forest	**which**	is very pretty.
Le château de Balleroy	**qui**	mérite une visite.
Balleroy castle	**which**	deserves a visit.
Les enfants	**qui**	jouent sur la plage.
The children	**who**	are playing on the beach.
Un ami	**qui**	habite dans le Midi.
A friend	**who**	lives in the South.

'Qui' is called the relative pronoun, and stands at the beginning of a relative clause. It can mean either 'who' or 'which', and it is always written in the same way.

'Qui' meaning 'who' or 'which' is the *subject* of the relative clause. If you look at the examples above , you will see that 'qui' replaces the subject of the verb:

qui [les enfants] jouent sur la plage
qui [le chateau] mérite une visite

(ii) 'Que'

Un ami	**que**	je connais depuis longtemps.
A friend	**(whom)**	I have known a long time.
Les collègues	**que**	vous invitez chez vous.
The colleagues	**(whom)**	you invite home.
Un restaurant	**qu'**	un ami m'a recommandé
A restaurant	**(which)**	a friend recommended to me.
La route	**qu'**	on prend pour aller à la côte.
The road	**(which)**	you take to go to the coast.

'Que' is also a relative pronoun, and also stands at the beginning of a relative clause. It can *also* mean either 'who' or 'which'. It is written 'qu'' when it comes before a vowel as in the examples above (qu'un ami...; qu'on...).

'Que' meaning 'who' or 'which' is the *object* of the relative clause. If you look at the examples above, you will see that 'que' replaces the object of the verb:

qu'on prend [on prend **la route**]
que vous invitez [vous invitez **les collègues**]

In English, the relative pronoun (direct object) can often be left out, for example, 'a friend (...) I have known for a long time'; 'the road (...) you take to go to the coast'. 'Qui' and 'que' can never be left out in French.

(b) *Indirect object pronouns (grammar ref. 4.1)*

Look again at the *explanations* in Chapter 10 which explained the use of *direct* object pronouns. Some verbs are followed by an *indirect* object. In French the preposition that indicates an indirect object is 'à'. For example:

Subject	*Verb*	*Direct object*	*Indirect object*
Je	donne	le livre	à mon ami.
Je	donne	le livre	à mes amis.

If the indirect object is replaced by a pronoun, these sentences change as follows:

Je **lui** donne le livre.	I give the book **to him**. (OR I give **him** the book.)
Je **leur** donne le livre.	I give the book **to them**. (OR I give **them** the book.)

Note that in English the word 'to' may be left out.

Apart from 'lui' (to him / to her) and 'leur' (to them), the indirect object pronouns are the same as the object pronouns. For example:

Un ami **me** recommande un restaurant.	A friend recommends a restaurant **to me**.
Qu'est-ce que vous **nous** proposez?	What do you suggest (**to us**)?

Once again, in this latter example, English does not express the indirect object, but leaves it to be understood or implied.

There are a number of French verbs which take an indirect object. You can spot them because the dictionary will tell you that 'à' comes between the verb and its object, for example:

plaire à quelqu'un	to please somebody
ressembler à quelqu'un	to look like somebody

This explains the following sentences:

Est-ce que ça **lui** plaît?	Does he/she like it?
Son fils **lui** ressemble.	His son looks like him.

(c) *'y'* *there*

You have already met 'y' in the phrase 'il y a'. The usual meaning of 'y' is 'there'. Note the use in the following examples:

J'**y** suis allé.	I went **there**.
On **y** mange bien.	You eat well **there**.
On pourra s'**y** arrêter.	We shall be able to stop **there**.

(d) *Expressions of quantity*

It has already been explained that expressions of quantity are normally followed by 'de', as in 'beaucoup **de** pain'. Note the following two exceptions which occur in this chapter:

Il y a **bien des** années.	**Many** years ago.
Il y a **plusieurs** possibilités.	There are **several** possibilities.

146 *MASTERING FRENCH*

Exercises

● *The key to these exercises begins on p.225.*

Parlez
(Speaking exercise)

Exercise 1   Visiting England

Now imagine that you have French friends staying with you and you are discussing a possible excursion. They will want to know the sort of things there are to see in the area. Use the prompts below to help you prepare for the conversation, but the details will depend on your own area. On p. 225 there is a sample answer for you to compare with your own, but which is based upon the author's own area of Exeter and surrounding country.

You: *(Ask your friends what they would like to do tomorrow.)*
Amie: Eh bien, on ne connaît pas du tout cette région de l'Angleterre. On aimerait beaucoup voir un peu le paysage / la ville, et il y a peut-être des châteaux ou des monuments qu'on aimerait visiter. Qu'est-ce que vous nous proposez?
You: *(Tell them about the town or village where you live. Anything to see there? Cathedral or church? Say something about the countryside round about. Anything else you would like them to see?)*
Amie: Mais ça paraît très intéressant. Et est-ce qu'on aura du beau temps demain?
You: *(Say that it's going to be fine, according to the weather forecast (selon la météo).)*

Lisez et écrivez
(Reading and writing exercises)

Exercise 2

Imagine you are asked a question. For example:

Vous connaissez la tapisserie?

You don't know which tapestry is being referred to, so you ask:

Quelle tapisserie?

You are then given an explanation which uses a relative pronoun. For example:

La tapisserie **qui** est à Bayeux.

Try writing out the sentences which correspond to the cues in English in the examples below. Decide whether you should use 'qui' or 'que'.

(a) Vous connaissez la cathédrale?	Quelle cathédrale?
(The cathedral which is in Bayeux.)	
(b) Vous connaissez la forêt?	Quelle forêt?
(The forest which is south of Bayeux.)	
(c) Vous avez le timbre?	Quel timbre?
(The stamp which you bought.)	
(d) Vous avez l'argent?	Quel argent?
(The money which I gave you.)	
(e) Vous connaissez mon ami?	Quel ami?
(The friend who lives in the Midi.)	
(f) Vous avez visité le château?	Quel château?
(The castle which is in the forest.)	

Exercise 3

In the following sentences you are asked to carry out an action. For example:

Donnez cette lettre à Madame Lebrun, s'il vous plaît.

You reply that you have already done so, changing the indirect object for a pronoun:

Je lui ai déjà donné la lettre.

Write answers to the following requests, following the same model.

(a) Donnez cette bouteille à Monsieur Smith, s'il vous plaît.
(b) Écrivez cette carte postale à votre ami, s'il vous plaît.
(c) Envoyez ce paquet à l'hôtelier, s'il vous plaît.
(d) Proposez une excursion à vos amis.
(e) Téléphonez aux enfants, s'il vous plaît.

Exercise 4

Imagine you spent two days in Paris last week. Opposite are pictures of the places you saw and visited. Write a short paragraph in French about what you did, using the following verbs:

arriver: to arrive
marcher: to walk
flâner: to stroll
se promener: to go for a walk

remonter: to walk up
monter: to go up
visiter: to visit
se reposer: to rest

You can start off:

La semaine dernière je suis allé(e) passer deux jours à Paris...

Then continue:

Le premier jour...
Le deuxième jour...

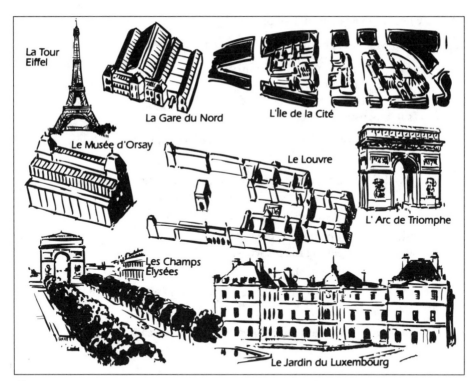

La Tour Eiffel
La Gare du Nord
L'Île de la Cité
Le Musée d'Orsay
Le Louvre
L'Arc de Triomphe
Les Champs Elysées
Le Jardin du Luxembourg

Écoutez
(Listening exercise)

Exercise 5 Spontaneous dialogue A birthday surprise

Saturday is Monsieur Desprès' birthday (l'anniversaire de papa). His wife and his daughter Silvie are planning a surprise for him. Will it be a surprise party with friends invited round, or will they take him out to celebrate? Listen and see if you can pick out the main points of their conversation.

(a) These celebrations should be special. Can you hear which birthday he is celebrating?

(b) The first idea suggested is 'une soirée surprise'. Who would be invited and what would they serve?

(c) Silvie is not really in favour of this first idea. She has several reasons. What are they? Complete the following sentences choosing phrases from the box.

D'abord, rappelle-toi …	mes examens à cette époque-là
Et puis, pense …	il n'aime pas tellement les grandes fêtes
Et moi je vais avoir …	tu fasses tout ça toute seule
Il faudra que …	au travail que ça va nous donner

Now write out the sentences in full and see if you can give an English version of each one.

(d) So what is Silvie's alternative proposal?

(e) What do we know about the place they now propose?

> Is it in the town or in the country?
> Has it a garden or not?
> Is the food reckoned to be good or mediocre?
> Is it expensive or cheap?

(f) Silvie mentions two things that will be ready when he arrives home (quand il rentrera). What are they?

(g) When will they spring the surprise on him and tell him he is going to a restaurant?

> When he is starting his champagne ☐
> When he has finished his champagne ☐
> When he is opening his presents ☐
> When he is given his presents ☐

(h) Where will they want to sit in the restaurant (une table avec vue sur le jardin)?

(i) Can you guess the meaning of 'un gâteau d'anniversaire'?

15 Quand j'étais à l'ecole... Describing how things used to be

 Dialogue

As their holiday draws to a close, the Smiths spend a pleasant evening together with the Lebruns and the Jacquiers. After a meal they chat about a variety of topics.

Pierre: Dites-moi, John, est-ce que vous vous êtes toujours intéressé à l'étude des langues?

John: Oui, même quand j'étais jeune, les langues m'intéressaient. Il y avait certaines difficultés pour moi à l'école. Ma famille n'était pas riche et nous habitions à la campagne. Alors, tous les jours je devais faire deux kilomètres à pied pour aller prendre l'autobus de l'école.

Pierre: Mais vous ne regrettez pas ces difficultés?

John: Bien sûr que non. Mes parents étaient si fiers quand j'ai passé l'équivalent anglais du baccalauréat. Et évidemment il y a beaucoup de satisfaction à poursuivre ses études. Mais vous aussi Pierre, vous aviez des difficultés à cette époque-là.

Pierre: Oui, surtout parce que j'étais aussi à la campagne comme vous, et on avait des problèmes de transport. Vous êtes caennais, Michel, ce n'était pas pareil pour vous en ville.

Michel: Non, ce n'était pas pareil. Surtout que je suis plus âgé que vous. J'étais à l'école primaire déjà en mil neuf cent quarante-quatre (1944), et on nous a évacués à la campagne avant l'invasion. Quand nous sommes revenus à Caen après les bombardements, c'était le chaos. Peu à peu on a commencé à rebâtir, mais pour les enfants c'était une période difficile. J'ai quitté l'école à l'âge de quinze ans pour commencer à travailler dans l'entreprise où je me trouve à présent.

John: Vous êtes resté plus de trente ans dans la même compagnie?

Michel: Oui, j'y étais très bien, alors, pourquoi changer? C'était la période de la reconstruction de Caen, parce que la ville était en ruines après les bombardements. Autrefois Caen était une ville de trente mille (30,000) habitants, mais depuis la guerre Caen est devenu peu à peu un des centres

Arromanches

régionaux les plus importants de France, avec plus de cent mille (100,000) habitants. La vie ici a beaucoup changé – mais c'est pareil aussi chez vous dans le Midi.

Anne-Marie: Oui, c'est certainement pareil dans les grandes villes et près des zones industrielles. Mais à la campagne, chez nous, beaucoup de choses ne changent pas vite. La vie est aussi paisible qu'avant, aussi lente que quand on était petit.

Mary: Pour moi, c'est le charme du Midi; on retrouve toujours le même rythme de vie qu'autrefois. J'y suis allée la première fois quand j'étais écolière et nous avons fait un échange scolaire. Je me rappelle que tout était plus calme, plus décontracté que chez nous.

Pierre: C'est peut-être à cause du soleil. À mon avis, on a besoin de conserver son énergie quand il fait tellement chaud.

John: C'est vrai que la chaleur du Midi, c'est peut-être l'impression la plus frappante pour un jeune Anglais qui visite la région pour la première fois.

Michel: Et c'est peut-être aussi à cause du climat du nord que les Normands étaient si énergiques dans le temps. Rappelez-vous que c'était la race la plus aventureuse de l'époque. On les retrouvait partout, en Angleterre, en Italie ...

Mary: Oui, mais il faut peut-être se méfier de trop généraliser. Regardez les Romains, eux venaient d'un pays chaud, après tout.

Nicole: L'influence du climat sur l'histoire, c'est peut-être le sujet le plus difficile à résoudre. Ça ressemble aux discussions sur les caractéristiques nationales. On n'en finit jamais.

Pierre: C'est vrai. Mais il faut quand même admettre que les Anglais et les

152　*MASTERING FRENCH*

Normands ont beaucoup de traits communs. Ils sont tous les deux plus flegmatiques que les gens du Midi ..., il faut bien le reconnaître!

John: Vous êtes contestataire, mon vieux Pierre. Vous savez bien qu'il y a des gens du Midi qui sont excessivement flegmatiques et des Normands qui sont même fougueux!

Nicole: Vous voyez, c'est exactement ce que je vous disais. On n'en sortira pas!

Vocabulary

(i) Useful expressions

bien sûr que non	certainly not
ce n'était pas pareil	it wasn't the same
peu à peu	little by little
dans le temps	in the old days
il faut se méfier de généraliser	one must be careful not to generalise
on n'en sortira pas	there's no end to it

(ii) Nouns – masc.   Nouns – fem.

un équivalent: equivalent
le baccalauréat: (see *explanations (c)*)
le transport: transport
le bombardement: bombing
le chaos: chaos
un habitant: inhabitant
le rythme: rhythm
un écolier: schoolboy
un échange: exchange
le nord: north
le Romain: Roman
le sujet: subject
le trait: feature

une étude: study
la langue: language (also 'tongue)
la difficulté: difficulty
la campagne: country
la satisfaction: satisfaction
une époque: period; era
une écolière: schoolgirl
une invasion: invasion
une entreprise: firm; company
la compagnie: company
la période: period
la reconstruction: rebuilding
la ruine: ruin
la guerre: war
la vie: life
l'énergie: energy
la race: race (of people)
une influence: influence
l'histoire: history; story
la discussion: discussion
la caractéristique: characteristic

(iii) Other words

s'intéresser à: to be interested in
jeune: young
riche: rich
habiter: to live
je devais (devoir): I had to
fier (fière): proud
passer (un examen): to take (an exam)
poursuivre: to pursue
caennais(e): native to Caen (see
  explanations (c) (ii)
pareil(le): similar
primaire: primary
évacuer: to evacuate
rebâtir: to rebuild
quitter: to leave
travailler: to work
à présent: now; at present
autrefois: in the old days
devenir: to become
régional(e): regional
paisible: peaceful

lent(e): slow
toujours: still
scolaire: educational
se rappeler: to remember
calme: quiet; calm
décontracté(e): relaxed
conserver: to preserve; to conserve
frappant(e): striking
énergique: energetic
aventureux (aventureuse): adventurous
partout: everywhere
se méfier de: to beware of ...; to take
  care not to ...
national(e): national
finir: to finish
admettre: to admit
commun(e): common; in common
flegmatique: phlegmatic
reconnaître: to recognise
contestataire: argumentative
excessivement: excessively

fougueux (fougueuse): fiery; impetuous

Explanations

(a) *The imperfect tense (grammar ref. 5.2 (b))*

There are three occasions when the imperfect is used in talking about the past.

(i) The action described was a regular habit:

Nous **habitions** à la campagne.	We **used to live** in the country.
J'**allais** tous les jours à l'école.	I **used to go** every day to school.

(ii) The action described was continuous, without a clear beginning and end:

J'**allais** à l'école quand j'ai vu mon ami Jean.	I **was going** to school when I saw my friend John.

In this sentence, 'I was going' is past continuous (= imperfect), but 'I saw' is past definite and recounts a single, completed event. This verb is therefore in the perfect tense in French. (See Chapter 12.)

(iii) There is a description of something in the past. The description might be a landscape or scene:

La ville **était** tout en ruines.

a state of affairs:

Ma famille **n'était pas** riche.

a state of mind:

Mes parents **étaient** si fiers.

You can expect to find perfect and imperfect tenses together both in spoken and written French. It depends on whether the speaker/writer is referring to a single, completed event (perfect) or a continuous, habitual event (imperfect). Look at the following short, amended extract from the text of the chapter, and see if you can give reasons for the choice of tense:

Je **suis allée** dans le Midi la première fois quand j'**étais** écolière et nous **avons fait** un échange scolaire. Tout **était** plus calme que chez nous.

(b) *Comparative and superlative of adjectives (grammar ref. 3.4)*

You learned about comparative and superlative of adjectives in Chapter 7. This chapter gives further examples:

Je suis **plus âgé que** vous.　　　　　I am **older than** you.
Le sujet **le plus difficile** à résoudre. **The most difficult** subject to resolve.
Un des centres régionaux **les plus**　 One of **the most important** regional
　importants de France.　　　　　　centres in France.

In this chapter there are examples of another way to make comparisons:

La vie	est	**aussi** paisible	**qu'**avant.
Life	is	**as** peaceful	**as** before.
La vie	est	**aussi** lente	**que** quand on était petit.
Life	is	**as** slow	**as** when one was small.

(c) *Notes on vocabulary*

(i) The 'baccalauréat' is the French equivalent of the A-level examination. A pass in the 'bac' (as it is called) gives right of entry to most university courses.

(ii) The adjective 'caennais' is used to describe someone who is a native of Caen, in the same way that 'parisien' is used for someone from Paris.

(d) *Talking about nationality*

Note that when referring to nationality or to being a native of a town or region:

(i) Adjectives have a small letter, for example:

la langue française; le paysage normand; le vin français; un passeport anglais

(ii) Nouns have a capital letter. They have the appropriate feminine or plural endings if they refer to women or to a group of people, for example:

un Anglais / une Anglaise; un Français / une Française; les Normands

Exercises

● *The key to these exercises begins on p.226.*

Parlez
(Speaking exercises)

Exercise 1

Here are some notes you might have jotted down to describe a few details of the life of some imaginary retired French lady you have interviewed. Using this

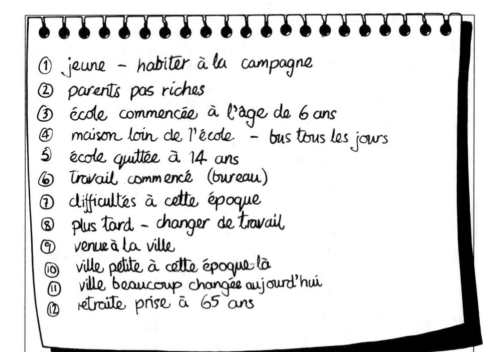

① jeune – habiter à la campagne
② parents pas riches
③ école commencée à l'âge de 6 ans
④ maison loin de l'école – bus tous les jours
⑤ école quittée à 14 ans
⑥ Travail commencé (bureau)
⑦ difficultés à cette époque
⑧ plus tard – changer de travail
⑨ venue à la ville
⑩ ville petite à cette époque-là
⑪ ville beaucoup changée aujourd'hui
⑫ retraite prise à 65 ans

information, tell the life story of this person. For example:

Quand cette dame était jeune, elle habitait à la campagne...

Choose carefully whether to use the imperfect or the perfect tense for each of the verbs.

Exercise 2

Now make notes about your own life in the same way and imagine telling someone about yourself, about your schooldays, your work and so on. Use the dialogue to help you formulate what you want to say.

Lisez et écrivez
(Reading and writing exercises)

Exercise 3

In Box 1 are a group of expressions of time. You would expect to find an imperfect tense after each one, because they introduce descriptions of past events. In Boxes 2–4 are the elements you need to build up sentences by selecting appropriate items. Write out as many meaningful sentences as you can, using one expression or phrase from each box. Remember to make adjectives agree, if necessary, and to put the verbs into the imperfect.

Examples: Autrefois les villages étaient plus calmes.
À cette époque-là Pierre s'intéressait aux langues.

Box 1
autrefois
dans le temps
tous les jours
à cette époque-là
quand il était jeune

Box 2	Box 3	Box 4
les villages	prendre	plus petit
la ville	être	à la campagne
les langues	habiter	plus paisible
mes parents	s'intéresser à	à l'école
la campagne	aller	plus calme
la vie		l'autobus
Pierre		les langues
il		

Exercise 4

Read the following article about the death of an immigrant living in the XXe arrondissement in Paris. Try to guess the meaning of words from the context, but look them up in a dictionary if you need further help.

La mort de Makome

Makome est arrivé en France à l'âge de 5 ans. Il vivait avec ses parents dans le XXe arrondissement – l'un des quartiers de Paris où la population immigrée est la plus importante. Dans les jours qui ont précédé son arrestation, il sortait peu: la police venait de lui confisquer son scooter parce qu'on l'accusait d'avoir volé un phare. Sa famille avait peur des problèmes avec la police, alors on lui conseillait de se tenir tranquille. Mais le 6 avril, à 4h 30 du matin, la police l'a arrêté avec deux de ses amis car il était en possession d'une cargaison de cigarettes d'une valeur de 20 000F. Tous trois sont mis au commissariat des Grandes-Carrières. À midi les deux amis étaient relâchés tandis qu'un inspecteur faisait subir à Makome un nouvel interrogatoire. Vers 16 heures, l'inspecteur a tiré une balle à bout portant dans la tête du jeune Zaïrois.

Adapted from the Guardian, 15 June 1993

(a) What do you learn about the XXe arrondissement in Paris?
(b) Why did Makome's parents advise him to lie low on the days preceding his arrest?
(c) What was the reason for Makome's arrest on 6 April?
(d) Until what time were Makome's two friends kept in custody?
(e) What happened to Makome after his friends had been released?

Écoutez

(Listening exercise)

Exercise 5 Spontaneous dialogue Childhood holidays

Hélène talks to Patrick about memories of childhood holidays. She talks about the time the journey used to take down to Nice and the old-fashioned hotel at Thouars where the family used to stop to break their journey, and how she has since tried to find the place again. Try to pick out the key items in the conversation and use the exercises to help your comprehension.

(a) Why is Hélène so keen to go to Nice?

Because she hasn't been there since she was 15. ☐
Because she lived there for 15 years. ☐
Because she hasn't been there for 15 years. ☐

(b) Patrick says:

Tu allais à Nice quand tu étais gamine.

What do you think the word 'gamine' means?

(c) Fill in the gaps in the following sentence spoken by Hélène:

On y allait .... les ans, au mois de ...., avec mon ...., ma sœur et .... parents.

158   *MASTERING FRENCH*

(d) There was no motorway in those days (à l'époque il n'y a pas d'autoroute), so how long did the journey take?

(e) Insert the verbs into the following gapped text. The infinitive forms are given in the box and you need to put them into the imperfect. Hélène is saying 'we used to...'.

On .... assez tôt le matin. On .... vers 11 heures. On .... des courses pour le piquenique du déjeuner.

partir = to set off   s'arrêter = to stop   faire = to do

(f) Patrick says he can't imagine something. His sentence begins:

Je ne peux pas imaginer...

What does he go on to say he can't imagine:

Hélène stopping to have a picnic ☐
Hélène's family having a picnic ☐
Hélène's father picnicking on the grass ☐

(g) Hélène's father tries to find excuses not to picnic. Hélène gives three excuses as examples. Two are insects and one refers to the weather. Can you guess at the meaning? Here are the excuses:

les moustiques
il y avait des guêpes
il faisait trop chaud

(h) What did he manage to do as an alternative to the picnic? Complete the sentence:

Naturellement, il optait toujours pour aller manger...

(i) Why did they always stay in the hotel at Thouars? Can you guess at the meaning of the phrase 'à mi-chemin entre Boulogne et Nice'?

(j) Here is Hélène's description of the hotel where they stayed in Thouars. Follow the description using the tape and the transcript below. Then cover up the transcript and see if you can write out the description by listening to the tape – like a sort of dictation. You may want to look up some words, but to help you you might like to note that 'poutres' refers to old-fashioned beams and the phrase 'd'époque' is what, in English, would be referred to as 'period'. (You will find some notes on the translation in the *key*.)

Et cet hôtel à Thouars était une très vieille maison mais très confortable, mais tu sais avec le charme ancien des vieilles maisons d'époque et classiques, si tu veux – avec des grosses poutres, c'était ravissant. Même dans les chambres il y avait toujours un petit détail, des meubles d'époque...

(k) Did the three children have separate rooms? (The key word to listen for is 'partager' (to share). Did they share or didn't they?)

(l) Hélène gives the following answer to a question from Patrick:

Oui, j'ai essayé, j'ai cherché dans la petite ville, parce que je ne me souvenais plus très bien où c'était.

What was Patrick's question?

(m) Complete the following sentence:

Figure-toi que j'ai reconnu la façade ancienne, mais évidemment...

(n) How did Hélène feel when she saw the old building?

nostalgic ☐
excited ☐
pleased ☐
disappointed ☐

Comme vous le savez...
A letter to friends

Letters

 Letter 1

John Smith writes a letter to friends they had hoped to visit during their stay.

Chers amis,

Comme vous le savez, nous avions l'intention de vous rendre visite pendant notre séjour en France. Maintenant que ces trois semaines touchent à leur fin, il est évident que nous n'aurons pas assez de temps pour faire le voyage. Nous le regrettons beaucoup, mais de toute façon nous allons nous revoir en automne quand vous viendrez passer quelques jours chez nous en Angleterre. Avec les enfants, les longs voyages ne sont pas faciles, et il y avait beaucoup à faire dans cette région.

Pendant les premiers jours de notre visite il faisait mauvais. Il y avait beaucoup d'averses et nous avons même dû acheter des coupe-vent et des imperméables! Heureusement nous nous y sommes habitués, et nous avons pu nous amuser quand même. Nous avons découvert la ville de Caen, ce qui était un vrai plaisir. Bien qu'une grande partie de la ville soit tout à fait nouvelle, à cause des bombardements de la guerre, il reste beaucoup de choses historiques à voir, et même les bâtiments modernes ne sont pas laids.

Mardi dernier nous avons fait une excursion d'une journée à Paris. Ce n'était pas très long, mais les enfants étaient contents de pouvoir y aller, et Mary et moi, nous étions ravis de revoir cette belle ville. Heureusement nous avons eu du soleil pour cette visite à Paris, et depuis, on n'a eu que quelques petits orages. Nous avons pu profiter des plages et de la campagne. Nous avons passé deux jours dans un camping tout près de la mer, et nous avons fait plusieurs excursions.

J'ai du mal à croire que nous sommes ici depuis déjà trois semaines; le temps a passé si vite. Mais lundi prochain je dois recommencer mon travail et les enfants aussi doivent rentrer à l'école. J'ai dû vous dire déjà que Mary a repris son travail, et elle aussi recommence dans quelques jours. Demain, c'est le premier septembre, et nous avons passé presque tout le mois d'août en France.

Nous attendons avec plaisir de vous revoir en octobre.

Bien amicalement.

John

The glass pyramid in the Louvre museum forecourt, Paris

Caen

 ## Letter 2

John receives a letter from the police relating to his witnessing the accident some days before.

Monsieur,

J'ai l'honneur de vous envoyer une copie d'un document rédigé à la suite de votre déclaration du 25 août concernant un accident de la circulation qui a eu lieu place Gambetta. Veuillez signer ce document et le renvoyer au commissariat de police. Ceci fait, nous n'aurons plus à vous déranger à ce sujet. Veuillez aussi remplir la section au bas du document afin de nous fournir quelques détails personnels.

Je vous prie d'agréer, Monsieur, l'expression de mes sentiments dévoués.

Déclaration de John Smith

Je me promenais le long du boulevard Bertrand en direction de la place Gambetta peu après neuf heures le matin du 25 août, mil neuf cent quatre-vingt-quatorze (1994). Je me suis arrêté à un passage clouté pour attendre un feu rouge. Soudain une voiture rouge a brûlé le feu rouge à pleine vitesse et est allée emboutir une voiture qui traversait la place.

.... *(signature)*

COMME VOUS LE SAVEZ ... 163

Nom .... John Smith
Date de naissance .... le 30 mai, mil neuf cent soixante et un (1961)
Nationalité .... anglaise
Domicile .... 3 London Road, Exeter, Devon, Angleterre
Raison de séjour
    à Caen .... vacances
Adresse à Caen .... Hôtel Beau Rivage
Date de départ .... le 2 septembre 1994

 Letter 3

John Smith's reply.

> Monsieur,
>   Je vous renvoie le document que vous m'avez prié de remplir. Les détails me paraissent être corrects. Je dois vous signaler que je rentre en Angleterre après-demain, le 2 septembre, et je ne serai donc plus en mesure de vous aider.
>   Je vous prie de croire, Monsieur, à l'expression de mes sentiments distingués.

Vocabulary

Letter 1

(i) Useful expressions

de toute façon	anyway
j'ai du mal à croire que	I find it difficult to believe that
bien amicalement	with friendly greetings (see *explanations (a) (iii)*)

(ii) Nouns – masc.   **Noun – fem.**

un ami: friend   une averse: shower of rain
l'automne: autumn
le travail: work
le mois: month

(iii) Other words

rendre visite à: to pay a visit to   évident(e): evident; obvious
toucher à la fin: to draw to a close   facile: easy

être habitué à: to be accustomed to
découvrir: to discover
bien que: although
nouveau (nouvelle): new
il reste: there remains
moderne: modern

laid(e): ugly
mardi: Tuesday (see *grammar ref. 9.2*)
content(e): pleased
profiter de: to take advantage of
lundi: Monday (see *grammar ref. 9.2*)
recommencer: to begin again

Letter 2

(i) Useful expressions

à la suite de
ceci fait
nous n'aurons plus à
veuillez
à pleine vitesse

in consequence of
when this has been done
we shall have no further need to
be so good as to
at full speed

(ii) Nouns – masc.

l'honneur: honour
le document: document
le commissariat: police station
le détail: detail
le sentiment: feeling
le domicile: home address
le départ: departure

Nouns – fem.

la copie: copy
la suite: sequel; result
la déclaration: statement
la section: section
une expression: expression
la vitesse: speed
la signature: signature
la date: date
la naissance: birth
la nationalité: nationality

(iii) Other words

rédiger: to draw up
concernant: concerning
avoir lieu: to take place
signer: to sign
renvoyer: to send back
remplir: to fill in
au bas de: at the bottom of

afin de: in order to
personnel(le): personal
agréer: to receive favourably
dévoué(e): devoted
soudain: suddenly
plein(e): full
emboutir: to crash into

Letter 3

prier: to request
paraître: to appear; to seem
correct(e): correct
signaler: to point out

après-demain: the day after tomorrow
en mesure de: in a position to
aider: to help
distingué(e): distinguished

Explanations

(a) *Writing letters*

Letters are probably the most likely context in which students in the early stages of language learning may need to write in the foreign language. This chapter contains an informal letter to friends and two more formal letters. The rules for letter writing may be briefly summarised as follows:

(i) Formal letters – beginnings

Formal letters usually begin 'Monsieur' or 'Madame'. If the person addressed has a title, this is usually included, for example: 'Monsieur le Directeur'.

(ii) Formal letters – endings

There are a number of possible ways to finish the letter, all of them sounding rather flowery and long-winded compared with 'yours faithfully'. Two possible endings are:

Veuillez agréer, Monsieur, l'expression de mes sentiments dévoués.
Je vous prie d'agréer, Madame, l'expression de mes sentiments les
    meilleurs.

(iii) Informal letters

Letters to friends begin: 'Cher Jean', 'Chère Marie', etc. They end: 'Amicalement', 'Amitiés', 'Meilleurs sentiments', etc. Informal letters may also have more lengthy ways of signing off, for example:

Je vous envoie l'amical souvenir de toute la famille.
Nous vous envoyons toutes nos amitiés.

(iv) Set phrases

In French, as in English, there are certain formulas of expression which crop up frequently in letters. Note the following expressions for use in *formal* letters:

J'ai l'honneur de vous rendre compte que...	I beg to inform you that....
Je vous serais très obligé de... Je vous serais très reconnaissant de... }	I should be grateful if...
J'ai le regret de vous informer que...	I regret to inform you that...
J'ai le plaisir de vous informer que...	I have pleasure in informing you that...

In *informal* letters you might find:

J'ai bien reçu votre lettre du...	I have received your letter of... (date)
Je vous remercie de votre lettre du...	Many thanks for your letter of...
Votre lettre du ... m'est bien arrivée.	Your letter of ... has arrived safely.
Je suis heureux de savoir que...	I'm glad to know that...

(b) *Use of 'devoir' (must, have to) (grammar ref. 5.8 (b))*

(i) Present tense

Je	**dois**	recommencer mon travail.
I	**must**	start work again.
Les enfants	**doivent**	rentrer à l'école.
The children	**must**	go back to school.

The present tense of 'devoir' (je dois, il doit, etc.) is followed by the *infinitive* of the French verb, as in the model sentences above.

(ii) Imperfect and perfect tenses

Nous	**avons dû**	acheter des coupe-vent.
We	**had to**	buy anoraks.
Je	**devais**	faire deux kilomètres à pied.
I	**had to**	walk two kilometres on foot.

The first of these sentences tells us of an event which happened on a single occasion and is complete, so French uses the perfect.

The second sentence tells us about something that took place regularly and habitually. It therefore uses the imperfect. In this case, the English 'I had to' could also be expressed as 'I used to have to'.

Finally, the perfect of 'devoir' also gives the sense of the English use of 'must have'.

> **J'ai dû** vous dire que Mary a repris son travail.
> I **must have** told you that Mary has started work again.

(c) *Subjunctive (grammar ref. 5.5)*

Use of the subjunctive is restricted in modern French. The main point to note is that there are certain expressions after which the subjunctive is used, for example: 'il faut que...'. This means, literally, 'it is necessary that...', but it would normally be translated into English as 'I must'. So, in practice, there is no difference in meaning between 'il faut que' and 'je dois'. Another expression which is followed by the subjunctive is 'bien que' (although).

Il faut que je m'en aille.	**I must** be going.
bien qu'une grande partie de	**although** a large part of the town
la ville soit nouvelle	is new

● *See the reference section for how to form the subjunctive.*

(d) *Relative pronouns: 'ce qui', 'ce que' (grammar ref. 4.3)*

Ça vous intéressera de savoir **ce que** nous avons fait.	You will be interested to know **what** we have been doing.
Nous avons fait la connaissance de la ville de Caen, **ce qui** était un vrai plaisir.	We got to know the town of Caen, **which** was a real pleasure.

In each of these sentences, 'what' and 'which' are relative pronouns, but they do not refer to a *single* word. They refer to the *whole* of the preceding idea. In the second sentence, 'ce qui' refers to the whole idea of getting to know the town. The rules for deciding whether to use 'ce qui' or 'ce que' are the same as for the use of 'qui' and 'que' explained in Chapter 14. It depends on whether the relative pronoun is subject or object of the clause.

Exercises

● *The key to these exercises begins on p.227.*

Lisez et écrivez
(Reading and writing exercises)

Exercise 1

Read the postcard on p. 169 which was sent by an English family who had called in on French friends in Normandy while driving down to the Midi. Now pick out the French equivalents for the following phrases:

    (a) We have arrived safely.
    (b) What a pleasure to see you all again!
    (c) A big thankyou for this unforgettable day.
    (d) Hoping to see you again very soon.

Exercise 2

Now write your own postcard. Invent some details of your own, but use some of the above phrases and thank friends in similar circumstances.

Exercise 3

Opposite is a letter written to reserve hotel rooms. Using this letter as a model, write another letter changing elements in the original letter to suit your own circumstances, for example, number of rooms, number of people, with or without bathroom, proximity to town centre, etc.

Note: 'le tarif' (the scale of charges); 'les arrhes' (deposit).

Chers amis,
Nous sommes maintenant bien arrivés
à Collioure.
La journée que nous avons passée
chez vous a été une halte si
agréable dans notre long voyage.
Quel plaisir de vous revoir tous!
Nous gardons un excellent souvenir
du sympathique déjeuner en famille,
dans votre jardin, sous les pommiers
de Normandie.
Un grand merci de la part de tous
les quatre pour cette journée inoubliable.
Grosses bises à toute la famille et
à très bientôt j'espère.
Avec toutes nos amitiés. Carolyn
        Mike, Helena & Chris

Famille Bovary
"La Vieille Auberge"
14 310 Villers-Bocage

---

le vendredi 24 mars 1995

Monsieur

Votre hôtel m'a été recommandé par un ami. Je vous écris pour réserver deux chambres avec salle de bains pour la période du 12 au 27 juillet. Nous serons quatre personnes, ma femme, mes deux enfants et moi-même. Pourriez-vous me renseigner sur vos tarifs et me dire s'il faut envoyer des arrhes? Je voudrais savoir aussi si l'hôtel est près de la plage, et s'il y a des possibilités de divertissements pour les enfants.

Je vous prie d'agréer, Monsieur, l'expression de mes sentiments les plus distingués.

Exercise 4

Now write an informal letter to a French friend to tell them how you spent the summer holidays. The details will depend on your own experiences, but you might like to use some of the following ideas.

Cher...
Nous sommes rentrés de nos vacances (dans le Midi / en Espagne / en Italie / dans le nord de l'Angleterre).

Nous avons eu des vacances très réussies (very successful) / très décevantes (very disappointing).

Nous avons beaucoup marché / passé la plupart du temps à la plage / visité des lieux intéressants.

Il faisait un temps magnifique. / Il a fait plutôt froid pour la saison. / Il a plu presque tous les jours.

Exercise 5

What have you got to do today?

Qu'est-ce que vous devez faire aujourd'hui?

Reply to the question using the notes below and using the verb 'devoir' to express the idea of 'must'.

Example: Je dois me lever de bonne heure (early).

de bonne heure	me lever
9h	aller au bureau
11h	faire les courses
12h 30	déjeuner avec un visiteur
15h	interviewer un client
16h 30	aller chercher les enfants à l'école
17h	rentrer à la maison

17 Quels sont les symptômes? Feeling unwell

Dialogues

 Dialogue 1   Une visite chez le médecin   A visit to the doctor

Both the children are feeling unwell. Mary decides to take them along to see the doctor.

Mary: Bonjour, docteur. Je viens pour les enfants. Ils ont tous les deux mal à la gorge et ils ont toussé toute la nuit. Ce n'est peut-être qu'un rhume, ou une grippe, mais je préfère en être sûre.

Médecin: Mais bien sûr, madame. Quel âge ont-ils?

Mary: Le garçon a huit ans et la fillette en a six.

Médecin: Eh bien, fais voir ta gorge, mon petit ... oui, comme ça c'est bien; tire ta langue. Oui, et toi aussi, ma petite. Bon. Maintenant, tousse plusieurs fois. C'est bien, merci. Oui, et toi aussi. Est-ce qu'ils ont de la fièvre et d'autres symptômes, madame?

Mary: Ils ont peut-être un peu de fièvre et en plus, ils n'ont pas d'appétit depuis deux jours. Ils ont tous les deux mal à la tête.

Médecin: Oui, bien sûr, ils ont un peu de fièvre, mais rien de sérieux. Vous leur avez donné des médicaments déjà?

Mary: Je leur ai donné de l'aspirine pendant la nuit.

Médecin: Ils sont tous les deux un peu enrhumés, mais ce n'est pas grave. Vous n'avez aucune raison de vous inquiéter. Je vais vous faire une ordonnance pour des comprimés et pour un sirop qui soulagera la toux. Donnez-leur les comprimés trois fois par jour, après les repas, et ne les laissez pas aller dans l'eau.

Mary: Non, sûrement pas. Ce n'est vraiment pas de chance que ça nous arrive, juste à la fin de nos vacances. Il ne nous reste qu'un jour à Caen.

Médecin: Ce n'est qu'un rhume, madame. On peut attraper un rhume n'importe quand.

Mary: Mais on s'y attend davantage en hiver ou au printemps, pas en été.

Médecin: Il fait quelquefois frais le soir. De toute façon, ça ne durera que deux ou trois jours. N'oubliez pas de leur donner les médicaments, et tout ira bien.

Mary: Merci beaucoup, docteur. Combien est-ce que je vous dois?

Médecin: Le prix de la consultation est cent francs. Je vais vous remplir la feuille de sécurité sociale et vous la ferez compléter par la pharmacie. Cela vous permettra de vous faire rembourser des soins.

Mary: Merci beaucoup, docteur.

Médecin: Au revoir, madame. Au revoir, les enfants.

 Dialogue 2   Au supermarché   At the supermarket

The children are taken back to the hotel to rest, and while John looks after them, Mary goes to meet up with Nicole Lebrun to do the last-minute shopping for the return journey.

Nicole: Alors, comment vont les enfants?

Mary: Ce n'est qu'un rhume, mais ils ne se sentent pas bien en ce moment. John est resté à l'hôtel avec eux. Je leur ai donné des médicaments, et j'espère qu'ils seront mieux demain.

Nicole: Et le docteur, qu'est-ce qu'il a dit?

Mary: Il m'a dit que ce n'était pas grave et que ce n'était qu'un mauvais rhume.

Nicole: Il n'a pas dit qu'il fallait les garder au lit?

Mary: Non, il a dit qu'il n'y avait vraiment aucune raison de s'inquiéter et qu'ils pourront faire le voyage demain.

Nicole: Les pauvres petits! Qu'est-ce qu'il vous reste à acheter? Votre panier est déjà plein.

Mary: Oui, il est assez lourd. J'ai déjà acheté pas mal de choses pour le piquenique pendant le voyage. Est-ce que je peux mettre ça dans votre voiture?

Nicole: Bien sûr, laissez-le là, sur le siège arrière. J'ai mon sac et un autre panier vide, si vous en avez besoin.

Mary: Il me faut encore des provisions pour le voyage, et John veut aussi que j'achète du vin.

Nicole: Allons au supermarché, alors. Il y a plus de choix ... Voilà, qu'est-ce qu'il veut comme vin?

Mary: Nous aimerions rapporter un peu de tout, mais nous devons nous limiter à six bouteilles à cause du manque de place dans la voiture.

Nicole: Regardez, celui-ci est très bon, c'est un bourgogne rouge que je peux vous recommander.

Mary: Et celui-ci, vous connaissez?

Nicole: C'est un blanc assez doux. Celui-là est plus sec, ça dépend des goûts.

Mary: Nous préférons le blanc sec en général, alors je vais prendre deux bouteilles de celui-là et une bouteille de vin doux pour le dessert.

Nicole: Et qu'est-ce qu'il vous faut encore?

Mary: Nous voulons emporter des fromages de la région.

Nicole: Gardez-les au frais, alors, jusqu'à votre départ. Ne les laissez pas au chaud, ou alors les autres passagers sur le bateau vont se plaindre!

Mary: Et puis, je voudrais aussi des petits pains pour le voyage.

Nicole: Eh bien, voilà le rayon de la boulangerie.

Mary: John m'a aussi demandé de lui acheter un journal, mais pour ça il faut aller ailleurs, je suppose.

Nicole: Oui, payons d'abord tout ça à la caisse, et puis on va chercher un marchand de journaux.

Vocabulary

Dialogue 1

(i) Useful expressions

ils ont mal à la gorge	they have a sore throat
fais voir	show me
ils ont mal à la tête	they've got a headache
aucune raison	no reason at all
ce n'est vraiment pas de chance	we're really out of luck
n'importe quand	any time at all

(ii) Nouns – masc.

le docteur: doctor (usually used as a title and as a form of address)

le médecin: doctor (general term for the practitioner)

Nouns – fem.

la gorge: throat (see *explanations (g)*)

la grippe: 'flu

la langue: tongue

la fièvre: fever; temperature

le mal: ache; pain
le rhume: cold
le symptôme: symptom
le médicament: medicine
le comprimé: tablet
le sirop: cough medicine
l'hiver: winter
le printemps: spring
le prix: price
le soin: (medical) care

la tête: head
une ordonnance: prescription
la toux: cough
l'eau: water
la consultation: consultation
la feuille de sécurité sociale: social
     security form
la pharmacie: chemist's

(iii) Other words

tousser: to cough
tirer: to put out (tongue); to pull
sérieux (sérieuse): serious
enrhumé(e): with a cold
aucun(e): not a single one
soulager: to relieve; to comfort
laisser: to let; to permit
     (see *explanations (g)*)
juste: just

attraper: to catch
davantage: more
frais (fraîche): cool; fresh
durer: to last
je dois (devoir): I owe
compléter: to finish filling in (a form)
permettre: to allow
rembourser: to reimburse

Dialogue 2

(i) Useful expressions

comment vont les enfants?
ce n'était que
qu'est-ce qu'il vous reste à acheter?
pas mal de
un peu de tout

how are the children?
it was nothing more than
what have you got left to buy?
quite a few
a little of everything

(ii) Nouns – masc.

le supermarché: supermarket
le piquenique: picnic
le panier: basket
le siège: seat
le siège arrière: back-seat
le choix: choice
le manque: lack
le bourgogne: Burgundy (the wine)
le goût: taste
le frais: cool (place)
le chaud: warm (place)
le passager: passenger
le petit pain: bread roll
le marchand: shopkeeper; merchant

Nouns – fem.

la provision: provision
la boulangerie: bakery
la Bourgogne: Burgundy (the
     province)

(iii) Other words

se sentir: to feel
il fallait: it was necessary
garder: to keep
pauvre: poor
lourd(e): heavy
mettre: to put
vide: empty

se limiter: to limit oneself
rapporter: to take back
doux (douce): sweet
sec (sèche): dry
emporter: to take away
se plaindre: to complain
ailleurs: elsewhere

Explanations

(a) *Reported speech*

Il a dit qu'il n'y avait aucun danger.   He said that there was no danger.
Il m'a dit que ce n'était pas grave.   He told me that it wasn't serious.

In English, reported speech begins with a phrase such as 'He says that...', or 'She told me that...'. French usage is exactly the same, as shown in the two examples above.

(b) *Object pronouns with the imperative*

When the imperative is *negative* (in English, 'Do not... !'), the pronoun comes immediately before the verb, as already explained in Chapter 10:

Ne **les** laissez pas aller dans l'eau.   Don't let them go into the water.
Ne **les** laissez pas au chaud.   Don't leave them where it is warm.

When the imperative is *affirmative,* the pronouns follow the verb:

Donnez-**leur** des comprimés.   Give them some tablets.
Gardez-**les** au frais.   Keep them in the cool.

Note that when the objects follow the verb in this way, they are linked to it by a hyphen.

(c) *This one / that one (grammar ref. 4.4)*

Prenez cette bouteille, et moi, je prends **celle-ci**.	You take that bottle and I'll take **this one**.
Ce vin est doux mais **celui-là** est plus sec.	This wine is sweet, but **that one** is drier.

'This one' is translated as 'celui-ci' or 'celle-ci', depending on whether the object referred to is masculine or feminine.

'That one' is translated as 'celui-là', or 'celle-là', again depending on whether the object referred to is masculine or feminine.

(d) *More about negatives (grammar ref. 5.10)*

(i)

rien de sérieux	**nothing** serious
rien de bon	**nothing** good

(ii) Note that 'ne...aucun' expresses a stronger negative than 'ne...pas':

Vous **n'**avez **pas** de raison de vous inquiéter.	There is **no** need for you to get worried.
Vous **n'**avez **aucune** raison de vous inquiéter.	There is **absolutely no** need for you to get worried.

(e) *Uses of 'en'*

(i) With numbers

You have already met 'en' on several occasions, particularly with numbers. For example:

Il y **en** a six.   There are six (**of them**).

(ii) With verbs followed by 'de'

Some verbs do not take a direct object but are followed by 'de'. For example:

Je suis sûr **de** l'heure du départ.
J'ai besoin **d'**une cuillère.

The nouns in these sentences may be replaced by a pronoun, and in these cases the pronoun 'en' replaces not only the noun but also 'de':

J'**en** suis sûr.	I'm sure **of it**.
J'**en** ai besoin.	I need one. (I have need **of one**.)

(f) Use of 'faire' + infinitive

When 'faire' is used with a following infinitive, it means 'to get something done' or 'to make someone do something'.

Vous la **ferez compléter**.	You will get it filled in (referring to filling in a form).
Cela vous permettra de vous **faire rembourser**.	In that way you will be able to get yourself reimbursed.

(g) Notes on vocabulary

(i) 'Laisser', meaning 'to let' or 'to permit', is followed by a direct infinitive:

Laissez-le **sortir**.   Let him leave.
Ne les laissez pas **aller** dans   Don't let them go into the water.
l'eau.

(ii) Masculine nouns ending in '-al' have an irregular plural ending in '-aux'. For example:

le journal → les journaux
le cheval → les chevaux

(iii) The preposition used with three seasons of the year is 'en':

en hiver
en automne
en été

The exception is '**au** printemps' (in spring).

(iv) 'Devoir' was introduced in Chapter 16 *explanations* in the sense of 'must'. When not used in this way it means 'to owe'. For example:

Combien est-ce que je vous **dois**?   How much do I **owe** you?

(v) Parts of the body are often referred to by the definite article:

Ils ont mal à **la** gorge.
Ils ont mal à **la** tête.

However, when the doctor addresses the children directly he says:

Fais voir **ta** gorge ... tire **ta**   Let me see your throat ... put
langue.   your tongue out.

Exercises

● *The key to these exercises begins on p.228.*

Parlez
(Speaking exercise)

Exercise 1   What did the doctor say?

Imagine that you are playing the role of someone who has taken a child
(Robert) to the doctor and is telling a friend about the doctor's comments.
Look at the dialogue below and use the English prompts to help you prepare
your role. Then turn on the recording and practise playing the part of the
parent.

Ami: Alors, qu'est-ce qu'il a dit, le docteur?
Parent: *(Tell your friend what the doctor said – that it wasn't serious and that there
was no reason to get worried.)*
Ami: Qu'est-ce que c'est, alors?
Parent: *(He said that the child had a bit of a cold and had a slight temperature.)*
Ami: It doit rester au lit?
Parent: *(No, but the doctor said that he must not go out.)*
Ami: Et il doit prendre des médicaments?
Parent: *(The doctor said that you must give him two tablets a day, and let him
sleep, if possible.)*

Lisez et écrivez
(Reading and writing exercises)

Exercise 2

Here is a list of items in pairs. Opposite each pair of items are two adjectives.
Practise the use of 'celui-ci', 'celui-là', 'celle-ci' and 'celle-là' by combining
items as shown in the example:

Example: deux paniers   lourd (heavy)   léger (light)
Answer: Voilà deux paniers. Celui-ci est lourd et celui-là est léger.

(a) deux vins   sec   doux
(b) deux sacs   plein   vide
(c) deux paniers   lourd   léger
(d) deux voitures   rouge   blanche
(e) deux routes   bonne   mauvaise

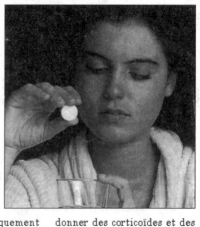

MÉDECINE GÉNÉRALE

L'allergie à l'aspirine, ça existe

L'aspirine est devenue un remède miracle. Mais, comme tous les médicaments, elle présente également des dangers.

Le Français consomme en moyenne 65 comprimés d'aspirine par an, contre 50 pour les autres Européens. Ce médicament est devenu un familier des armoires à pharmacie!

Chez une minorité d'individus, l'aspirine produit des troubles qui peuvent dans certains cas être graves. On estime à 4% la proportion des personnes allergiques. Les symptômes apparaissent le plus souvent entre 30 et 40 ans, mais touchent aussi les enfants et les adolescents. Déclenchée par la prise de petites quantités d'aspirine, cette intolérance peut atteindre pratiquement tous les organes. Les réactions varient selon les personnes: asthme, chute de la tension, douleurs abdominales... L'irritation de l'estomac se manifeste par des ulcères, mais également, dans une minorité des cas, par des hémorragies digestives. Le traitement d'urgence lors d'une allergie médicamenteuse consiste à donner des corticoïdes et des antihistaminiques. Mais l'arrêt total et définitif de prise d'aspirine et de ses dérivés constitue la mesure préventive essentielle. Pour être sûr du diagnostic, un test peut être pratiqué en milieu hospitalier donc sous surveillance médicale, afin d'éviter tout accident grave.

Isabelle Decaux

Adapted from Femme Actuelle

Exercise 3

Read the article and then tick to show whether the following statements are *true* or *false* (T or F).

(a) The French use less aspirin than other Europeans. T ☐ F ☐

(b) For the majority of people, aspirin in reasonable doses is well tolerated. T ☐ F ☐

(c) It is mainly children who suffer from allergy caused by aspirin. T ☐ F ☐

(d) One of the symptoms of aspirin allergy is stomach pain. T ☐ F ☐

(e) If there are signs of allergy it is best to stop taking aspirin straight away. T ☐ F ☐

Écoutez

(Listening exercise)

Exercise 4   Spontaneous dialogue   At the doctor's

Annette pays a visit to the doctor. Some of the vocabulary is a little technical, but you hear the usual sort of questions you'd expect in such a situation. Use the exercises to help you with the difficult bits.

(a) Complete the following statement made by Annette to the doctor:

J'ai été...

She then says, 'Je ne me sens toujours pas d'aplomb'. Can you have a guess at what this means?

(b) The doctor's next question is:

Vous avez mal au cœur, envie de vomir?

Look up the meaning of these phrases, or see if you can guess what they mean from the context.

(c) Where does Annette say that she has pains (des douleurs)?

dans le dos ☐
dans le bas du ventre ☐
dans la tête ☐
dans la poitrine ☐

(d) The doctor wants Annette to lie down to be examined. How does she say this? Complete the sentence:

Si vous voulez bien...

(e) How would you say in French, 'It really hurts when you press just there'? (Note that the French for 'to press' is 'appuyer'.)

(f) The doctor explains her diagnosis. The following paragraph is a transcription of what she says with some key words missing. Listen to the section of the tape and fill in the gaps choosing words from the box. Then see if you can write out an English version of what the doctor says.

Bon, écoutez, ça .... être une appendicite. Bien sûr, il est fort .... que ça ne soit pas ça. Mais, vous avez probablement une .... Ça arrive très souvent en périodes de grosse .... Enfin, comme on ne sait ...., et pour être tout à fait ...., je vais vous faire un ...., une prise de .... qui nous dira s'il s'agit d'une ....

| sang | pourrait | appendicite | probable | chaleur | jamais |
| | indigestion | | sûre | test | |

(g) What question is put by Annette to obtain the following reply from the doctor?

Oh, c'est très rapide; demain matin certainement.

(h) There are two reasons why Annette has to see the secretary. What are they?

(i) What time does the secretary suggest for the next appointment?

4.30 pm ☐
3.00 pm ☐
2.30 pm ☐
11.00 am ☐

Si vous aviez plus de temps!
Taking your leave

Menu

Nicole has asked the Smiths and the Jacquiers to come and have a meal on the last evening of the holiday. This is the menu she has prepared, with some notes from her cookery book.

Soupe à l'oignon
1½ litres de bouillon, 250g d'oignons, 60g de beurre, 80g de farine, sel, poivre.

Soufflé de poisson
200g de poisson cuit, 50g de beurre, 70g de farine, 3dl de lait, 4 œufs.

Poulet sauté chasseur
1 poulet, 1dl de bouillon, 2dl de vin blanc, 1dl de cognac, 50g de beurre, 50g de farine, 125g de tomates fraîches, sel, poivre, estragon, cerfeuil, 40g d'échalotes. Avant de mouiller avec le vin blanc, mettre le cognac et faire flamber. Ajouter le bouillon. Saler. Poivrer. Couvrir. Laisser cuire 30 minutes. Incorporer alors les tomates. Cuire encore 10 minutes. Terminer la sauce avec ½ cuillère à café d'estragon et de cerfeuil hachés finement. Bien mélanger sans faire bouillir.

Fromages: camembert, livarot, pont l'évêque

Dessert: bavaroise au chocolat
½ litre de lait, 250g de crème, 150g de chocolat, 5 œufs, 100g de sucre, 20g de feuilles de gélatine, 3 cuillerées d'eau froide.

Dialogues

 Dialogue 1   Une dernière rencontre   A final get-together

After the meal, the friends sit and talk, before the Smiths have to go back to their hotel.

Michel: Alors, les vacances se terminent. Mais il y a encore beaucoup à voir, vous savez! Si vous aviez plus de temps vous pourriez visiter la vallée de la

Seine, les montagnes de la Suisse Normande, ou même aller jusqu'au Mont St-Michel.

John: Ah oui, si on avait le temps ... Mais il y a vraiment un embarras de richesses dans cette région, et comme vous savez, il faut bien gagner sa vie.

Anne-Marie: C'est bien vrai, ce que vous dites; nous aussi, nous allons bientôt partir et la semaine prochaine on recommence le travail.

Mary: Ces vacances étaient vraiment réussies. On a passé un excellent séjour. Mais nous espérons beaucoup vous revoir chez nous en Angleterre. Vous avez bien notre adresse?

John: Et le numéro de téléphone aussi, je vous l'ai donné, Michel, non?

Michel: Oui, oui, vous me l'avez donné, et je vous assure qu'on va faire notre possible pour vous rendre visite. Merci beaucoup pour l'invitation.

John: C'est nous qui vous remercions pour votre accueil.

Nicole: Mais c'est normal, voyons. Si nous étions en Angleterre, vous feriez la même chose pour nous sans doute.

Mary: C'est sûr. Et Anne-Marie et Pierre savent bien où nous trouver aussi.

John: Alors, à la santé de tous, et à la prochaine fois.

Tous: À la vôtre, et à la prochaine fois.

Dialogue 2 Départ de l'hôtel *Leaving the hotel*

Hôtelier: Alors, Monsieur Smith, c'est déjà le départ. Voilà votre note.

John: Merci. C'est tout compris, taxes et service aussi?

Hôtelier: Oui, monsieur. Taxes et service sont compris.

John: Excusez-moi, monsieur, mais il y a peut-être une petite erreur ici. Les boissons pour le 24 août. Je ne m'en souviens pas bien.

Hôtelier: Montrez-moi ça, monsieur. Oui, c'est le soir où vous êtes rentrés avec votre ami, après le voyage à Paris.

John: Mais, oui, bien sûr. Excusez-moi, j'avais oublié. Alors, c'est correct. Voilà, et merci.

Hôtelier: C'est moi qui vous remercie, monsieur. J'espère que vous êtes satisfait de votre séjour.

John: Oui, très satisfait. S'il ne fallait pas recommencer le travail, nous aimerions rester encore quelques jours.

Hôtelier: Alors, bon voyage, monsieur. Bon retour chez vous et au plaisir de vous revoir.

John: Merci, monsieur, et au revoir.

Dialogue 3 Au garage *At the garage*

John: Je vais faire le plein de super. Mais je voudrais aussi que quelqu'un vérifie le niveau d'huile et la pression des pneus. Nous allons prendre le bateau et je ne veux pas tomber en panne.

Garagiste: Faites toujours le plein, monsieur, et je suis avec vous dans 5 minutes.

(5 minutes plus tard)

Garagiste: Vous êtes en route pour Le Havre, alors?
John: Oui, mais nous ne sommes pas pressés. Nous avons le temps de nous
    arrêter un peu en route.
Garagiste: Il vous faut pas mal d'huile, monsieur.
John: Ça m'étonne un peu.
Garagiste: Et regardez les bougies. Celle-ci est sale et huileuse.
John: Ah, mon Dieu! Qu'est-ce que cela veut dire?
Garagiste: Je ne crois pas que ça soit grave. Mais il vaut mieux être sûr.
    Autrement, vous allez certainement tomber en panne. Est-ce que vous
    pouvez nous laisser la voiture pour une demi-heure?
John: Mais oui; heureusement on a le temps. Nous allons nous promener en
    attendant.

                              ★ ★ ★ ★

Garagiste: Voilà, monsieur. Tout est en ordre maintenant. Nous avons trouvé
    une petite fuite d'huile. Rien de grave, mais il vaut mieux que ça soit réparé.
John: Oui, alors. Combien est-ce que je vous dois?
Garagiste: 165F pour trente litres de super; 53F pour deux litres d'huile, et
    94F pour la réparation. Ça fait 312F en tout, monsieur. Merci, et bonne
    route.
John: C'est moi qui vous remercie. Au revoir.

Vocabulary

Menu

(i) Nouns – masc.

un oignon: onion
le bouillon: stock
le sel: salt
le soufflé: soufflé
le poisson: fish
le chasseur: hunter
le poulet: chicken
l'estragon: tarragon
le cerfeuil: chervil
le sucre: sugar

Nouns – fem.

la soupe: soup
la farine: flour
la tomate: tomato
une échalote: shallot
la sauce: sauce; gravy
la cuillère à café: coffee spoon
la bavaroise: mousse
la feuille: leaf
la gélatine: gelatine
la cuillerée: spoonful

(ii) Other words

sauter: to fry and toss (also 'to jump')
ajouter: to add
saler: to add salt
poivrer: to add pepper
couvrir: to cover
mouiller: to wet; to soak
flamber: to set light to
cuire: to cook
incorporer: to mix in; to incorporate

alors: then
terminer: to finish
hacher: to chop up
finement: finely
fin(e): fine; refined; best quality
mélanger: to blend; to mix
faire bouillir: to bring to the boil
froid(e): cold

Dialogue 1

(i) Useful expressions

un embarras de richesses
gagner sa vie
nous allons faire notre possible
voyons!
à la vôtre

too much to choose from
to earn one's living
we shall do everything possible
come now!
cheers!; good health!

(ii) Nouns – masc.

le mont: mount
un embarras de: too much; too many
un accueil: welcome

Nouns – fem.

la rencontre: get together; meeting
la vallée: valley
la montagne: mountain; hill
la Suisse: Switzerland
la richesse: wealth
une invitation: invitation
la santé: health

(iii) Other words

se terminer: to come to an end
gagner: to earn; to win
réussi(e): successful

assurer: to assure
normal(e): normal

Dialogue 2

(i) Useful expressions

j'avais oublié
bon retour chez vous
au plaisir (de vous revoir)

I had forgotten
safe journey home
I hope we shall meet again

(ii)

Nouns – fem.

la note: bill
la taxe: tax
une erreur: mistake

(iii) Other words

se souvenir de: to remember

Dialogue 3

(i) Useful expressions

faites toujours le plein
tomber en panne
qu'est-ce que cela veut dire?
il vaut mieux être sûr
en attendant
en ordre
bonne route

just carry on filling up
to break down
what does that mean?
it's better to be sure
while waiting
in order
have a good drive

(ii) Nouns – masc.

le garage: garage
le garagiste: garage owner
le plein: full tank
le super: 4-star petrol
le niveau: level
le pneu: tyre

Nouns – fem.

l'huile: oil
la pression: pressure
la panne: breakdown
la bougie: spark plug
la fuite: leak
la réparation: repair

(iii) Other words

faire le plein: to fill up
tomber: to fall
sale: dirty
huileux (huileuse): oily

vouloir dire: to mean
laisser: to leave
réparer: to repair

Explanations

(a) Conditional sentences ('If...') (grammar ref. 5.2 (d))

The word 'si', meaning 'if', introduces a condition into the sentence. For example:

> **Si** vous veniez à Caen, vous **verriez** le château.
>
> **If** you came to Caen, you **would see** the castle.

There is a rule about the sequence of tenses. The imperfect in the 'if' clause is followed by the conditional in the second half of the sentence. Look at these examples from the text of this chapter:

Si vous aviez plus de temps, vous **pourriez** visiter...

If you had more time, you **would be able** to visit...

Si nous étions en Angleterre, vous **feriez** la même chose.

If we were in England you **would do** the same thing.

See the *reference section* for how to form the conditional.

(b) Use of the infinitive when giving instructions

Instructions and commands are usually given in the *imperative*. *But* instructions in books, for example in recipes, often use the *infinitive*:

Ajouter le bouillon.
Terminer la sauce.

(c) More about the subjunctive (grammar ref. 5.5)

This chapter contains two further examples of the use of the subjunctive.

(i) In a clause beginning with 'que', following a statement in the negative:

Je ne crois pas que ça **soit** grave.   I don't think that it is serious.

(ii) In a clause beginning with 'que', and following the expression 'il vaut mieux':

Il vaut mieux que ça **soit** réparé.   It's better to have it repaired.

(d) Use of 'c'est' to give emphasis

If you want to emphasise a particular word in a sentence, you can do so by using 'c'est' at the beginning of the sentence. A good example of this is when somebody thanks you and you thank them in return:

> **C'est moi** qui vous remercie.
> **C'est nous** qui vous remercions de votre accueil.

(e) *Notes on vocabulary*

(i) Note that the plural of 'pneu' is 'pneus'.

(ii) 'Laisser' was introduced in Chapter 17 with the meaning 'to let', or 'to permit'. It can also mean 'to leave behind', as in the following example:

Vous pouvez nous **laisser** la voiture pour une demi-heure?	Can you **leave** your car with us for half an hour?

(iii) Note the French way of saying 'the evening when...' or 'the morning when...':

le soir **où**...
le matin **où**...

(iv) 'Avant de' is followed by an infinitive. For example:

avant de **partir**   before leaving

(v) Note the phrase:

Qu'est-ce que ça **veut dire**?   What does that **mean**?

(vi) 'Voyons' is difficult to translate into English. It has a note of reproach about it, as when used by parents scolding a child:

Mais ne fais pas ça, **voyons**.

In the text of this chapter, Nicole strikes this slightly reproachful note when she says:

Mais c'est normal, **voyons**.

Exercises

● *The key to these exercises begins on p.229.*

Parlez
(Speaking exercise)

Exercise 1   The national lottery

You can always dream! In the role play below, a friend asks you what you would do if you won the jackpot (le gros lot) on the Loterie Nationale. Your reply begins 'Si je gagnais...' and you must then make up sentences in the conditional. If you don't like the suggestions below, make up some of your own. Here is some vocabulary to help you:

faire le tour du monde
manger dans les meilleurs
   restaurants

acheter un château sur la Côte d'Azur
pouvoir aller souvent au théâtre
aller en France tous les ans

habiter à la campagne   passer l'hiver dans un climat chaud
avoir une grande voiture

Ami: Dites-moi, qu'est-ce que vous feriez si vous gagniez le gros lot de la
Loterie Nationale?

You: *(Say that if you won the jackpot you would probably go on a tour of the world.
Perhaps you would buy a castle on the Côte d'Azur. You would eat in the best
restaurants, live in the country and have a big car. You would be able to go to the
theatre often, you would go to France every year and you would spend the winter
in a warm climate.)*

Lisez et écrivez
(Reading and writing exercises)

Exercise 2

What if you had to prepare 'poulet sauté chasseur'? In the box below are your
instructions from the cookery book. Write out sentences beginning 'Si je devais
préparer ce poulet...' (If I had to prepare this chicken...) and complete the
sentences with the verbs in the conditional.

Example: Si je devais préparer ce poulet, je mettrais le cognac.

Si je devais préparer ce poulet, je...

> ajouter le cognac
> faire flamber le cognac
> ajouter le bouillon
> laisser cuire 30 minutes
> terminer la sauce
> mélanger bien les ingrédients

Exercise 3

You read the interview on p. 190 with two young people in a French magazine.
Read the statements below and indicate whether you think that they are *true* or
false (T or F).

(a) The journalist wants to know if Nathalie and Jean
like the jobs they are doing.   T ☐ F ☐
(b) Nathalie would like to have the chance to work in a
team.   T ☐ F ☐
(c) Jean already know how to organise the financial side
of a tour.   T ☐ F ☐
(d) Nathalie knows that the hours are sometimes difficult.   T ☐ F ☐
(e) Jean's favourite pastime is travelling.   T ☐ F ☐
(f) The journalist would love to be able to change her job.   T ☐ F ☐

Journaliste
Supposons qu'on vous offre maintenant le travail que vous désirez. Que choisiriez-vous?
Nathalie
Moi, sans hésiter, je deviendrais journaliste, comme vous! Interroger les gens, être au courant de tout ce qui se passe, travailler en équipe, je suis vraiment sûre que j'adorerais ça! En plus, il faut bien dire que j'aime beaucoup écrire. Je sais que c'est un métier aux horaires parfois difficiles, mais dans lequel je ne m'ennuierais jamais et surtout qui me donnerait la chance d'apprendre plein de choses. J'ai raison, non?
Journaliste
Oui, tout à fait. D'ailleurs, si j'avais de nouveau à faire un choix c'est encore le métier que je choisirais! Mais parlons maintenant de vous, Jean. Qu'est-ce qui vous plairait?
Jean
Moi, je choisirais tout de suite le métier de voyagiste. Pour moi, ce serait le rêve; être payé pour faire ce que j'aime le plus – voyager. J'organiserais des voyages pour différents types de clients, avec des intérêts différents. Bien sûr, pour faire ce métier, il faudrait aussi savoir calculer les budgets, obtenir des réductions...mais ça, j'apprendrais vite, j'en suis sûr. Et puis, enfin, j'irais sur place pour tester la qualité des hôtels, les circuits à proposer, les visites à faire... Je ne sais pas ce que je donnerais pour avoir un travail comme ça!

Exercise 4

Look through the interview again and underline all the verbs in the conditional. Then think how you would express those statements in English. Write out a translation of the whole phrase in which the conditional appears.

Écoutez
(Listening exercise)

Exercise 5   Spontaneous dialogue   Expressing appreciation

Having returned home to England, Mary rings her French friend Françoise to thank her and her husband for their hospitality. She invites Françoise and her husband to come and visit them next time. Listen to the ways of saying thank you and expressing appreciation.

(a) After a stop at Abbeville, what problem did they have on the return journey?

They couldn't persuade the children to leave. ☐
They couldn't get the car to start again. ☐
They couldn't find their ferry tickets. ☐
They couldn't find where they had parked the car. ☐

(b) Why was their crossing very quick? To get this answer you have to remember that French has borrowed an English word for the journey via the tunnel.

(c) How do you say the following phrases in French?

(i) It was so nice of you to welcome us.

(ii) We spent some fantastic days with you.

(iii) It was a pleasure.

(iv) We were delighted to welcome you.

(d) What is Françoise's response when Mary says that they must come and visit them in England? The key words here are 'prendre des congés' meaning 'to take holidays'. Note also the beginning of the sentence where Françoise says 'Mais justement...'. This might be translated, 'Well, yes, that's just what I was going to say...'

(e) What is Mary going to send when she writes to Françoise?

19 De si bons souvenirs! Expressing gratitude

Letters

 Letter 1

John Smith writes to thank the Lebruns for their help during the family's stay in Caen.

Chers amis,

Ça fait déjà trois jours que nous sommes rentrés et les vacances paraissent déjà loin. Nous avons de si bons souvenirs de cette visite et nous vous sommes très reconnaissants de tout ce que vous avez fait pour nous accueillir. Le contact avec vous nous a aidés à mieux connaître la ville et la région.

Notre voyage de retour n'a pas été une réussite. Heureusement les enfants allaient mieux et n'étaient plus aussi enrhumés. Nous étions donc partis de bonne heure, et nous pensions que ce serait un voyage sans problèmes. Nous avons d'abord eu des problèmes avec la voiture, puis nous avons pris du retard à cause de la circulation. Nous avions pensé que les petites routes ne seraient pas encombrées, mais c'était une erreur! Mais nous sommes enfin arrivés au Havre et nous avions juste le temps de prendre un snack avant d'embarquer. La traversée était calme, et nous avons pu nous asseoir sur le pont au soleil. Nous voilà de retour, les enfants sont rentrés à l'école, et pour Mary et moi, le travail a recommencé aussi. Mais nous gardons un très bon souvenir de notre visite en Normandie, et nous attendons avec plaisir de vous recevoir chez nous.

En vous remerciant encore, nous vous envoyons toutes nos amitiés.

Letter 2

Some articles have been left behind ... John writes to the hotel.

Monsieur,

En quittant l'hôtel jeudi dernier, nous avons dû oublier plusieurs articles. Si vous avez trouvé ces articles, je vous prie de bien vouloir nous les renvoyer, et je vous rembourserai, bien sûr, les frais de port. Ma femme a oublié une écharpe de soie blanche et les enfants ont laissé quelques jouets et une balle noire.

Je vous remercie à l'avance et je vous prie d'accepter l'expression de mes sentiments les meilleurs.

 Letter 3

To the Jacquiers.

Chers amis,

Quel plaisir de vous revoir en Normandie! Nous sommes heureux d'avoir pu vous rencontrer lors de votre passage. Nous espérons que votre voyage de retour s'est bien passé. En passant, je peux vous dire que le nôtre n'a pas été une réussite! Mais je ne vais pas vous ennuyer avec les détails. L'important, c'est que nous sommes maintenant bien rentrés chez nous et qu'il y a beaucoup à faire dans la maison et dans le jardin. En travaillant pendant tous nos moments libres, nous arriverons peut-être à y remettre de l'ordre, mais ça sera difficile. Quant au travail, le mien a déjà commencé avec la rentrée des classes hier, et Mary retourne demain au bureau. Les enfants se font un plaisir de raconter à tous leurs amis tout ce qu'ils ont fait, et même de dire quelques mots en français. La prochaine fois nous devrions peut-être essayer de les faire parler davantage. Mon français s'est certainement amélioré pendant la visite. On a toujours besoin de parler une langue étrangère, et la seule façon c'est de se rendre dans le pays. Et puis, comme vous le savez bien, apprendre une langue c'est aussi se familiariser avec toute une nouvelle culture. Étant anglais de naissance, je ne pense pas être jamais capable de me sentir tout à fait français, mais il est possible quand même de partager un peu de la culture et de la façon de vivre des Français, et il est certain que cela représente un élément d'enrichissement personnel. C'est pour cette raison que je suis tellement en faveur des jumelages entre communes françaises et anglaises. La nôtre va bientôt signer une charte de jumelage avec un village français et cela va créer des possibilités de contacts personnels qui révèlent, non seulement les différences entre les pays et les peuples mais aussi les similarités. Le grand avantage de ces jumelages, c'est qu'ils offrent la possibilité d'entrer directement dans un foyer français, de connaître les gens chez eux, et c'est ce contact humain qui manque quelquefois si on visite un pays seulement en tant que touriste. Mais le tourisme est aussi un élément important dans l'entente cordiale, alors, ne le critiquons pas.

Vous m'excuserez de la longueur de cette lettre. De retour chez moi, je réfléchis, comme ça m'arrive quelquefois, aux avantages de connaître une langue étrangère.

En attendant le plaisir de vous lire, et de vous revoir tous, je vous envoie l'amical souvenir de toute la famille.

Vocabulary

Letter 1

(i) Useful expressions

ça fait déjà trois jours que	it's already three days since
les enfants allaient mieux	the children felt better
nous avons pris du retard	we were held up
nous voilà de retour	here we are, back again

(ii) Nouns – masc.

le contact: contact
le snack: snack
le pont: deck

Nouns – fem.

la réussite: success
la circulation: traffic
la traversée: crossing
une amitié: friendship

(iii) Other words

reconnaissant de: grateful for
accueillir: to welcome
encombré(e): crowded

embarquer: to go on board
recevoir: to receive

Letter 2

(i) Useful expression

je vous prie de bien vouloir

would you please be so kind as to

(ii) Nouns – masc.

un article: article
les frais de port: postal charges
le jouet: toy

Nouns – fem.

une écharpe: scarf
la soie: silk
la balle: ball

(iii) Other words

jeudi: Thursday (see *grammar ref. 9.2*)
rembourser: to reimburse

noir(e): black

Letter 3

(i) Useful expressions

lors de votre passage	when you were passing through
nous arriverons à	we shall manage to
les enfants se font un plaisir de	the children take a delight in
étant anglais de naissance	being English by birth
non seulement ... mais aussi	not only ... but also

(ii) Nouns – masc.

un ordre: order
le mot: word
un élément: element
un enrichissement: enrichment
le jumelage: twinning
le peuple: people
un avantage: advantage
le foyer: home

Nouns – fem.

la réussite: success
la maison: house
la rentrée: return; start of term
la classe: class
la culture: culture
la faveur: favour
la commune: commune; parish
la charte: charter
la différence: difference
la similarité: similarity
une entente: understanding
la longueur: length

(iii) Other words

rencontrer: to meet
lors de: at the time of
ennuyer: to bore
remettre: to bring back; to put back
quant à: as for
    raconter: to relate
s'améliorer: to improve
étranger (étrangère): foreign
se rendre dans: to go to
se familiariser: to get to know
capable: capable; able
se sentir: to feel
partager: to share

vivre: to live
représenter: to represent
signer: to sign
créer: to create
révéler: to reveal
offrir: to offer
humain(e): human
manquer: to be missing; to be lacking
cordial(e): cordial
critiquer: to criticise
réfléchir: to reflect
lire: to read
amical(e): friendly

Explanations

(a) *Pluperfect tense (grammar ref. 5.2 (f) (iii))*

Compare the following sentences from this chapter with their English equivalents:

Nous **avions** pensé que les petites routes ne seraient pas encombrées.	We **had** thought that the little roads would not be crowded.
Nous **étions** partis de bonne heure.	We **had** set out early in the morning.

The tense used here, in both French and English, is the pluperfect, which expresses an action which took place even further back in the past than action expressed in the perfect tense. In English you can always recognise the pluperfect by the auxiliary verb 'had'. In French, the rules for forming the tense and making agreements are similar to those for the perfect, with either 'avoir' or 'être' as the auxiliary verb. (See the examples above.) The auxiliary verb is in the imperfect tense.

(b) Conditional of 'devoir' (grammar ref. 5.8 (b))

In Chapter 16 there was an explanation of the use of 'devoir' to express 'must', 'have to'. There is one further tense to add to that explanation. The conditional of 'devoir' is used with the sense of 'ought to':

La prochaine fois nous **devrions** essayer...	Next time we **ought to** try...

(c) Present participle (grammar ref. 5.2 (e))

In English the present participle is that part of the verb which ends in '-ing' (e.g., 'reading', 'writing'). The present participle is not as widely used in French as in English, and is never used as a noun. It is often used in combination with 'en'. For example:

en passant   in passing
en attendant   while waiting

Note the examples from the texts of this chapter:

En vous **remerciant** encore, nous vous envoyons toutes nos amitiés.	**Thanking** you once more, we send you friendly greetings.
En **quittant** l'hôtel, nous avons dû oublier plusieurs articles.	On **leaving** the hotel we must have forgotten several items.
étant anglais de naissance	**being** English by birth

(d) Order of object pronouns (grammar ref. 4.1 (a) and (c))

In the second letter of this chapter you read the following sentence:

Je vous prie de **nous les** renvoyer.	Please send **them** back **to us**.

When there is more than one object pronoun with the verb there are rules about the order in which they should come.

(e) *Possessive pronouns*

Consider the following sentences from the texts:

Nous espérons que votre voyage de retour s'est bien passé. **Le nôtre** n'a pas été une réussite.	We hope that you had a good return journey. **Ours** was not a success.
Quant au travail, **le mien** a déjà commencé.	As far as work is concerned, **mine** has already started.

The possessive pronoun is the form which occurs in English as 'mine', 'ours', 'yours', 'theirs'. It is used to refer to an act of possession without repeating the noun. In the sentences above, for example, 'ours' stands for 'our journey'; 'mine' stands for 'my work'.

(f) *Some uses of the infinitive*

(i) In some cases, French uses an infinitive where English is more likely to use a present participle:

Apprendre une langue c'est aussi se familiariser avec une autre culture.	**Learning** a language is also a matter of getting to know another culture.

(ii) The following sentence is an example of the past infinitive:

Nous sommes heureux d'**avoir pu** vous rencontrer.	We are happy **to have been** able to meet you.

A past infinitive is most usually found in French after the preposition 'après':

après **être rentré**	after returning
après **avoir vu**	after seeing

(g) *Some notes on vocabulary*

(i) The relative pronoun after 'tout' is always 'ce qui' or 'ce que'. For example:

tout **ce qu'**ils ont fait   all **that** they have done

(ii) 'Peuple' refers to 'people' in the sense of 'nation' (le peuple français). 'Gens' is used to mean 'people' in the more everyday sense of 'a group of individuals'.

(iii) Note the uses of 'manquer':

C'est ce contact qui **manque**.   It's this contact which **is lacking**.

Mon ami me **manque** beaucoup.   I **miss** my friend very much.

Ne **manquez** pas de me rendre visit.   Don't **miss** paying me a visit. (= Make sure you come and see me.)

Exercises

● *The key to these exercises begins on p.230.*

Parlez
(Speaking exercise)

Exercise 1

Now see if you can develop your side of a conversation about learning French. Look at the English prompts below and use the French suggestions to help you prepare what you want to say. Of course, your answers will be personal to you, so if the suggestions don't help you, try to phrase what you want to say without help.

Quand est-ce que vous avez commencé à apprendre le français?

(I began at school.)	J'ai commencé à l'école.
(I began a year ago.)	J'ai commencé il y a un an.
(I began three years ago.)	J'ai commencé il y a trois ans.
(I began at school but never learned to speak.)	J'ai commencé à l'école mais je n'ai jamais appris comment parler.
(I never learned at school but I attended evening classes.)	Je n'ai jamais appris à l'école mais j'ai assisté à des cours du soir.

Pourquoi est-ce que vous avez choisi le français et non pas une autre langue?

(I always spend holidays in France.)	Je passe toujours les vacances en France.
(I have many French friends and I wanted to speak to them.)	J'ai beaucoup d'amis français et je voulais leur parler.
(I've always liked the sound of French.)	J'ai toujours aimé le son du français.
(I wanted to read French books.)	Je voulais lire des livres français.

Est-ce que vous trouvez facile d'apprendre les langues étrangères?

(No, not at all, I have to work hard.)	Non, pas du tout, je dois travailler dur.

(Not really, but I enjoy it.)	Pas vraiment, mais ça me fait plaisir.
(I find it easy to read, but listening and speaking are more difficult.)	Je trouve facile de lire, mais écouter et parler sont plus difficiles.
(My memory isn't as good as when I was younger.)	Ma mémoire n'est pas aussi bonne que quand j'étais plus jeune.

Est-ce que vous croyez que c'est important de passer du temps dans le pays?

(It's the most important thing.)	C'est la chose la plus importante.
(It's very important to immerse yourself in the language.)	C'est très important de vous plonger dans la langue.
(Yes, because the people and the culture are an important part of language learning.)	Oui, parce que les gens et la culture sont une partie importante de l'apprentissage d'une langue.

Lisez et écrivez
(Reading and writing exercises)

Exercise 2

A French magazine has asked its readers to send letters telling the story of their first meeting with their partner. Here is an extract from one of these letters. Read the letter and then indicate whether the statements below the text are *true* or *false* (T or F). Try to guess the meaning of words from the context but look them up in a dictionary if you need further help.

COUP DE FOUDRE

C'était en juillet et je me souviens qu'il avait fait chaud pendant tout le mois. Ma meilleure amie, Oriane, avait organisé une soirée pour ses 20 ans. Malheureusement, j'avais attrapé la veille un très gros rhume et je me sentais plutôt mal. J'avais donc décidé de ne pas y aller. J'étais en train de téléphoner à Oriane pour m'excuser quand on a sonné à la porte. Quand j'avais raccroché, ma mère m'a expliqué que c'était un garçon pour moi, qu'elle ne le connaissait pas mais qu'elle l'avait fait entrer dans le salon. Pendant que je téléphonais, il lui avait expliqué qu'il avait été invité à la soirée d'Oriane mais comme il n'avait pas de voiture il ne pouvait pas y aller. Quelqu'un lui avait donné mon adresse et lui avait dit que j'allais à cette soirée. Par simple curiosité, j'ai regardé par la porte du salon. Et là, je l'ai vu qui parlait et riait avec mon petit frère. Je n'oublierai jamais cet instant. Ça a été immédiat! Je me suis dit: il faut que j'aille à cette soirée, que je rencontre ce garçon. Il me plaît terriblement. Et nous sommes allés ensemble à cette soirée. Et à beaucoup d'autres depuis 20 ans que nous sommes mariés.

Charlotte

(a) Charlotte met her future husband at a party.   T ☐ F ☐

(b) On the day she met him she was not feeling well.   T ☐ F ☐

(c) He came to invite her to Oriane's party.   T ☐ F ☐

(d) Charlotte was on the phone when he came in.   T ☐ F ☐

(e) He came to ask if she wanted a lift to the party.   T ☐ F ☐

(f) For Charlotte, it was love at first sight.   T ☐ F ☐

Exercise 3

The letter from Charlotte in the previous exercise is full of pluperfect tenses. Write out the phrases containing a pluperfect and give an English translation.

Example: Je me souviens qu'il avait fait chaud pendant tout le mois.
               I remember that it had been hot all month.

Exercise 4

Compose a letter of thanks to friends in France, taking the first letter of the chapter as a guide, and using the following suggestions as an outline:

(Tell your friends that it is already more than a week since you returned home. Time goes so quickly. You have a lot of happy memories of your time in France. Tell them you are grateful for their welcome. Tell them a little about the return journey – whether it went without incident or whether you had any problems. Now the holidays are over and you will soon start work again. Tell your friends you are looking forward to a visit from them, and finish by thanking them again and sending them your best wishes.)

Exercise 5

The aim of this exercise is for you to write sentences using verbs in the pluperfect tense. Combine the elements in each sentence following the model of the example:

Example: Il / partir / je / rencontrer son père.
Answer: Il était déjà parti quand j'ai rencontré son père.
              (He had already left when I met his father.)

(a) Nous / prendre du retard / nous / arriver au port.

(b) Elle / arriver à la gare / nous / aller la chercher.

(c) Il / recommencer son travail / sa femme / retourner au bureau.

(d) L'hôtelier / renvoyer les articles / je / lui écrire.

(e) Mon ami / apprendre la langue / il / visiter le pays.

(Note that 'prendre du retard' means 'to lose time'.)

Écoutez

(Listening exercise)

Exercise 6   Spontaneous dialogue   Learning foreign languages

Isabelle and Édouard talk about learning foreign languages. He started learning at school, but has some particular ideas about how to start by adjusting one's ear to the foreign sounds.

(a) Complete the following sentence:

Je me demande comment tu es arrivé à...

(b) What happened when Édouard was 11 years old?

(c) Édouard thinks there is a certain gift, but a lot of hard work as well. What sort of work? Fill in the gaps.

Afin d'apprendre ...., d'étudier la .... et .... aussi dans la langue.

(d) How does Isabelle phrase her question to ask what is the most important thing in learning a language?

(e) For Édouard, the most important thing, especially at the beginning, is:

listening a lot	☐
speaking a lot	☐
visiting the country	☐
reading newspapers	☐

(f) How does Édouard describe his own approach to language learning?

(g) In what ways do children learn their mother tongue, according to Isabelle?

C'est d'ailleurs ce que font les enfants, ils...

(h) What advantages will now be offered by having access to foreign TV channels? Complete the sentence.

Et puis maintenant, avec l'accès aux chaînes de télévision étrangères...

⟨20⟩ *Supplementary listening material*

This book has given you plenty of opportunity to hear people talking in French. But there are many other occasions, besides conversations, when listening to the language and understanding what you hear are important everyday skills.

Information may be given over loudspeakers, on telephone answering machines, on the radio or television. You may hear announcements in shops or on the beach. The following extracts are authentic listening tasks which you might face in situations such as these.

There will be quite a lot of words and phrases that you will not have met previously in the book, but use the setting and the context of the extract to help you guess at what is said, and don't be put off by particular words you don't know. Read the opening title and explanation and then listen several times, trying to get the gist of what is being said, particularly if there are times and dates involved. Then write answers to the English questions on each extract. The *key* to this chapter contains the French transcription and a translation of each extract. You can check your answers to the questions by using these translations, and you can clarify any problems in understanding the French by comparing the recording with the written French text and looking up in a dictionary any words which are unfamiliar.

1 Le répondeur téléphonique   The telephone answering machine

You try ringing the home number of Monsieur and Madame Lefèvre, but they are not at home, and there is a message on the answering machine.

(a) What three things are you asked to record on the answering machine?

(b) When will they call you back?

2 *Prévisions météorologiques* *Weather forecast*

Not very good weather in the North, but better in the South, except when muggy weather leads to thunderstorms in some areas.

(a) Give more information about the weather in the North. Will there be rain? Will it be windy? Where will the wind be particularly strong?

(b) What will temperatures in the North be like compared with the average for this time of year?

(c) What are temperatures going to be in the South?

(d) What is threatened for the Pyrenees and the Basque coast?

3 *Dans le hall de la gare* *On the station concourse*

The train to Rouen is about to leave, but another train is arriving late (most unusual for SNCF).

(a) Give the platform and time of departure of the train to Rouen.

(b) Which train is 20 minutes late and at which platform will it arrive?

4 *Aux Galeries Lafayette* *At the Galeries Lafayette*

Special offers on underwear at the department store.

(a) What is on offer in the underwear department?

(b) Where is the department situated?

5 *Sur la plage* *On the beach*

Dangers announced, and a little girl has got lost.

(a) How are the bathing limits indicated on the beach at Biarritz?

(b) What are the dangers for swimmers outside these limits?

(c) Describe the little girl who has got lost.

(d) Where should she be taken by anyone finding her?

6 *Musée: renseignements enregistrés* *Recorded information at the museum*

Opening times and other information on the museum answering machine.

(a) On which day of the week is the museum closed?

(b) What are the opening hours on every day except Saturday, Sunday and public holidays?

(c) What number must you ring if you want information on exhibitions?

7 Publicité à la Radio Radio advertising

Publicity for a firm selling electrical goods for the home.

(a) What guarantees do you get if you buy equipment with a well-known brand name (according to this radio advertisement)?

(b) How many different brands does this store have in stock?

(c) What is guaranteed by the technicians working for Darty?

8 Annonce de grande surface Hypermarket announcement

'Grande surface' is a term often used to mean a large hypermarket. One of the chains is Auchan, and here it's 'white week' and household linen is reduced.

(a) Can you give three types of household linen in the sale?

(b) How much will a complete set of bed linen cost you?

(c) When will the sale finish?

9 Sécurité routière Road safety

It's the end of the holidays and the traffic is streaming home. This announcement attempts to warn drivers before they run into a jam at Lyon.

(a) When, apparently, did most motorists start their journey home?

(b) How long is the jam at the entrance to the Fourvières tunnel?

(c) What advice is given to drivers to enable them to avoid this delay?

10 Informations santé sur France-Info Health information on France-Info

Radio information about the best sort of sleep to help get over late night parties at Christmas and New Year.

(a) What sort of sleep is best for getting over physical fatigue?

(b) Why is a siesta recommended?

(c) If the first night's sleep helps you to get over physical fatigue, what does the second night's sleep do for you?

(d) What is particularly beneficial according to the last statement in this broadcast?

Translations of dialogues in Chapters 1-5

Chapter 1

Dialogue 1

Policeman: Good morning, sir. Your passport, please.
John Smith: Good morning. Here's my passport.
Policeman: Thank you, sir. Are you John Smith?
John: Yes, that's right. And this is my wife and my two children.
Policeman: Good morning, madam.
Mary: Good morning.
Policeman: How long are you staying in France?
John: Three weeks.
Policeman: Right, sir. Here's your passport. Goodbye and have a nice trip.
John: Thanks. Goodbye.

Dialogue 2

John: Good afternoon. I'm Mr Smith. You have a room for my family.
Hotelier: Ah yes! Good afternoon, Mr Smith; good afternoon, Mrs Smith.
Mary: Good afternoon. And here are our two children, Catherine and Robert.
Hotelier: Hello, children. Now, Mr Smith, you are staying three weeks, that's right, isn't it?
John: Yes, that's right.
Hotelier: Good, well it's room number five. Here is your key.
John: Thank you.
Hotelier: Goodbye, sir, goodbye, madam.

Dialogue 3

John: Excuse me, is Mr Lebrun in please? My name is John Smith.
Secretary: Ah, yes, you're Mr Smith. Mr Lebrun is in. Just a moment please.

Lebrun: Good afternoon, Mr Smith, I am very pleased to meet you.
John: Good afternoon, Mr Lebrun. May I introduce my wife, Mary, and our two children, Catherine and Robert.
Lebrun: Delighted to meet you, Mrs Smith. Hello, children. Well, are you free this evening? Can you have dinner with us?
John: We'd be delighted.
Mary: That's very kind of you.
Lebrun: Right, then. We'll see you at seven o'clock this evening.
John: Many thanks and goodbye.
Lebrun: Goodbye, Mr Smith. Goodbye, Mrs Smith. Goodbye, children. See you later.

Dialogue 4

Lebrun: Good evening, Mr Smith. Good evening, Mrs Smith. How are you?
John: Very well, thank you. And you?
Lebrun: I'm very well, thanks. Do come in, please. Nicole, Mr and Mrs Smith and the children are here.
Madame L: Good evening, Mr Smith. Good evening, Mrs Smith.
John: How do you do, Mrs Lebrun. And these are our two children, Catherine and Robert.
Madame L: Good evening, children.

Chapter 2

Dialogue 1

Bank employee: Good morning, sir. Can I help you?
John: Good morning. Can I change fifty pounds into francs, please?
Employee: Certainly, sir. You can change cash or cash a cheque. You can also use your credit card in the cashpoint and enter your personal number. In that way you can get cash. Which would you prefer?
John: Can I cash an English cheque?
Employee: You can cash an English eurocheque if you present your bank card.
John: Good. Well, here's my card and a eurocheque for 500F.
Employee: Thank you, sir. May I see your passport, please?
John: Here is my passport.
Employee: Thank you sir. That's fine, will you step along to the cash-desk, please?

Dialogue 2

Waitress: Good morning, sir. What would you like?
John: I'd like white coffee.
Mary: And I'd like black coffee. And two Oranginas for the children.

206   *MASTERING FRENCH*

Waitress: So that's one white coffee, one black coffee and two Oranginas. Will that be all?

John: Will you also bring two ices for the children, please?

Waitress: Yes, sir. Which flavour? There is vanilla, strawberry or chocolate.

Mary: Chocolate, please.

Waitress: Certainly, madam.

John: Miss, the bill, please.

Waitress: Yes, sir, well, two coffees, that's 14 francs, two Oranginas, that's 20 francs, and two ice-creams 24 francs. So that comes to 58 francs.

John: Is the service included?

Waitress: Yes, sir. Service is included.

John: There you are. Thank you.

Waitress: Thank you, sir. Goodbye, sir. Goodbye, madam.

Dialogue 3

John: Excuse me. Can I have the key to room number five, please?

Hotelier: Here you are, sir. I am sorry, but there is a small problem.

John: Why?

Hotelier: Because your room is not quite ready. The chambermaid is making the beds.

John: It doesn't matter. Can we have lunch?

Hotelier: I'm very sorry, sir. Lunch is not quite ready.

John: Oh really? What's happening? It's already half past midday.

Hotelier: We've got a problem with the electricity. But it's not serious.

John: It's a breakdown probably, is it?

Hotelier: Yes but everything is working again now. In two minutes your room is all yours.

John: Good.

Chapter 3

Dialogue 1

John: Good morning. We are in Caen for the first time. Have you any information on the town, please?

Lady: Certainly, sir. Here is a town plan and here is the official guide. Would you like information about the main sights?

John: Yes, please.

Lady: Well, on the plan you can see the castle here. In front of the main entrance to the castle you can see the church of St Pierre.

Mary: Is that the church with the tall spire?

Lady: That's right, madam. Well now, follow St Pierre Street and Écuyère Street, cross over Fontette Square and St Étienne church is on the left.

John: Oh yes, that's very well-known. And near the church, what's that?

Lady: That's the town hall. You can also visit the port of Caen.
Mary: Is there a port here at Caen?
Lady: Yes, madam, there is a very important port. The Botanical Gardens are also very interesting.
John: Good, thank you very much.
Lady: You're welcome, sir. Have a nice stay in Caen.

Dialogue 2

John: Excuse me. How do I get to St Étienne church, please?
Passer-by: St Étienne church, well, you go straight on, cross over Fontette Square, take the first street on the right and the church is on your left.
John: Is it far from here?
Passer-by: Oh no. Ten minutes on foot, that's all.
John: Thanks very much.
Passer-by: Don't mention it.

Dialogue 3

John: Excuse me, how do I get to the castle please?
Passer-by: The castle. It's quite a long way.
John: Oh, really?
Passer-by: Yes, on foot you'll need half an hour, at least, especially with the children. Take the bus.
John: That's a good idea. Where is the bus stop?
Passer-by: Over there, in front of the town hall.
John: Many thanks. That's very kind of you.
Passer-by: You're welcome.

Dialogue 4

John: Two adults and two children, please.
Driver: Where are you going?
John: To the castle.
Driver: That'll be twelve francs forty. Thank you. Don't forget to stamp your tickets. Here is your change.
John: Thank you.

Dialogue 5

John: Excuse me. Do you know where the port is?
Passer-by: I'm sorry, sir. I don't know. I don't come from here.
John: Excuse me, how do I get to the port, please?
Lady: Go straight on, cross over Courtonne Square and the St Pierre docks are on your right.

John: Thank you. Is it far from here?
Lady: No, not at all. About two hundred metres away.
John: Thank you.
Lady: You're welcome.

Chapter 4

Dialogue 1

Man on the phone: Hello, this is the municipal swimming pool, Caen.
John: Good morning. When is the swimming pool open?
Man: This morning the pool is open from 9 o'clock until midday.
John: Is it open in the afternoon as well?
Man: Yes, in the afternoon the pool is open from 2 till 6.
John: Are the times of opening the same every day?
Man: The times are the same from Monday to Friday. On Saturdays the pool is open until 9 pm and on Sundays from 9.45 until 5.30.

Dialogue 2

John: Hello, is that the Museum of the D-Day Landings?
Man: Hello, yes, this is the D-Day Landings Museum at Arromanches.
John: I'd like to know when the museum is open.
Man: The museum is open every day from 9 till midday and from 2 pm until 7 pm.
John: Thank you.

Dialogue 3

Lady on the phone: Hello, Tourist Information Centre, Lisieux.
John: Good morning. I am coming to Lisieux with my family and I'd like to know if there is a guided visit to the Basilica of St Teresa.
Lady: Yes, sir, there are guided tours every day from 9 until midday and from 2 pm until 4.30 pm.
John: Good. And when is the Son et Lumière performance at the Basilica?
Lady: The Son et Lumière performance is presented every evening except Friday, at 9.30 pm.
John: Thank you.
Lady: You're welcome.

Dialogue 4

Mary: Good morning. Have you got two seats for the Tuesday evening performance?
Lady at the cash-desk: I'm sorry, madam. We're full up on Tuesday.

Mary: What a pity! How about Wednesday?
Lady: Wednesday as well. I'm sorry but we're fully booked. There are some seats left at 120 francs for Thursday evening.
Mary: Good. What time does the play begin?
Lady: At 7.15, madam. There is an interval at 8.45.
Mary: Do you take Visa?
Lady: Certainly, madam.

Chapter 5

Dialogue 1

Lebrun: Good morning, everybody. Enjoy your meal. How are things?
John: Good morning, Michel. How nice to see you again. We are fine, thanks. How are you?
Lebrun: I'm very well too. How is your stay in Caen going?
Mary: Very well. We're delighted with our visit.
Lebrun: Good. Well, forgive me for disturbing your breakfast, but what have you got planned for today?
John: This morning we are going to do some shopping.
Mary: Yes, this morning we want to buy some clothes for the children. After that, we don't know yet.
Lebrun: If you are free at midday I would like to invite you to join my wife and me for lunch in a restaurant.
John: We'd be delighted. How kind of you. The children as well?
Lebrun: Of course. Right then, we'll have lunch at the 'Cultivateurs' near the Avenue of 6 June. Do you know the street?
John: Yes I know the street, but where is the restaurant?
Lebrun: Well, you go down the street in the direction of the river and the restaurant is on the right on the Quai de Juillet. When shall we meet?
John: We are at your disposal.
Lebrun: Right then, half past twelve, is that all right?
John: Yes, that's fine.
Lebrun: Fine, see you later. Goodbye.
John: Goodbye and thank you.

Dialogue 2

Hotelier: Do you like this weather, sir?
John: Certainly not! We are out of luck. It's raining again. Isn't it ever fine in Caen?
Hotelier: Oh yes! Usually it's fine in summer. Sometimes it's even very warm. But the sea isn't very far away, you know. We have a maritime climate like you in England, and it rains from time to time.
John: Do you think it will be fine later on?

Hotelier: That's possible. The weather changes quickly here. Look! You can already see a bit of blue sky. The sun will be back, just you wait and see.
John: You're an optimist. But I think we shall go and buy anoraks for the children all the same. You never know, that's quite right.
Hotelier: Good luck, all the same. Enjoy yourselves.

Key to exercises

Chapter 1

Exercise 1
Here are some model answers for John Smith's part of the conversation:
Bonjour, monsieur. Je suis John Smith. / Voilà. / C'est bien ça. / Merci. / Merci, monsieur. À bientôt.

Exercise 3
Bonjour, monsieur. Je vous présente ma femme, Mary. / Bonjour, monsieur. / Oui, avec plaisir. / Oui, ça va bien. / Merci, monsieur. Au revoir et à bientôt.

Exercise 4
(a) Je m'appelle Colette. Et vous?
(b) Anne, je vous présente Monsieur Dupont.
    Bonjour, monsieur.
    Enchanté.
(c) Bonjour Anne. Vous êtes libre ce soir? Vous pouvez dîner chez nous?
    Vous êtes très gentil. Avec plaisir.
(d) Je m'appelle Carole.
(e) Bonjour Madame Dupont. Comment allez-vous?
    Très bien, merci. Et vous?

Exercise 5
(a) Vous êtes Mary Smith? (OR Est-ce que vous êtes Mary Smith?)
(b) Vous pouvez dîner chez nous? ('Oui, avec plaisir' could be a response to lots of other possible questions and invitations.)
(c) Comment allez-vous?
(d) (Est-ce que) Monsieur Lebrun est là?
(e) This could be a response to a variety of queries, for example:
    Vous êtes bien Monsieur Smith?
    Vous restez trois semaines?

Exercise 6
(a) Oui, c'est ma clef.
(b) Oui, c'est ma chambre.
(c) Oui, c'est mon enfant.
(d) Oui, c'est mon passeport.
(e) Oui, c'est ma famille.

Exercise 7
(a) Réservation.
(b) Trois semaines.
(c) C'est cela, oui.
(d) Are you sure it's a family room?
(e) Fiche.
(f) Voilà.
(g) 5
(h) Key.
(i) Je vous souhaite un bon séjour.

Chapter 2

Exercise 1
Je voudrais un café et une glace vanille, s'il vous plaît. / Oui, c'est tout. / Merci. / Mademoiselle, l'addition, s'il vous plaît. / Voilà … merci.

Exercise 3
(a) (Est-ce que) je peux déjeuner?
(b) (Est-ce que) je peux aller à ma chambre?
(c) (Est-ce que) je peux avoir un café?

Exercise 4
(a) Welcome to our service. ('Bienvenue' means 'welcome'.)
(b) Please enter your personal number. ('Touche' means 'key' (on a computer).)
(c) The word for 'cash' is 'espèces'.
(d) The word for 'request' is 'demande'.
(e) 'Billets' is the French for 'banknotes' and 'carte' is the French for 'card'.

Exercise 5
The following are possible answers, but you might have a different preference.
(a) Je préfère de l'argent liquide, s'il vous plaît.
(b) Je préfère un thé, s'il vous plaît.
(c) Je préfère fraise, s'il vous plaît.

Exercise 6
(a) Parce que je veux un café.
(b) Parce que je veux déjeuner.
(c) Parce qu'il y a un petit problème.

Exercise 7
(a) Mesdames, messieurs, bonjour, qu'est-ce que vous désirez?
(b) Woman: un grand chocolat chaud; un crossiant; Man: un café au lait; un croissant.
(c) Un café – 7 francs; un grand chocolat – 14 francs; deux croissants – 10 francs; Total = 31 francs.
(d) Is service included? (Le service est compris?)

Chapter 3

Exercise 1
Pour aller au château s'il vous plaît? / Oui, je suis à pied. / C'est loin d'ici? / Est-ce qu'il y a un bus? / Où est l'arrêt d'autobus? / Merci beaucoup, monsieur.

Exercise 2
You can use any of the ways for asking the way, for example:
Pardon, madame, pour aller au château, s'il vous plaît?
où est le Jardin des Plantes, s'il vous plaît?
l'église Saint-Étienne, s'il vous plaît?
pour aller à l'Hôtel de Ville, s'il vous plaît?

Exercise 3
Syndicat d'initiative.

Exercise 4
The cathedral.

Exercise 5
(a) Oui, c'est un port important.
(b) Oui, c'est une église intéressante.
(c) Oui, c'est un château connu.
(d) Oui, j'ai le guide officielle.
(e) Oui, je vois l'entrée principale.

Exercise 6
(a) A town plan (un plan de la ville).
(b) Vous tournez à droite; première à gauche.
(c) Is it very far?
(d) Une très belle cathédrale.
(e) Take the first on the right, then first on the left and you arrive at the cathedral.
(f) I wish you an excellent day.

Chapter 4

Exercise 1
Bonjour, madame. Quand est-ce que le château est ouvert, s'il vous plaît? /
Est-ce qu'il y a des visites guidées? / Est-ce qu'il y a un spectacle Son et
Lumière au château? / Merci, madame.

Exercise 3
(a) Il est sept heures moins cinq. (6h 55)
(b) Il est dix heures moins le quart. (9h 45)
(c) Il est une heure vingt-cinq. (1h 25)
(d) Il est huit heures vingt. (8h 20)
(e) Il est midi vingt. (12h 20)
(f) Il est minuit dix. (12h 10)

Exercise 4
(a) No. Open mornings only in January.
(b) Tomorrow morning.

Exercise 5
Here are some possibilities, but your own suggestions are equally valid:
lundi – le château / mardi – le musée / mercredi – le théâtre / jeudi – le spectacle
Son et Lumière / vendredi – la piscine / samedi – le port / dimanche – l'église.

Exercise 6
Here are some further possibilities to add to those given on p. 41:
Je voudrais aller à Caen. Je voudrais voir le château. Je voudrais visiter le musée.
Je voudrais visiter Paris. Je voudrais voir Notre-Dame. Je voudrais visiter le
Louvre.

Exercise 7
(a) Salle 1 – *Manon des Sources*; Salle 2 – *Cyrano de Bergerac;* Salle 3 *Germinal.*
(b) 2 pm, 4 pm, 6 pm, 8.30 pm.
(c) *Cyrano de Bergerac.*
(d) 8.30 pm.

Chapter 5

Exercise 1
Ce matin je vais visiter le château. / Je vais déjeuner au restaurant. Est-ce que
vous connaissez un bon restaurant? / C'est une bonne idée. Vous croyez qu'il va
faire beau? / Après le déjeuner je crois que je vais faire des courses en ville. /
Merci bien. Au revoir.

Exercise 2

Lundi matin je vais visiter le château.

Mardi matin je vais voir le port. **Mardi après-midi** je vais visiter le musée.

Mercredi matin je vais aller à la basilique. **Mercredi soir** je vais aller au théâtre.

Jeudi matin je vais visiter le Musée du Débarquement. **Jeudi après-mid**i je vais voir la tapisserie de Bayeux et **jeudi soir** je vais aller au cinéma.

Vendredi matin je vais faire des courses. **Vendredi après-midi** je vais déjeuner au restaurant.

Samedi matin je vais aller à la piscine. **Samedi soir** je vais dîner chez des amis.

Dimanche matin je vais aller à l'église Saint-Étienne.

Exercise 3

Where you are replying for yourself with a partner or family, use the same pattern as in Exercise 2 but use 'nous allons' instead of 'je vais'. For example: **Lundi matin** nous allons visiter le château.

Exercise 4

(a) True (pluvieux le matin).

(b) False (vent modéré).

(c) True (quelques éclaircies (bright periods) l'après-midi).

(d) True (les éclaircies reviennent = bright periods return).

(e) True (vent modéré).

(f) True (températures maximales 18–21).

Exercise 5

(a) Je crois qu'il va faire mauvais.

(b) Je crois qu'il va faire froid.

(c) Je crois qu'il va pleuvoir.

Exercise 6

(a) Maljasset.

(b) Encore une heure.

(c) She shows surprise. It means 'As long as that!'

(d) The key word is 'tard', meaning 'late'. The rain is coming 'plus tard' (later).

(e) She says 'parce que la mer n'est pas loin' (because the sea is not far away).

(f) You get used to it.

(g) She says that they are English and in England it rains quite often. (En Angleterre aussi il pleut assez souvent.)

(h) She is saying she prefers a temperate climate. (Je préfère un climat plus tempéré.)

(i) The important thing is to be prepared for bad weather.

(j) Bonne promenade.

Chapter 6

Exercise 1
Oui, il fait encore mauvais.Vous croyez qu'il va faire beau plus tard? / Oui, il pleut beaucoup en Angleterre. Je n'ai pas de chance, mais il va y avoir du soleil plus tard, peut-être. / On ne sait jamais. Je crois que je vais visiter un musée aujourd'hui. / Merci beaucoup. Au revoir.

Exercise 2
There are various possibilities. Here are some suggestions:
le pullover de Monsieur Lebrun / le port de Caen / l'entrée du château / la voiture du monsieur / la clef de la chambre / le numéro de la chambre / l'imperméable de l'enfant / la piscine de la ville / les vêtements des hommes

Exercise 3
(a) 2 (librairie = bookshop).
(b) RC (droguerie = hardware and household goods).
(c) SS (alimentation = food).
(d) 1 (confection = clothing).
(e) 3 (tout pour le jardin = everything for the garden).
(f) RC (électroménager = household electrical goods).

Exercise 4
The answers will depend on your personal preferences.

Exercise 5
(a) Oui, c'est pour elle.
(b) Oui, c'est pour lui.
(c) Mais si, c'est pour lui.
(d) Oui, il est avec eux.
(e) Oui, il est avec elle.
(f) Oui, elle est avec eux.

Exercise 6
(a) Bonjour, madame. Je peux vous aider?
(b) Do you want a one-piece or a two-piece costume?
(c) She chooses a one-piece because she wants it for swimming.
(d) Là-bas, au fond (over there, at the back of the shop).
(e) Because there is an unbelievable choice.
(f) (i) Which colour do you want?(ii) Do you prefer a single colour? (iii) Do you want stripes? (iv) ...or perhaps a print?
(g) She chooses a single, dark colour.
(h) Size 40–42.
(i) Peut-être que je peux l'essayer?
(j) Fitting rooms.

Chapter 7

Exercise 1

The choice of apéritif and menu will depend on your own preference. Here is one possible answer:

Comme apéritif, je voudrais un kir. Et donnez-moi le menu, s'il vous plaît. / Alors, je commence avec des huîtres. Après, le steak au poivre. Puis, du fromage et, pour terminer, une crème caramel. / Apportez-moi une bouteille de pomerol, s'il vous plaît. / Monsieur, l'addition, s'il vous plaît.

Exercise 2

(a) False (fromage ou pâtisserie = cheese OR pastry).
(b) False (service compris = service included).
(c) False (boissons en sus = drinks extra).
(d) True (potage = soup).

Exercise 3

(a) 3 (de belles spécialités alsaciennes = specialities from Alsace).
(b) 1 (la superbe terrasse de verdure = splendid 'terrasse' in a setting of green foliage).
(c) 4 (tout Paris à vos pieds vu du Tour Eiffel = all of Paris at your feet from the top of the Eiffel Tower).
(d) 2 (faux-filet grillé avec ... pommes allumettes).

Exercise 4

(a) Le climat français est meilleur que le climat anglais.
(b) Le Jardin des Plantes est plus intéressant que le port.
(c) La couleur rouge est plus chic que la couleur jaune.
(d) Dans le Midi il fait plus chaud qu'en Angleterre.
(e) Le livarot est plus fort que le camembert.
(f) Le théâtre est plus intéressant que le cinéma.
(g) Mon imperméable est plus beau que votre coupe-vent.
(h) Catherine est plus belle que son frère.

Exercise 5

(a) Vous aimeriez un apéritif avant le repas?
(b) Un kir royal (champagne with a dash of blackcurrant liqueur (cassis)).
(c) Les crevettes grillées; les escargots; la blanquette de veau; la sole meunière.
(d) They decide to have half a bottle of white (sancerre) and a bottle of red (bordeaux).

Chapter 8

Exercise 1

Avec plaisir, je ne suis pas pressé. / Oui, c'est ma première visite à Caen. / Je viens d'Angleterre. / Non, je suis dans un hôtel. / Je suis ici avec ma femme et mes deux enfants. / Je suis professeur. / On se promène en ville, on visite les monuments, etc. / Je suis ravi, et ma femme aussi. Les gens sont accueillants et nous aimons la ville. / De rien. Au revoir.

Exercise 2

(a) No (sans permis = without licence).
(b) The Loire valley.
(c) 350 km.
(d) 2–12 persons.
(e) Castles, manor houses, abbeys, many typical villages.
(f) Horse-riding (équitation); fishing (pêche); cycling (vélo); bathing (baignade).

Exercise 3

Here are some possible answers, but your own times may be different.
(a) Je me réveille à sept heures.
(b) Je me lève à sept heures et demie.
(c) Je me lave à huit heures.
(d) Je me prépare pour sortir à neuf heures du matin.
(e) Je me promène en ville à dix heures du matin.
(f) Je me repose à huit heures du soir.
(g) Je me couche à dix heures du soir.

Exercise 4

Questions can be phrased using either 'à quelle heure?' OR 'quand?' Here are some examples, but there are other possibilities.
À quelle heure est-ce que vous vous réveillez?
Quand est-ce que vous vous levez?
Quand est-ce que vous vous promenez en ville?
À quelle heure est-ce que vous vous couchez?

Exercise 5

(a) Je vais à l'église. Je vais au Jardin des Plantes. Je vais au port. Je vais à Caen. Je vais au syndicat d'initiative. Je vais au château. Je vais en France. Je vais en Normandie. Je vais en Bretagne. Je vais en Angleterre.
(b) Je viens de France. Je viens du château. Je viens de l'Hôtel de Ville. Je viens de Normandie. Je viens de l'école. Je viens d'Angleterre.

Exercise 6
(a) Je vous présente mon amie et ma cousine Juliette.
(b) Tu habites par ici?
(c) Her father is English, her mother is French and she lives in England.
(d) London.
(e) Qu'est-ce que tu fais? Tu es étudiante?
(f) Je fais des études de droit.
(g) She is bilingual.
(h) Nous, on va aller à la plage cet après-midi. They are going to the beach.
(i) Dans une demi-heure. In half an hour.

Chapter 9

Exercise 1
Je voudrais une livre de beurre, un kilo de pommes de terre et du pain. / Deux baguettes. Je voudrais aussi deux bouteilles de lait. Qu'est-ce que vous avez comme charcuterie? / Alors, cinq tranches de jambon. Est-ce que vous avez du cidre? / Non, je ne veux pas de bière. Alors je prends une bouteille de limonade pour les enfants. Ça fait combien?

Exercise 2
There are a number of possibilities. Here are some examples:
Je voudrais une bouteille de vin rouge.
Je voudrais une boîte d'allumettes.
Je voudrais un paquet de cigarettes.
Je voudrais des œufs (une douzaine d'œufs = 12 eggs).
Je voudrais beaucoup de croissants.

Exercise 3
There are a number of possibilities. Here are some examples:
C'est possible d'acheter de la bière.
Il faut arriver à huit heures.
Je vais rester six jours.
Nous voulons acheter un apéritif.
Je peux visiter l'église.

Exercise 4
(a) Une pincée de; fondre; fromage (gruyère) râpé; nappez avec la sauce.
(b) Cooking (time); vegetables; oven; serve immediately after taking out of the oven.

Exercise 5

(a) A barbecue; Cédric has a grill, a few bricks and some wood.
(b) Verres; couteaux; plastique; serviettes.
(c) Du vin (wine), de la bière (beer), de la limonade (lemonade).
(d) Des hamburgers (hamburgers), du poulet (chicken), des saucisses (sausages).
(e) Des bananes cuites (grilled bananas).
(f) 6.30 au parking de la plage.

Chapter 10

Exercise 1

On verra certainement Notre-Dame et on visitera le Louvre. / Oui, alors on fera certainement une excursion en bateau-mouche. / Oui, on verra la Tour Eiffel et aussi l'Arc de Triomphe. / On n'aura pas le temps de manger dans un bon restaurant, alors on prendra sans doute des sandwichs. / Merci. Il fera beau, j'espère.

Exercise 2

(a) Non, ils ne le connaissent pas encore.
(b) Oui, on le prendra à sept heures du matin.
(c) Oui, nous les aimons beaucoup.
(d) Oui, on la fera pendant l'après-midi.
(e) Non, je ne l'aime pas du tout.

Exercise 3

(a) Money (argent).
(b) Give good advice (donner un bon conseil).
(c) Good luck and self-discipline (chance et auto-discipline).
(d) Find love (rencontrer l'amour).
(e) This evening (la soirée).

Exercise 4

(a) On pense partir vendredi.
(b) Honfleur.
(c) Il faut compter trois heures de route.
(d) Go to the market (marché).
(e) They would take the tunnel if they were in a hurry, but they have plenty of time.
(f) Voyage / élèves / prochain / passera / dire.
(g) Je vous souhaite un bon voyage de retour.

Translation of extracts from guide-book given on p. 96.

The Avenue of the Champs-Élysées

From the Concorde to the Rond-Point
Go up towards the Étoile following the drives of chestnut trees lining the avenue. It's the part of the walk where there are most people. There are lots of children there, attracted by the little shops, the swings.

From the Rond-Point to the Étoile
Stroll up the avenue. One should walk on the right-hand side. It is the liveliest and the most typical. A street, a café and a cinema bear the name Colisée. One arrives at the Place de l'Étoile, at the base of the majestic arch.

The Eiffel Tower
This is the most universally known of the sights of Paris. Ascent: Every day from 10.45 am until 6.00 pm (in July and August from 9.30 am until 6.00 pm). For the visitor who climbs to the top, the view can extend as far as 67 kilometres.

The Basilica of the Sacré Cœur
The tall white silhouette now forms part of the Parisian landscape. The ascent to the dome (from 10.00 am to 1.00 pm and from 2.00 pm to 5.00 pm) offers a magnificent panorama.

Paris, seen from its river
There are regular services of pleasure boats every day from 1 April until 5 October. In winter there is one service per day at 3.15 pm. Embarcation point: Solferino Bridge.

Chapter 11

Exercise 1
Pardon, monsieur, est-ce que ces places sont libres? / Vous permettez? / Il y a tellement de monde dans la ville aujourd'hui. / Non, nous passons une journée à Paris en famille. / Nous espérons visiter le Louvre, et Notre-Dame. Nous espérons aussi faire une excursion en bateau-mouche.

Exercise 2
Quatre adultes aller-retour pour Paris, s'il vous plaît.
Combien est-ce que je vous dois?
Quand est-ce que le prochain train va partir? Et de quelle voie?
Quand est-ce que le train va arriver?

Exercise 3
(a) 941.
(b) 14.04.
(c) 3 hours and 1 minute.
(d) Restaurant service, but for 1st-class passengers and with a reservation only.

Exercise 4

(a) La Préfecture de Police se trouve en face de la cathédrale.
(b) La cathédrale de Notre-Dame se trouve près du pont Saint-Louis.
(c) Le Palais de Justice est situé en face de la Préfecture de Police.
(d) La rue de la Cité est située à côté de la place du Parvis Notre-Dame.
(e) Le Marché aux Fleurs se trouve à côté de la Préfecture de Police.
(f) La place du Parvis Notre-Dame se trouve devant la cathédrale.

Exercise 5

(a) Ce train est très confortable.
(b) C'est pour les enfants, cette visite.
(c) Ce grand bâtiment est le Louvre.
(d) Cette deuxième île s'appelle l'Île Saint-Louis.
(e) Cet agent de police est devant la Préfecture.
(f) Ces touristes aiment visiter Paris.

Exercise 6

(a) Vous êtes ici pour combien de temps?
(b) The most pleasant and the prettiest road.
(c) Première / droite / chemin / vélos / long / agréable / plat / parfait.
(d) Une forêt (a forest).
(e) Agréable randonnée.

Chapter 12

Exercise 1

Oui, nous avons passé une bonne journée. On a beaucoup marché. / Tout d'abord, nous avons pris le métro pour aller à l'Île de la Cité et nous avons visité Notre-Dame. Puis nous avons pris un café et après nous sommes allés au Louvre. / Non, il n'y avait pas assez de temps. Nous avons mangé des sandwichs. / Pas beaucoup. Les enfants ont eu juste assez de temps pour acheter des souvenirs. / Oui, on a eu de la chance. Il a fait beau toute la journée.

Exercise 3

(a) On the map you can hardly see it.
(b) A croissant.
(c) Only one – by boat.
(d) 20 minutes or so.
(e) It's another world, silent and peaceful.
(f) They are single storey (sans étages), whitewashed (blanchies à la chaux) and with blue shutters (équippées de volets bleus).
(g) Very little.
(h) By bike (vélo) or horse-drawn carriage (calèche).
(i) No. There are only 200 inhabitants.

Exercise 4

J'ai pris le train. / Ma femme a eu le temps de se reposer. / Mon ami Michel a fait une visite à Paris. / Mon ami Michel a vu la Tour Eiffel. / Nous avons eu un choc. / Vous avez été souvent à Paris. / Mes enfants ont pu voir la cathédrale. / Les Lebrun ont repris le bus.

Exercise 5

(b) En Suisse Romande.
(c) À pied.
(d) Bourgogne.
(e) Beaune; Dijon.
(f) On n'a jamais aussi bien mangé de notre vie. (Note that the negative 'n'' is often not pronounced in speech. See *grammar ref. 5.10 (a)*.)
(g) On a dû prendre tous les deux au moins dix kilos.
(h) Visité / monuments / flâner / terrasse.
(g) That really makes me want to set off when I hear all that you are saying.

Chapter 13

Exercise 1

Oui, j'ai vu l'accident. / Je suis sortie de l'hôtel vers 9h 05. / Oui, je suis allée à pied. Je suis arrivée à la place vers 9h 15. / Une voiture ne s'est pas arrêtée au feu rouge (une voiture a brûlé le feu rouge) et est rentrée dans une autre voiture qui passait.

Exercise 2

These answers will depend on your personal experiences.

Exercise 3

The three main routes are as follows:

(a) Assuming that a man is speaking:
    Je suis sorti de l'hôtel. Je suis allé à la gare. J'ai pris le train. Je suis arrivé à Paris. J'ai visité les monuments. Je suis allé au théâtre. Je suis rentré à minuit.

(b) Assuming that a woman is speaking (verbs have feminine agreements if they take the auxiliary 'être'):
    Je suis sortie de l'hôtel. Je suis allée au bureau. J'ai travaillé toute la matinée. Je suis sortie déjeuner au restaurant. Je suis retournée au bureau. Je suis rentrée à six heures.

(c) Assuming that someone is speaking about a group of people (verbs have plural agreements if they take the auxiliary 'être'):
    Nous sommes sortis de l'hôtel. Nous nous sommes promenés dans la rue. Nous avons acheté un journal. Nous sommes retournés à l'hôtel. Nous sommes sortis pour la journée. Nous avons fait une excursion. Nous sommes rentrés très tard.

Exercise 4

(a) It was raining so hard that they sometimes had to stop.
(b) About 2 am.
(c) Because of the noise made by the storm.
(d) There was a tremendous clap of thunder (un effroyable coup de tonnerre) and a terrible noise (un bruit terrible).
(e) The large window opening onto the garden was wide open; a beautiful Chinese vase and a large mirror were smashed to pieces on the floor.

Exercise 5

(a) La route de retour.
(b) Tout à coup.
(c) Effroyable.
(d) En bas.
(e) Je ne pouvais en croire mes yeux.
(f) Grande ouverte.

Exercise 6

(a) Nous sommes partis / on a quitté / on a pris / on est arrivé / on est parti.
(b) It broke down (tomber en panne).
(c) He telephoned a garage and a colleague.
(d) Plus d'une heure.
(e) You were fantastically lucky that the other driver was able to come like that, straight away.
(f) The employee was kind enough to let us embark because I explained the situation to him.
(g) Les enfants ont trouvé l'aventure amusante. (They were amused.)

Chapter 14

Exercise 1

This is a possible answer, but your own answer will depend on the area you are talking about:

Eh bien, qu'est-ce que vous voudriez faire demain? / Alors, ici, dans le village où j'habite, il y a une belle église. C'est un village anglais assez typique. Le paysage autour est joli et très varié, et la mer n'est pas loin. On pourrait faire un petit tour vers la mer. Il y a aussi la ville d'Exeter qui n'est pas loin. C'est une ville avec une très belle cathédrale, et un Hôtel de Ville très ancien. Il y a aussi un musée intéressant. / Il va faire beau, selon la météo.

Exercise 2

(a) La cathédrale qui est à Bayeux.
(b) La forêt qui est au sud de Bayeux.
(c) Le timbre que vous avez acheté.
(d) L'argent que je vous ai donné.
(e) L'ami qui habite dans le Midi.
(f) Le château qui est dans la forêt.

Exercise 3

(a) Je lui ai déjà donné la bouteille.
(b) Je lui ai déjà écrit la carte postale.
(c) Je lui ai déjà envoyé le paquet.
(d) Je leur ai déjà proposé une excursion.
(e) Je leur ai déjà téléphoné.

Exercise 4

La semaine dernière je suis allé(e) passer deux jours à Paris. Le premier jour, je suis arrivé(e) à la Gare du Nord ... J'ai marché jusqu'à l'Île de la Cité. Ensuite, j'ai visité le musée du Louvre ... J'ai remonté l'Avenue des Champs-Élysées et j'ai vu l'Arc de Triomphe...
Le deuxième jour, j'ai visité le Musée d'Orsay ... L'après-midi, je suis monté(e) tout en haut de la Tour Eiffel ... Puis, pour me reposer, je suis allé(e) me promener au Jardin du Luxembourg.

Exercise 5

(a) It is his 40th birthday.
(b) They would invite friends and serve a buffet (une soirée surprise avec des amis et un buffet).
(c) D'abord, rappelle-toi, il n'aime pas tellement les grandes fêtes. (Firstly, remember, he doesn't very much like big celebrations.) / Et puis, pense au travail que ça va nous donner. (And then, think of the work that it will make for us.) / Et moi je vais avoir mes examens à cette époque-là. (And I shall have my exams at that time.) / Il faudra que tu fasses tout ça toute seule. (You will have to do all that on your own.)
(d) Take him out to a restaurant.
(e) In the country (à la campagne); it has a very pretty garden (un très joli jardin); excellent food (la cuisine est excellente); it's rather expensive (un peu cher).
(f) Le champagne, les cadeaux.
(g) When he has finished his champagne.
(h) At a table with a view of the garden.
(i) A birthday cake.

Chapter 15

Exercise 1

Quand cette dame était jeune, elle habitait à la campagne. Ses parents n'étaient pas riches. Elle a commencé l'école à l'âge de 6 ans. Sa maison était loin de l'école, alors elle prenait le bus tous les jours. Elle a quitté l'école à 14 ans et elle a commencé à travailler dans un bureau. Elle avait des difficultés à cette époque. Plus tard, elle a changé de travail et elle est venue à la ville. La ville était petite à cette époque-là, mais elle a beaucoup changé aujourd'hui. La dame a enfin pris sa retraite à 65 ans.

Exercise 3

There are a number of possibilities. Here are some examples:

Autrefois les villages étaient plus paisibles.

À cette époque-là la ville était plus petite.

Dans le temps mes parents habitaient à la campagne.

Quand il était jeune il s'intéressait aux langues.

Tous les jours Pierre allait à l'école.

Tous les jours Pierre prenait l'autobus.

Exercise 4

(a) It's an area with a large immigrant population.

(b) Because they were afraid of problems with the police.

(c) He was in possession of a load of cigarettes worth 20,000 francs.

(d) Until midday.

(e) He was interrogated and shot.

Exercise 5

(a) Because she hasn't been there for 15 years.

(b) A little girl / a small child / a kid.

(c) Tous / juillet / frère / les.

(d) Three days.

(e) Partait / s'arrêtait / faisait.

(f) He can't imagine Hélène's father picnicking on the grass.

(g) Mosquitoes (moustiques), wasps (guêpes), the heat (il faisait trop chaud).

(h) He always chose to go and eat in a restaurant. (Naturellement, il optait toujours pour aller manger dans un petit restaurant.)

(i) Because it lies half way between Boulogne and Nice.

(j) It was an old place, but very comfortable, with big beams (avec des grosses poutres), and antique furniture (des meubles d'époque) in the bedrooms.

(k) No, the three children shared a bedroom.

(l) Tu as essayé de retrouver cet hôtel? (What he actually says is 'T'as essayé...')

(m) ... ce n'était plus un hôtel.

(n) Disappointed (déçu(e)).

Chapter 16

Exercise 1

(a) Nous sommes bien arrivés.

(b) Quel plaisir de vous revoir tous!

(c) Un grand merci pour cette journée inoubliable.

(d) À très bientôt, j'espère.

Exercises 2, 3 and 4

The answers will depend upon your personal choices.

Exercise 5

Je dois me lever de bonne heure. / Je dois aller au bureau à 9 heures. / Je dois faire les courses à 11 heures. / Je dois déjeuner avec un visiteur à midi trente (OR midi et demi). / Je dois interviewer un client à trois heures de l'après-midi. / À quatre heures et demie je dois aller chercher les enfants à l'école. / Je dois rentrer à la maison à cinq heures.

Chapter 17

Exercise 1

Il a dit que ce n'était pas sérieux et qu'il n'y avait pas de raison de s'inquiéter. / Il a dit que l'enfant était un peu enrhumé et qu'il avait un peu de fièvre. / Non, mais le docteur a dit qu'il ne devait pas sortir. / Le docteur a dit que je devais lui donner deux comprimés par jour et le laisser dormir, si possible.

Exercise 2

(a) Voilà deux bouteilles de vin. Celui-ci est sec et celui-là est doux.
(b) Voilà deux sacs. Celui-ci est plein et celui-là est vide.
(c) Voilà deux paniers. Celui-ci est lourd et celui-là est léger.
(d) Voilà deux voitures. Celle-ci est rouge et celle-là est blanche.
(e) Voilà deux routes. Celle-ci est bonne et celle-là est mauvaise.

Exercise 3

(a) False (le Français consomme 65 comprimés d'aspirine par an contre 50 pour les autres Européens).
(b) True (chez une minorité d'individus, l'aspirine produit des troubles).
(c) False (les symptômes apparaissent le plus souvent entre 30 et 40 ans).
(d) True (l'irritation de l'estomac).
(e) True (l'arrêt total et définitif de prise d'aspirine...constitue la mesure préventive essentielle).

Exercise 4

(a) J'ai été malade toute la nuit dernière. / I still don't feel quite right.
(b) Do you feel sick? Do you want to be sick?
(c) Dans le bas du ventre.
(d) Si vous voulez bien vous allonger sur la table.
(e) Ça fait vraiment très mal quand vous appuyez là.
(f) Pourrait / probable / indigestion / chaleur / jamais / sûre / test / sang / appendicite.
(g) Et quand est-ce que vous auriez un résultat?
(h) To settle the bill and to fix another appointment.
(i) 2.30 pm.

Chapter 18

Exercise 1
Si je gagnais le gros lot, je ferais probablement le tour du monde. J'achèterais peut-être un château sur la Côte d'Azur. Je mangerais dans les meilleurs restaurants, j'habiterais à la campagne et j'aurais une grande voiture. Je pourrais aller souvent au théâtre, j'irais en France tous les ans et je passerais l'hiver dans un climat chaud.

Exercise 2
Si je devais préparer ce poulet,...
j'ajouterais le cognac / je ferais flamber le cognac / j'ajouterais le bouillon / je laisserais cuire 30 minutes / je terminerais la sauce / je mélangerais bien les ingrédients.

Exercise 3
(a) False; she is asking them about what they would like to do.
(b) True (travailler en équipe).
(c) False (j'apprendrais vite = I would learn quickly).
(d) True (un métier aux horaires difficiles).
(e) True (ce que j'aime le plus – voyager).
(f) False; she says that if she had to make the choice again she would choose the same job.

Exercise 4
Que choisiriez-vous? (What would you choose?)
Je deviendrais journaliste. (I would become a journalist.)
J'adorerais ça! (I would love that!)
Je ne m'ennuierais jamais. (I would never get bored.)
qui me donnerait la chance d'apprendre (which would give me the chance to learn)
le métier que je choisirais (the profession that I would choose)
Qu'est-ce qui vous plairait? (What would you like to do? (*literally* What would please you?))
Je choisirais tout de suite le métier de voyagiste. (I would immediately choose a job as a tour operator.)
Ce serait le rêve. (It would be a dream.)
J'organiserais des voyages. (I would organise journeys.)
Il faudrait aussi savoir calculer les budgets. (It would also be necessary to know how to calculate budgets.)
J'apprendrais vite. (I would learn quickly.)
J'irais sur place. (I would go to the places themselves.)
Je ne sais pas ce que je donnerais pour avoir un travail comme ça! (I don't know what I would give to have a job like that.)

Exercise 5
(a) They couldn't get the car to start again.
(b) They travelled by the Shuttle.
(c) (i) C'était si gentil de votre part de nous accueillir.
    (ii) On a passé des journées fantastiques avec vous.
    (iii) C'était un plaisir.
    (iv) Nous étions ravis de vous avoir reçus.
(d) They are going to arrange to take their holidays in England.
(e) The photos of their visit.

Chapter 19

Exercise 1
The answers to this exercise will be found in the phrases suggested on pp. 198–9, or they will be personal to yourself.

Exercise 2
(a) False; she met him at home before going to a party.
(b) True (j'avais attrapé un très gros rhume).
(c) False; he came hoping for a lift to the party.
(d) True.
(e) False; he didn't have a car himself.
(f) True (un coup de foudre).

Exercise 3
Il avait fait chaud pendant tout le mois. (It had been hot all month.)

Ma meilleure amie, Oriane, avait organisé une soirée pour ses 20 ans. (My best friend Oriane had organised a party for her 20th birthday.)

Malheureusement, j'avais attrapé la veille un très gros rhume. (Unfortunately, I had caught a heavy cold on the day before.)

J'avais donc décidé de ne pas y aller. (I had therefore decided not to go.)

Quand j'avais raccroché, ma mère m'a expliqué que c'était un garçon pour moi. (When I had hung up, my mother explained that it was a boy for me.)

Elle l'avait fait entrer dans le salon. (She had asked him to go into the sitting room.)

Il lui avait expliqué qu'il avait été invité à la soirée d'Oriane. (He had explained to her that he had been invited to Oriane's party.)

Quelqu'un lui avait donné mon adresse et lui avait dit que j'allais à cette soirée. (Someone had given him my address and had told him that I was going to this party.)

Exercise 4

Ça fait déjà plus d'une semaine que nous sommes rentrés. Le temps passe tellement vite. Nous avons beaucoup de bons souvenirs de notre séjour en France. Nous vous sommes très reconnaissants de votre accueil. Le voyage de retour s'est bien passé. (OR On a eu quelques problèmes pendant le voyage de retour.) Les vacances sont finies maintenant et je vais recommencer mon travail. Nous attendons avec plaisir de vous recevoir chez nous. Merci encore une fois et nous vous envoyons toutes nos amitiés.

Exercise 5

(a) Nous avions déjà pris du retard quand nous sommes arrivés au port.
(b) Elle était déjà arrivée à la gare quand nous sommes allés la chercher.
(c) Il avait déjà recommencé son travail quand sa femme est retournée au bureau.
(d) L'hôtelier avait déjà renvoyé les articles quand je lui ai écrit.
(e) Mon ami avait déjà appris la langue quand il a visité le pays.

Exercise 6

(a) ...parler aussi bien la langue.
(b) He started learning French at school.
(c) Le vocabulaire / grammaire / lire.
(d) D'après toi, qu'est-ce qui est le plus important dans l'apprentissage d'une langue?
(e) Listening a lot.
(f) Getting used to the music and rhythm of the language, listening to cassettes and repeating sounds even if he doesn't fully understand what is being said.
(g) Ils commencent par écouter et puis ils répètent (by listening and repeating).
(h) It will be easier to have opportunities for hearing languages. (Finalement ça va devenir de plus en plus facile d'avoir des occasions d'écouter différentes langues.)

Chapter 20

1 Le répondeur téléphonique   The telephone answering machine

Vous êtes bien au 31 21 33 81. Monsieur et Madame Lefèvre ne peuvent pas pour le moment répondre à votre appel. Si vous voulez bien laisser votre nom, votre numéro de téléphone et un bref message après la tonalité, nous vous rappellerons aussitôt que possible. Merci.

This is 31 21 33 81. Monsieur and Madame Lefèvre cannot answer your call at the moment. If you would like to leave your name, your telephone number and a short message after the tone, we shall call you back as soon as possible. Thank you.

2 *Prévisions météorologiques*   *Weather forecast*

Pour ce week-end, temps instable sur la majeure partie de la France. Des averses accompagnées de vents pouvant devenir assez violents sur le littoral sont à craindre sur la moitié nord du pays. Les températures seront en général inférieures à la moyenne.

Dans le Sud, au contraire, les éclaircies deviendront plus fréquentes en fin de week-end avec des températures estivales pour la saison.

Néanmoins, dans le Sud-Ouest, ce temps chaud deviendra de plus en plus lourd dans la journée de dimanche, avec des risques d'orage en fin de journée surtout sur les Pyrénées et la Côte Basque.

For this weekend, unsettled weather over most of France. Showers, together with winds which could become quite strong on the coast, are to be feared in the northern half of the country. In general, temperatures will be below average.

In the South, on the other hand, bright spells will become more frequent at the end of the weekend, with temperatures which will feel summery for the season.

Nevertheless, in the South West, this warm weather will become more and more muggy during Sunday, with a risk of thunderstorms at the end of the day, especially over the Pyrenees and the Basque coast.

3 *Dans le hall de la gare*   *On the station concourse*

Le train à destination de Rouen partira de la voie numéro 7 à 15h 45. Ce train desservira les gares de Lisieux et Evreux. Le train en provenance de Poitiers arrivera quai numéro 12 avec 20 minutes de retard. La SNCF vous prie de bien vouloir excuser ce retard dû à un incident mécanique.

The train for Rouen will leave platform 7 at 15.45. This train will stop at Lisieux and Evreux. The train from Poitiers will arrive 20 minutes late at platform 12. The SNCF apologises for the late running of this train, which is due to a mechanical failure.

4 *Aux Galeries Lafayette*   *At the Galeries Lafayette*

Mesdames, aujourd'hui c'est la fête de la lingerie aux Galeries Lafayette. Toute la journée et sur tous les articles de lingerie féminine une remise de 20% vous est offerte.

Alors, vite, n'attendez pas un instant. Allez au premier étage des Galeries Lafayette et profitez, vous aussi, de cette offre exceptionnelle.

C'est vrai, il se passe toujours quelque chose aux Galeries Lafayette.

Ladies, today is a festival of underwear at the Galeries Lafayette. All day, and on all articles of ladies' underwear you are offered a price reduction of 20%. So be quick, don't wait a moment. Go to the first floor of the Galeries Lafayette and you too can benefit from this exceptional offer. It's true! There's always something happening at the Galeries Lafayette.

5 Sur la plage   On the beach

Les sauveteurs de la Grande Plage de Biarritz vous rappellent qu'il est formellement interdit de se baigner en dehors des limites de bains signalées par les deux drapeaux verts. En dehors de cette zone la présence de forts courants entraînant vers le large représente un réel danger pour les nageurs. Nous vous remercions de votre co-opération.

Allô, allô. Une petite fille âgée d'environ trois ans, blonde et portant un maillot de bain rose à pois blancs s'est égarée sur la plage. Nous demandons à toute personne qui la rencontrera de bien vouloir la ramener au Poste de Secours où ses parents l'attendent.

The lifesavers of the Grande Plage at Biarritz remind you that it is strictly forbidden to bathe outside the bathing limits marked by the two green flags. Outside this area there are strong currents which are a real danger for swimmers and could force them out towards the open sea. Thank you for your co-operation.

Your attention please. A little girl of about three years old, blond and wearing a pink bathing costume with white spots, has wandered off on the beach. We ask anyone who meets her, please to bring her back to the First Aid Post, where her parents are waiting for her.

6 Musée: renseignements enregistrés   Recorded information at the museum

La direction du musée vous souhaite la bienvenue. Elle vous signale que le musée est ouvert tous les jours de 12 heures à 22 heures sans interruption sauf le mardi, jour de fermeture hebdomadaire. Le samedi, le dimanche et les jours fériés, le musée est ouvert de 10 heures à 22 heures. Pour tous renseignements concernant les prix, les forfaits à la journée, les tarifs groupes, ainsi que pour les renseignements concernant les programmes et les expositions hebdomadaires, téléphonez au 42 77 11 12.

The management of the museum is pleased to welcome you. They would like to inform you that the museum is open every day from noon until 10 pm continuously, apart from Tuesday, when it is closed. On Saturday, Sunday and holidays, the museum is open from 10 am until 10 pm. For all information concerning prices, special daily rates, group rates and all information about programmes and weekly exhibitions, telephone 42 77 11 12.

7 Publicité à la radio   Radio advertising

En télévision, électroménager, vidéo, acheter un appareil de grande marque, c'est une garantie, une garantie de qualité, de fiabilité, de technologie. En télévision, vidéo, électroménager, acheter cet appareil chez Darty, c'est la garantie des prix par le remboursement de la différence, la garantie du choix par 200 grandes marques, la garantie du service après-vente par les interventions des techniciens Darty 7 jours sur 7. Darty, c'est le contrat de confiance.

Whether it's TV, household electrical goods, or video, buying equipment with a well-known brand name is a guarantee, a guarantee of quality, reliability, technology. Whether it's TV, video or electrical equipment for the home, buy the appliance at Darty, where you get a price guarantee which will refund any difference, a guarantee of 200 brand names, a guarantee of after-sales service by Darty technicians, on 7 days out of 7. Darty is a contract with confidence.

8 Annonce de grande surface   Hypermarket announcement

Aujourd'hui et toute la semaine, c'est la semaine du blanc à Auchan. Draps, taies d'oreiller, serviette de toilettes, tout le linge de la maison est à des prix imbattables. Un exemple. La parure de lit complète pour 229F. Profitez-en vite. La semaine du blanc à Auchan, c'est seulement jusqu'au 30 janvier.

Today and all this week, it's 'white week' at Auchan. Sheets, pillowslips, towels, all the household linen is offered at unbeatable prices. One example. A complete set of bed linen for 229F. Take advantage of this quickly. White week at Auchan lasts only until 30 January.

9 Sécurité routière   Road safety

Comme chaque année à la même date, voici revenu le temps des grands retours vers les villes. Aujourd'hui encore, journée rouge sur les routes et autoroutes du retour. Malgré les conseils de la Sécurité routière, la plupart des automobilistes semblent avoir repris la route en début de matinée. On nous signale déjà un bouchon de 4km à Lyon à l'entrée du tunnel de Fourvières. Si vous roulez en direction de Lyon, on vous conseille de quitter l'autoroute à la sortie 'Vienne Nord' et de suivre l'itinéraire de délestage qui a été mis en place à cet endroit et vous évitera la traversée de Lyon. Toute la journée nous ferons le point sur l'état des routes.
À tous les automobilistes donc: 'Prudence et Patience'.

Like every year at the same date, here we are back to the time of the mass return to the towns. Today again, it's a red alert day on the roads and motorways for the return home. In spite of the advice of the road safety authorities, most motorists seem to have started off early in the morning. Already we have information about a 4km tailback at Lyon at the entrance to the Fourvières tunnel. If you are travelling towards Lyon, we advise you to leave the motorway at the exit 'Vienne Nord' and to follow the relief route which has been set up and which will help you avoid going through Lyon. We shall bring you up to date on the state of the roads all day long. So, to all drivers it's: 'Take care; be patient'.

10 *Informations santé sur France-Info* *Health information on France-Info*

Les nuits de fêtes, de Noël et du Nouvel An, sont souvent courtes, trop courtes. Et tous les spécialistes sont d'accord. Se lever très tard le matin, faire ce qu'on appelle la grasse matinée pour compenser les heures de sommeil perdues le soir, n'est pas suffisant, car le repos du matin comporte peu de sommeil lent, profond. Or, c'est ce type de sommeil seulement qui permet de récupérer de la fatigue physique.

La sieste, en revanche, est riche en sommeil lent, profond et donc plus propice à la récupération. Pourtant, peu de gens prennent le temps de faire la sieste. Dans ses conseils, le Comité français d'éducation pour la santé souligne aussi que la première nuit suivant une veille prolongée permet de compenser la fatigue physique, alors que c'est seulement la deuxième nuit qui nous permet de rattraper le retard pris sur le temps de sommeil et d'éliminer la fatigue physique et ceci grâce au sommeil avec rêves.

Party nights at Christmas and the New Year are often short, too short. And all the specialists agree that getting up late in the morning, having what is called a long lie-in to make up for the hours of sleep lost the night before, is not enough, because morning rest does not include enough slow, deep sleep. Now it is only this type of sleep which allows one to recuperate from physical fatigue.

The siesta, on the other hand, is rich in sleep which is slow, deep and therefore more suitable for recuperation. However, few people take time for a siesta. In its advice the French Health Education Committee also underlines the fact that the first night after a late night out allows one to compensate for physical fatigue but it is only the second night which allows us to catch up on the loss of sleeping time and to eliminate mental fatigue, and this is thanks to sleep with dreams.

Grammar reference section

This summary of the main points of French grammar does not make any claim to be complete. The purpose of the summary is to provide a reference section for the grammatical points that are dealt with in this book. Readers wishing to extend their knowledge beyond the outline given here should consult one of the grammars listed in the bibliography.

Contents

1 The article

1.1 The definite article

(a) Forms

Masculine	le; l'	
Feminine	la; l'	equivalent to English 'the'.
Plural	les	

(b) Uses

Some cases where French uses the article and English does not:

  (i)   Before nouns with a general sense, for example:

       J'aime les enfants.   I like children.

  (ii) Expressing price, for example:

       soixante francs la boîte   sixty francs a box

  (iii) With names of countries and provinces, for example: 'la France'; 'la Normandie' (but not after 'en', for example: 'en France').

(iv) With names of days of the week, when talking about habitual actions, for example:

Le lundi, je vais au bureau. On Mondays, I go to the office.

1.2 The indefinite article

(a) Forms
Masculine un ⎫
Feminine une ⎬ 'a', 'an'
Plural des 'some'

(b) Uses
As a general rule, the indefinite article is used much as in English, but note the following cases where French does not use the article.

(i) After 'quel', for example:

Quel dommage! What a pity!

(ii) With 'cent' and 'mille', for example:

cent kilomètres a hundred kilometres

1.3 The partitive article

The partitive article is used to express a portion or undetermined quantity and may not be omitted in French.

(a) Forms
Masculine du; de l' ⎫
Feminine de la; de l' ⎬ equivalent to English 'some', 'any'
Plural des ⎭

(b) Examples
Je voudrais du pain, de la farine, des cigarettes et de l'ail (garlic).

(c)
The form of the partitive article becomes 'de' in the following cases:

(i) When following a negative verb, for example: 'Je n'ai pas de pain.'
(ii) In expressions of quantity, for example: 'beaucoup de fromage', 'une bouteille de vin'. (But there are certain exceptions to this last rule, notably: 'bien des enfants' (many children); 'la plupart du temps' (most of the time); 'encore du pain' (more bread).)

2 Nouns

2.1 Gender

All words in French are either masculine or feminine gender. Getting the correct gender is largely a matter of experience, and words should always be learned with their gender.

(a) Masculine
The following are masculine:

 (i) Names of males and male occupations, for example: 'le père'; 'le médecin'.

 (ii) Languages, for example: 'le français'.

 (iii) Days, months, seasons.

 (iv) Metric system, for example: 'le mètre'; 'le litre'.

 (v) Nouns ending in '-er', for example: 'le panier'.

 (vi) Nouns ending in '-al', for example: 'le cheval'.

 (vii) Nouns ending in '-ent', for example: 'un accident' (but 'la dent' (tooth)).

 (viii) Nouns ending in '-eau', for example: 'le tableau'. (But note two exceptions: 'la peau' (skin); 'l'eau' (water).)

 (ix) Nouns ending in '-eur', for example: 'le moteur'.

 (x) Nouns ending in '-acle', for example: 'le spectacle'.

(b) Feminine
The following are feminine:

 (i) Names of females and female occupations, for example: 'la mère', 'la vendeuse'.

 (ii) Names of countries ending in '-e', for example: 'la France'.

 (iii) Nouns ending in '-ace', '-oire', '-ière', '-tion', '-sion', '-cion', for example: 'la glace'; 'une histoire'; 'la bière'; 'la prononciation'.

(c) Masculine and feminine
Some words can be of either gender, and their meaning changes accordingly. The only words in this book with the possibility of either gender are:

la livre pound
le livre book
la tour tower
le tour tour

(d) Formation of the feminine of nouns (including professions)
There are a variety of ways in which nouns form the feminine, including the female version of professions.

 (i) The most common change is to add '-e' to the masculine form, for example: 'le marchand' (merchant, shopkeeper) / 'la marchande'.

 (ii) Masculine nouns ending in '-x' change '-x' to '-se', for example: 'époux' / 'épouse' (husband / wife)

 (iii) Professions ending in '-at' or '-ant' add '-e', for example: 'avocat' / 'avocate'; 'gérant' / 'gérante'.

 (iv) Professions ending in '-er' change this ending to '-ère', for example: 'boulanger' / 'boulangère'; 'fermier' / 'fermière'.

 (v) Professions ending in '-teur' change this ending to '-trice', for example: 'administrateur' / 'administratrice'; 'inspecteur' / 'inspectrice'.

 (vi) Professions ending in '-eur' usually change to '-euse', for example: 'vendeur' / 'vendeuse'; 'serveur' / 'serveuse'.

(vii) Professions ending in '-en' or '-ien' double the 'n' and add '-e', for example: 'chirugien' / 'chirurgienne'.
(viii) Professions which end in '-e' in the masculine do not change the form of the noun, but the masculine or feminine article is used as appropriate, for example: 'le concierge' / 'la concierge'; 'un artiste' / 'une artiste'.
(ix) Some professions have only the masculine form of the noun, but the article may change to show the gender difference, for example: 'le professeur' / 'la professeur'.

It is not always easy, in modern French, to know when it is appropriate to use the feminine form. For example, although, grammatically speaking, it is correct to say of a woman, 'elle est chirurgienne', or 'elle est avocate', it is quite normal for you to be told: 'l'avocat vous attend'; 'le chirurgien vous verra tout de suite', even when referring to a woman practitioner. When addressing a doctor, whether man or woman, you would say 'docteur', and when addressing a lawyer, man or woman, you would always use the correct form of address, 'maître'. And if ever there was a doubt as to which form to use, you could always say, 'monsieur' or 'madame'. Sometimes, if there is a possibility of misunderstanding, you might hear, for example, 'une femme-docteur'.

2.2 Plural

(a)
The general rule is to add '-s' to the singular form.

(b)
Nouns ending in '-x' do not change in the plural, for example: 'les toux'.

(c)
Nouns ending in '-al' change '-al' to '-aux', for example: 'le cheval' (horse) / 'les chevaux'. (But note 'le bal' / 'les bals'(dances).)

(d)
Nouns ending in '-au', '-eau', '-eu', 'œu' all add '-x' in the plural, for example: 'les châteaux', 'les jeux'.

(e)
A few nouns ending in '-ou' add '-x', for example: 'les bijoux' (jewels).

(f)
Note the irregular plurals:

un œil / les yeux (eyes)
le ciel / les cieux (skies; heavens)
le travail / les travaux (road works)

(g)
With family names, there is usually no indication of the plural, for example:

les Lebrun   the Lebruns

(h)

Some nouns are used only in the plural, for example:

les environs   the surroundings
les frais   fees; expenses

(i)

Nouns made up of two hyphenated words do not change in the plural: 'des coupe-vent'; 'des croque-monsieur'.

3 Adjectives

3.1 Formation of the feminine

(a)

The general rule is to add '-e' to the masculine form, for example: 'petit' / 'petite'. When the adjective already ends in '-e' there is no change, for example: 'jeune'.

(b)

Adjectives ending in '-er', '-ier' change their ending to '-ère', '-ière', for example: 'léger' / 'légère'.

(c)

Adjectives ending in '-as', '-eil', '-el', '-en', '-on' double the final consonant and add '-e', for example: 'parisien' / 'parisienne'; 'bon' / 'bonne'; 'bas' / 'basse'.

(d)

Adjectives ending in '-et' change to '-ète', for example: 'inquiet' / 'inquiète'.

(e)

Adjectives ending in '-f' change to '-ve', for example: 'neuf '/ 'neuve' (brand new).

(f)

Adjectives ending in '-x' change to '-se', for example: 'jaloux' / 'jalouse' (jealous).

(g)

Adjectives ending in '-c' change to '-che', for example: 'blanc' / 'blanche'.

3.2 Formation of the plural

(a)

The general rule, as with nouns, is to add '-s' to the singular form.

(b)

Adjectives ending in '-s' and '-x' remain unchanged.

(c)

Adjectives ending in '-eau' add '-x', for example: 'nouveau' / 'nouveaux'.

(d)

Most adjectives ending in '-al' change to '-aux', for example: 'égal' / 'égaux' (equal). But note the exception: 'final' / 'finals' (final).

3.3 Position of adjectives

(a)
The general rule is that the adjective in French follows the noun it qualifies.

(b)
Certain common adjectives *always precede* the noun, notably: 'beau', 'bon', 'gentil', 'jeune', 'joli', 'long', 'mauvais', 'petit', 'vaste', 'vieux'.

(c)
Certain adjectives *always follow* the noun, namely:

    (i)   Adjectives of nationality, for example: 'une femme française'.
    (ii)   Participles used as adjectives, for example: 'une église connue'.
    (iii)   Adjectives of colour and other physical qualities (shape, temperature, and so on), for example: 'un pantalon gris'; 'un jour chaud'.

(d)
Certain adjectives vary in meaning according to whether they precede or follow the noun. Note the following examples:

un **cher** ami	un repas **cher**
a dear friend	an expensive meal
le **dernier** jour	la semaine **dernière**
the last day	last week
un **grand** homme	un homme **grand**
a great man	a tall man
la **pauvre** femme	la femme **pauvre**
the poor (i.e. unfortunate) woman	the poor (i.e. penniless) woman
la **seule** solution	une personne **seule**
the only solution	a person who is alone

3.4 Comparative and superlative

(a) Regular forms

joli	plus joli	le plus joli
pretty	prettier	the prettiest
joli	moins joli	le moins joli
pretty	less pretty	the least pretty

aussi joli que...	as pretty as...
...n'est pas si joli que...	...isn't as pretty as...
moins joli que...	less pretty than...

(b) Irregular forms

bon	meilleur	le meilleur (OR la meilleure, les meilleurs, etc.)
good	better	the best
mauvais	pire	le pire
bad	worse	the worst

3.5 Possessive adjectives

(a) Forms

	Masculine	Feminine	Plural
my	mon	ma	mes
your (familiar)	ton	ta	tes
his	son	sa	ses
her	son	sa	ses
its	son	sa	ses
one's	son	sa	ses
our	notre	notre	nos
your	votre	votre	vos
their	leur	leur	leurs

(b)

The possessive adjective agrees with the object possessed, and *not with the possessor*, thus 'sa table' may mean 'his table' or 'her table', and so on.

(c)

All nouns beginning with a vowel or mute 'h-' take the masculine form of the possessive adjective, for example: 'son école'.

3.6 Demonstrative adjectives

(a) Forms

	Singular	Plural
Masculine	ce, cet	ces
Feminine	cette	ces

(b)

'Cet' is used before masculine singular nouns beginning with a vowel or mute 'h-', for example: 'cet homme'.

(c)

The French demonstrative adjective can mean either 'this' or 'that'. If it is necessary to stress the notion of 'that one over there', in order to draw a contrast, '-là' can be added, for example: 'cette église-là' (that church over there).

3.7 Interrogative adjectives

(a) Forms

	Singular	Plural
Masculine	quel	quels
Feminine	quelle	quelles

(b)

The interrogative adjective is used:

  (i)   In the sense of 'which...?' or 'what...?' when these words qualify a noun, for example: 'Quelle est votre profession?'
  (ii) In exclamations, for example: 'Quel plaisir!'; 'Quel dommage!'.

3.8 Indefinite adjectives

These are a group of various adjectives representing unspecified amounts:

(a) 'Chaque'
chaque année   every year

(b) 'Quelque', 'quelques'
Je suis ici depuis quelques jours.   I have been here for a few days.

(c) 'Plusieurs'
Elle a plusieurs enfants.   She has several children.

(d) 'Tel', 'telle', 'tels', 'telles'
un tel accident   such an accident
une telle personne   such a person
de tels accidents   such accidents

(e) 'Tout', 'toute', 'tous', 'toutes'
tout mon argent   all my money
toute la famille   all the family
tous les gens   all the people

4 Pronouns

4.1 Personal pronouns

(a) Unstressed pronouns

Subject	Direct object	Indirect object	Reflexive
je	me	me	me
tu	te	te	te
il	le	lui	se
elle	la	lui	se
nous	nous	nous	nous
vous	vous	vous	vous
ils	les	leur	se
elles	les	leur	se

Note also: 'y' (there)
'en' (of it, of them) – see 4.1 (d) below.

Unstressed pronouns precede the verb, for example:

Je la vois.   I see her.
Il lui offre un verre.   He offers (to) him a glass.

(b) Use of 'tu' and 'vous'
Whereas English has the single form 'you' for addressing other people, French has two pronouns, 'tu' and 'vous'. Throughout this book, 'vous' has been used in the dialogues at the start of each chapter, because this is the form most likely to be heard and used by English people travelling on holiday or on business. It

is the polite form, used not only with strangers and acquaintances, but often also between people who have known each other for years but have not felt the degree of intimacy necessary for using 'tu'. 'Tu' is used within the family, when addressing children and animals and between close friends. It is used among students and young people as a matter of course but must be used with more care amongst older people. In the office or school staff-room, for example, 'vous' is often used among colleagues who have worked together for years, so as to maintain a certain detachment. In the dialogues for Chapters 14 and 15, a group of people who have known each other for some time use 'vous'. 'Tu' might be considered more usual in these circumstances, but 'vous' is not impossible. In the taped spontaneous dialogues there are examples of 'tu' being used by mother and daughter (Chapter 14) and by young people (Chapter 8). In speech, 'tu' is sometimes shortened to 't'' when it occurs before a vowel. For example, at the end of the taped dialogue in Exercise 5 of Chapter 15, you will hear: 'T'as essayé de retrouver l'hôtel?'.

(c) Order of unstressed pronouns before the verb
When there is more than one pronoun preceding the verb, they always appear in the following order:

me				
te	le	lui	y	en
se	la	leur		
nous	les			
vous				

For example:

Je vous le donne.	I give it to you.
Il n'y en a pas.	There isn't any (of it).
Elle la lui offre.	She offers it to him.

Note that where a verb is followed by the infinitive of another verb, the pronouns precede the infinitive, for example:

Je veux le voir.   I want to see him.

(d) Order of unstressed pronouns after the imperative
Where the verb is in the imperative mood, pronouns follow the verb in the following order:

	moi		
le	toi		
la	lui	y	en
les	nous		
	vous		
	leur		

For example:

Donnez-le-moi.	Give it (to) me.
Donnez-m'en.	Give me some (of it).

Note that in the written form the pronoun is linked to the verb by a hyphen, and the following pronouns are similarly linked.

When the imperative is used in the negative, pronouns precede the verb in the normal way, for example:

Ne le lui donnez pas.   Don't give it (to) him.

(e) Use of 'en'
   (i)   As can be seen from two of the above examples, 'en' is used in French where no equivalent is required in English, for example:

   Donnez-m'en.   Give me some (of it).

   The same is true when 'en' is used with numerals, for example:

   Combien en avez-vous? ⎱   How many have you got (of
   Vous en avez combien? ⎰   them)?
   J'en ai trois.   I've got three (of them).

   (ii)   'En' is also used as a pronoun in cases where a verb is followed by a dependent 'de', for example:

   Je me souviens de mes vacances. → Je m'en souviens.
   Est-ce que vous êtes sûr de la route? → Oui, j'en suis sûr. (Yes, I'm sure of it.)

(f) Stressed (disjunctive) pronouns
   Singular   Plural
   moi   nous
   toi   vous
   lui   eux
   elle   elles

(g) Uses of stressed pronouns
   (i)   Used after preposition, for example: 'avec eux'; 'sans moi'.
   (ii)   Used in double subject, for example: 'Son père et lui vont à l'église.'
   (iii) Used for emphasis, for example: 'Moi, je n'y vais pas.'
   (iv)   Used to give a one word answer, for example: 'Qui est là? – Moi!'

4.2 Relative pronouns

(a) Forms
   Subject   qui
   Object   que, qu'

The relative pronoun cannot be omitted in French, as it often is in English.

(b) Uses
   (i)   As subject of a relative clause, for example:

   l'homme qui me connaît   the man who knows me

(ii)　As object of a relative clause, for example:

l'homme que je connais　　the man (whom) I know

(iii)　After a preposition, when referring to people, for example:

la femme à qui je donne la lettre　the woman to whom I give the letter

(c) Use of 'quoi'
De quoi est-ce que vous parlez?　　What are you talking about?

(d) Use of 'où' in relative clauses
le parc où elle se promène　the park where she goes walking

4.3 Compound relative pronouns

(a) Forms
ce qui
ce que

(b) Uses
(i)　To translate 'what' as used in the phrase 'Do you know what I mean?':

Est-ce que vous savez ce que je veux dire?

(ii)　To translate 'what' in phrases such as 'What amuses me is...'

Ce qui m'amuse, c'est...

4.4 Demonstrative pronouns

(a) Forms

	Singular	**Plural**
Masculine	celui	ceux
Feminine	celle	celles

(b) Uses
This pronoun never stands alone. It is followed by:

(i)　'-ci', or '-là', for example:

Voilà deux voitures; est-ce que vous préférez celle-ci ou celle-là?
(That is, 'this one' or 'that one'.)

(ii)　The relative pronoun, for example:

Voilà deux maisons; celle qui est à gauche est la plus jolie.

(iii)　The preposition 'de', for example:

mon auto et celle de mon ami　　my car and my friend's

4.5 Possessive pronouns

(a) Forms

	Masculine	Feminine	Plural	
mine	le mien	la mienne	les miens	les miennes
yours	le tien	la tienne	les tiens	les tiennes
his				
hers	le sien	la sienne	les siens	les siennes
its own				
one's own				
ours	le nôtre	la nôtre	les nôtres	les nôtres
yours	le vôtre	la vôtre	les vôtres	les vôtres
theirs	le leur	la leur	les leurs	les leurs

(b) Uses

The possessive pronoun in French agrees with the thing possessed and not with the possessor, for example:

Cette maison est la mienne.
Ce sac est le sien.

5 Verbs

5.1 Verb forms

(a) Regular verbs

Infinitive	donner	choisir	attendre
Present tense	je donne	je choisis	j'attends
	tu donnes	tu choisis	tu attends
	il donne	il choisit	il attend
	elle donne	elle choisit	elle attend
	nous donnons	nous choisissons	nous attendons
	vous donnez	vous choisissez	vous attendez
	ils donnent	ils choisissent	ils attendent
	elles donnent	elles choisissent	elles attendent
Imperfect	je donnais	je choisissais	j'attendais
	tu donnais	tu choisissais	tu attendais
	il donnait	il choisissait	il attendait
	elle donnait	elle choisissait	elle attendait
	nous donnions	nous choisissions	nous attendions
	vous donniez	vous choisissiez	vous attendiez
	ils donnaient	ils choisissaient	ils attendaient
	elles donnaient	elles choisissaient	elles attendaient

Future	je donnerai	je choisirai	j'attendrai
	tu donneras	tu choisiras	tu attendras
	il donnera	il choisira	il attendra
	elle donnera	elle choisira	elle attendra
	nous donnerons	nous choisirons	nous attendrons
	vous donnerez	vous choisirez	vous attendrez
	ils donneront	ils choisiront	ils attendront
	elles donneront	elles choisiront	elles attendront
Conditional	je donnerais	je choisirais	j'attendrais

(and so on, adding the endings of the imperfect to the infinitive of the verb)

| **Present participle** | donnant | choisissant | attendant |
| **Past participle** | donné | choisi | attendu |

(b) Spelling variations in regular verbs

There are a number of verbs which are regular except that they undergo certain small changes in pronunciation and spelling. The most frequent are:

(i) The stem of the infinitive of '-er' verbs ends in 'c', for example: 'commencer'. To maintain the soft pronunciation of 'c', it must be written with a cedilla before 'a' and 'o', for example: 'il commençait', 'nous commençons'. (See *guide to pronunciation*, p. 268.)

(ii) The stem of the infinitive ends in 'g', for example: 'manger'. To maintain the soft pronunciation of 'g', it must be written 'ge' before 'a' and 'o', for example: 'il mangeait', 'nous mangeons'.

(iii) The infinitive ends in 'e' + consonant +'er', for example: 'mener' (to lead). The 'e' of the stem of the infinitive changes to 'è' in all forms of the present tense except 'nous' and 'vous', for example: 'je mène' but 'nous menons'. The same change occurs throughout the future tense, for example: 'je mènerai', 'nous mènerons'.

(iv) The infinitive ends in 'é' + consonant +'er', for example: 'préférer' (to prefer), 'espérer' (to hope). The 'é' of the stem of the infinitive changes to 'è' in all forms of the present tense except 'nous' and 'vous', for example: 'je préfère', 'nous préférons'; 'j'espère', 'nous espérons'.

(v) The infinitive ends in '-oyer' or '-uyer', for example: 'employer' (to use). In these cases, the 'y' of the infinitive changes to 'i' in all forms of the present tense except 'nous' and 'vous', for example: 'j'emploie', 'nous employons'. The same change occurs throughout the future tense, for example: 'j'emploierai', 'nous emploierons'.

(vi) Most verbs ending in '-eler' and '-eter', for example: 'appeler' (to call), 'jeter' (to throw). The 'l' and 't' respectively are doubled in all forms of the present tense except 'nous' and 'vous', for example: 'j'appelle', 'nous appelons'; 'je jette', 'nous jetons'. The same change takes place throughout the future tense, for example: 'j'appellerai'; 'je jetterai'.

(c) 'Être' and 'avoir'

These are the most important irregular verbs, so it is worth giving their forms in full. (Forms for 'il' and 'elle' are the same.)

	être	avoir
Present tense	je suis	j'ai
	tu es	tu as
	il est	il a
	nous sommes	nous avons
	vous êtes	vous avez
	ils sont	ils ont
Imperfect	j'étais	j'avais
	tu étais	tu avais
	il était	il avait
	nous étions	nous avions
	vous étiez	vous aviez
	ils étaient	ils avaient
Future	je serai	j'aurai
	tu seras	tu auras
	il sera	il aura
	nous serons	nous aurons
	vous serez	vous aurez
	ils seront	ils auront
Conditional	je serais etc.	j'aurais etc.
Present participle	étant	ayant
Past participle	été	eu

(d) Principal parts of other common irregular verbs

Infinitive	Present tense	Present participle	Past participle
aller (to go)	je vais, tu vas, il va, nous allons, vous allez, ils vont	allant	allé
s'asseoir (to sit)	je m'assieds, tu t'assieds, il s'assied, nous nous asseyons, vous vous asseyez, ils s'asseyent	s'asseyant	assis
boire (to drink)	je bois, tu bois, il boit, nous buvons, vous buvez, ils boivent	buvant	bu
conduire (to drive)	je conduis, tu conduis, il conduit, nous conduisons, vous conduisez, ils conduisent	conduisant	conduit
connaître (to know)	je connais, tu connais, il connaît, nous connaissons, vous connaissez, ils connaissent	connaissant	connu
courir (to run)	je cours, tu cours, il court, nous courons, vous courez, ils courent	courant	couru
croire (to believe)	je crois, tu crois, il croit, nous croyons, vous croyez, ils croient	croyant	cru

Infinitive	Present tense	Present participle	Past participle
devoir (to owe, to have to)	je dois, tu dois, il doit, nous devons, vous devez, ils doivent	devant	dû
dire (to say)	je dis, tu dis, il dit, nous disons, vous dites, ils disent	disant	dit
dormir (to sleep)	je dors, tu dors, il dort, nous dormons, vous dormez, ils dorment	dormant	dormi
écrire (to write)	j'écris, tu écris, il écrit, nous écrivons, vous écrivez, ils écrivent	écrivant	écrit
faire (to make; to do)	je fais, tu fais, il fait, nous faisons, vous faites, ils font	faisant	fait
joindre (+ **rejoindre**) (to join)	je joins, tu joins, il joint, nous joignons, vous joignez, ils joignent	joignant	joint
lire (to read)	je lis, tu lis, il lit, nous lisons, vous lisez, ils lisent	lisant	lu
mettre (to put)	je mets, tu mets, il met, nous mettons, vous mettez, ils mettent	mettant	mis
offrir (to offer)	j'offre, tu offres, il offre, nous offrons, vous offrez, ils offrent	offrant	offert
plaire (to please)	je plais, tu plais, il plaît, nous plaisons, vous plaisez, ils plaisent	plaisant	plu
pleuvoir (to rain)	il pleut *(only used in the 3rd person singular)*	pleuvant	plu
pouvoir (to be able)	je peux, tu peux, il peut, nous pouvons, vous pouvez, ils peuvent	pouvant	pu
prendre (to take)	je prends, tu prends, il prend, nous prenons, vous prenez, ils prennent	prenant	pris
recevoir (to receive)	je reçois, tu reçois, il reçoit, nous recevons, vous recevez, ils reçoivent	recevant	reçu
savoir (to know)	je sais, tu sais, il sait, nous savons, vous savez, ils savent	sachant	su
sortir (to go out)	je sors, tu sors, il sort, nous sortons, vous sortez, ils sortent	sortant	sorti
tenir (to hold)	je tiens, tu tiens, il tient, nous tenons, vous tenez, ils tiennent	tenant	tenu
venir (to come)	je viens *(like tenir)*	venant	venu
vivre (to live)	je vis, tu vis, il vit, nous vivons, vous vivez, ils vivent	vivant	vécu
voir (to see)	je vois, tu vois, il voit, nous voyons, vous voyez, ils voient	voyant	vu
vouloir (to want)	je veux, tu veux, il veut, nous voulons, vous voulez, ils veulent	voulant	voulu

5.2 Using verbs and participles

(a) Present tense

   (i)   The French present tense can be rendered in three possible ways in English, for example: 'je vais' can mean 'I go', 'I am going', or 'I do go'.

   (ii) The present tense is used with 'depuis' in sentences such as:

        Il est ici depuis une heure.   He has been here for an hour.

(b) Imperfect tense

The imperfect tense can be formed by taking the stem of the present participle and adding the endings already given in 5.1 (a) above, for example: present participle 'allant', of which the stem is 'all-', and the imperfect is therefore 'j'allais' and so on. Only two verbs in the language do not fit into this pattern of forming the imperfect, namely 'avoir' (j'avais) and 'savoir' (je savais). The imperfect tense is used in the following circumstances:

   (i)   To describe a continuous action in the past, for example:

        Lundi dernier il pleuvait sans cesse.   ...it went on and on raining.

   (ii) To describe a habitual action in the past, for example:

        Quand j'étais jeune, j'allais tous les jours à l'école.   ...I used to go...

   (iii) To express description in the past, for example:

        C'était une grande maison mais le jardin était petit.

   (iv) After 'si' (if) used with a conditional, for example:

        S'il venait me voir, je resterais   If he came... I would stay...
        à la maison.

(c) Future tense

The future tense is formed by taking the infinitive of the verb and adding the future endings already shown in 5.1 (a) above. There are a few irregular futures, notably:

être	je serai	faire	je ferai	tenir	je tiendrai
avoir	j'aurai	pouvoir	je pourrai	venir	je viendrai
aller	j'irai	recevoir	je recevrai	voir	je verrai
courir	je courrai	savoir	je saurai	vouloir	je voudrai

As will be seen from many examples in the dialogues, there is a tendency in contemporary French to use the construction 'aller' + infinitive instead of the future.

(d) Conditional

The conditional is formed by adding on to the infinitive the same endings as for the imperfect. The irregular forms are the same as those given for the future. The conditional has two main uses:

   (i)   In conditional 'si' clauses, for example:

        Si j'avais assez d'argent, j'irais à Paris.

(ii) To express a polite form of request or statement, for example:

Je voudrais du pain, s'il vous plaît.   I would like...
Est-ce que je pourrais payer par chèque?   Could I possibly pay...

(e) Present participle

The present participle has two main uses:

(i) Certain present participles are commonly found as adjectives, for example: 'charmant' (charming); 'fatigant' (tiring).

(ii) With a verbal function similar to the English present participle, for example: 'en passant' (in passing). French also uses the present participle where English might prefer a clause, for example:

En sortant du bureau, j'ai vu mon   As I was leaving the office...
ami

(iii) Note that the only preposition which can precede the present participle is 'en'. With other prepositions, French usage is different from English, for example:

avant de partir   before leaving
après avoir vu   after seeing

(f) Past participle

The past participle is used to form the perfect and pluperfect tenses. Each of these tenses is formed by combining an auxiliary verb ('être' or 'avoir') with the past participle. Note the following points:

(i) *Auxiliary verbs.* The majority of verbs in French use 'avoir' as the auxiliary verb, for example: 'j'ai mangé'. A number of verbs use 'être' as auxiliary, notably, all reflexive verbs, for example: 'je me suis levé', and verbs of motion:

aller	monter	retourner	tomber
arriver	partir	revenir	venir
descendre	rentrer	sortir	

Note also 'devenir' (to become). When a verb takes 'être' as its auxiliary, the past participle agrees with the subject of the verb, as follows:

le père est revenu   la mère est revenue
les garçons sont revenus   les fillettes sont revenues

Agreement with the subject is not required when the auxiliary verb is 'avoir'. Verbs with the auxiliary 'avoir' only agree if a feminine or plural direct object precedes the verb, for example: 'je les ai vus'.

(ii) *Perfect tense.* This is formed by the forms of the present tense of the auxiliary verb plus the past participle. The perfect tense in French is used to convey both the sense of English past definite and English perfect, thus 'je suis venu' might be translated 'I came' or 'I have come' according to context. Note these examples:

Quand est-ce que vous êtes arrivé en France?	When did you arrive...?
Je suis arrivé la semaine dernière.	I arrived last week.
J'ai déjà écrit deux fois.	I have already written twice.

(iii) *Pluperfect tense.* This is exactly equivalent to the English pluperfect, that is, it conveys the meaning of something that happened in the more remote past, for example:

J'étais déjà parti quand elle est arrivée.	I had already left when she arrived.
J'avais écrit la lettre avant de partir.	I had written the letter before leaving.

The pluperfect is formed by combining the imperfect of the auxiliary verb with the past participle. The rules for the use of 'être' and 'avoir' are the same as explained in (i) above.

(iv) *Position of pronouns.* Note that in the perfect and pluperfect tenses the pronouns always precede the auxiliary verb, for example:

je le lui ai donné
il leur a parlé
je lui avais donné le livre

5.3 Reflexive verbs

(a) Forms
The forms of reflexive verbs in the various tenses are identical with those already described for all other verbs, with the additional element of the reflexive pronoun, for example:

Je **me** lève.
Est-ce que vous **vous** souvenez?

The forms of the reflexive pronouns are given in 4.1 (a).
Note the following points of usage:
(i) The imperative of reflexive verbs includes the reflexive pronoun, for example: 'Levez-vous!'
(ii) In the perfect and pluperfect tenses, the auxiliary verb 'être' is used, with agreement of the past participle, as explained in 5.2 (f)(i).

(b) Uses
Note that although many reflexive verbs are equivalent to English reflexives, there are a number of French reflexive verbs which are expressed by a simple verb in English. The most common are:

s'arrêter	to stop	se promener	to go for a walk
s'endormir	to fall asleep	se réveiller	to wake up
se lever	to get up	se servir de	to use
se plaindre	to complain	se souvenir de	to remember

5.4 The passive voice

(a) Forms
The passive voice in French is formed, as in English, by combining the tense of the verb 'to be' (être) with the past participle, for example:

Active Le garçon ferme la porte.
Passive La porte est fermée par le garçon.

(b) Uses
This course has made little use of the passive voice, since it is not as much used in French as in English, and there are a number of ways in which its use can be avoided, that is:

(i)   By using the active form of expression, as in the example above.
(ii) By using the pronoun 'on', for example:

Ici on parle français.   French is spoken here.

(iii) By using a reflexive verb, for example:

Les œufs se vendent au marché.   Eggs are sold in the market.

5.5 The subjunctive mood

(a) Forms
The present subjunctive is formed by taking the stem of the 3rd person plural and adding the endings given below, using 'donner' as an example:

3rd person plural: **donnent**
stem of 3rd person plural: **donn-**
stem + endings: je donne, tu donnes, il donne, nous donnions, vous donniez, ils donnent

There are a number of irregular subjunctives, of which the most common are:

aller (j'aille, nous allions)   pouvoir (je puisse)
avoir (j'aie)   savoir (je sache)
être (je sois, nous soyons)   venir (je vienne, nous venions)
faire (je fasse)

(b) Uses
The subjunctive is not widely used in modern French, and it can often be avoided, or else the forms of the verb are identical with the ordinary present tense. The only forms of use introduced in this book are the most common, thus:

(i)   After 'il faut que...', for example:

Il faut que je m'en aille.
Il faut qu'il fasse son travail.

(ii) After 'je veux que...' and 'je préfère que...', for example:

Je veux qu'il fasse un effort.

(iii) After 'bien que' (although), for example:

bien qu'il soit riche

5.6 Impersonal verbs

These are verbs which are only found in the form of the 3rd person singular, in particular:

(i) 'Il fait', to express aspects of the weather, for example:

Il fait beau.
Il fait froid.

(ii) Other verbs describing weather conditions, for example:

Il pleut.
Il neige.

(iii) 'Il est' + certain adjectives, for example:

Il est nécessaire de partir.
Il est possible de voir.

(It should be noted that there is a tendency in modern spoken French to use 'c'est' instead of 'il est' in such expressions.)

(iv) 'Il y a' (there is / there are).

(v) 'Il est' in stating the time, for example:

Il est trois heures.

(vi) 'Il faut' to express necessity, for example:

Il faut partir.   We must leave. / I must leave.

5.7 The infinitive

There are many occasions when a verb is followed by an infinitive. There are three patterns for linking the verb to the following infinitive. The infinitive may follow directly after the first verb; the preposition 'à' may act as a link between the verb and the following infinitive; the preposition 'de' may act as a link between the verb and the following infinitive.

(a) Verbs followed directly by an infinitive

(i) After verbs of motion, for example: 'venir', 'aller'.

Je suis venu voir la maison.   I came to see the house.
Je vais fermer la porte.   I am going to shut the door.

(ii) After certain verbs of perception, for example: 'écouter', 'regarder', 'voir'.

Je le vois venir.   I see him coming.

(iii) After the following verbs used as auxiliaries: 'devoir' (vous devez aller), 'faire', 'laisser', 'pouvoir', 'savoir', 'vouloir'. (See the examples in 5.8 below.)

(iv) After verbs expressing hope or belief, for example: 'croire', 'espérer'.

J'espère vous voir avant les vacances.   I hope to see you before the holidays.

(b) Verbs linked to a following infinitive by 'à'
These verbs are followed by 'à' when used in an expression requiring a following infinitive: 'apprendre à', 'commencer à', 's'intéresser à', 'inviter à', 'se mettre à' (to begin), 'penser à', 'se préparer à'. For example:

Il apprend à nager.   He's learning to swim.
Je vous invite à déjeuner chez nous. I invite you to have lunch at our house.

(c) Verbs linked to a following infinitive by 'de'
These verbs are followed by 'de' when used in an expression requiring a following infinitive: 'continuer de', 'décider de', 'essayer de', 'finir de', 'oublier de'. For example:

Il a continué de travailler.   He carried on working.
J'ai oublié de vous le dire.   I forgot to tell you about it.

(d) Infinitive after 'pour' and 'sans'
For example:

pour aller à la gare   in order to go to the station
sans dire un mot   without (saying) a word

(e) Other constructions with the infinitive
(i)   'demander à quelqu'un de faire quelque chose', for example:

Je lui ai demandé de venir. I asked him to come.

(ii)   'dire à quelqu'un de faire quelque chose', for example:

Dites-lui de partir!   Tell him to leave!

(iii) 'venir de' + infinitive, for example:

Il vient de partir.   He has just left.

5.8 Modal auxiliary verbs

Besides the common auxiliary verbs 'être' and 'avoir' used to form the perfect and pluperfect tenses, there are a number of other verbs commonly used as auxiliaries in conjunction with infinitives, notably:

(a) 'Aller' expressing future intention

Je vais visiter la Normandie.

(b) 'Devoir' expressing compulsion

Je dois bientôt partir.

Note the English equivalents of the tenses of 'devoir':

je dois	I must / I have to
je devrai	I shall have to
je devrais	I ought to / I should
je devais	I had to ('habitual', that is, 'I used to have to...')
j'ai dû	I had to / I have had to / I must have
j'avais dû	I had had to
j'aurais dû	I ought to have

(c) 'Faire'   to make, to have something done
Faites-le parler!   Make him speak!
Il se fait couper les cheveux.   He's having his hair cut.

(d) 'Laisser'   to let, to allow
Laissez-le entrer!

(e) 'Pouvoir'   to be able
Est-ce que je peux sortir?   Can I go out?
Je pourrai vous voir demain.   I shall be able to see you tomorrow.

(f) 'Savoir'   to know about something
Je sais nager.   I know how to swim.

(g) 'Vouloir'   to express wishes
Je veux partir demain.

Note the use of other tenses, for example:

J'ai toujours voulu visiter la Normandie. I have always wanted to...
Je voudrais du pain, s'il vous plaît.   I should like...

5.9 Verbs and their objects

(a)
Verbs requiring a direct object in French but used with a preposition in English:

approuver	to approve of	écouter	to listen to
attendre	to wait for	espérer	to hope for
chercher	to look for	regarder	to look at
demander	to ask for		

(b)
Verbs requiring a direct object in English, but requiring 'à' in French:

convenir à	to suit	promettre à	to promise
permettre à	to permit	répondre à	to answer
plaire à	to please		

(c)
Verbs requiring a direct object in English, but requiring 'de' in French:

s'approcher de	to approach	se servir de	to use
avoir besoin de	to need	se souvenir de	to remember
partir de	to leave		

(d)

Verbs requiring 'de' in French but a different preposition in English:

se moquer de   to laugh at   remercier de   to thank for
profiter de   to profit from

(e)

Some verbs such as 'demander' and 'présenter' require both a direct and an indirect object, for example:

Il demande un bonbon à sa mère.   He asks his mother for a sweet.
Je vous présente ma femme.   I introduce my wife to you.

5.10 Negatives

(a)

When used with a verb, the following negative forms all have 'ne' before the verb and the second part of the negative after the verb, for example:

ne ... pas   Je ne le vois pas. (I don't see him.)
ne ... plus   Elle ne voit plus son ami. (She doesn't see her friend any more.)
ne ... rien   Je n'ai rien à déclarer.   (I have nothing to declare.)
ne ... personne   Je ne connais personne à Caen. (I don't know anyone in Caen.)
ne ... jamais   Je ne suis jamais allé en France. (I've never been to France.)
ne ... ni ... ni   Chez l'épicier il n'y a ni pommes ni poires. (At the grocer's there are neither apples nor pears.)
ne ... aucun(e)   Vous n'avez aucune raison de vous inquiéter. (You have absolutely no reason to worry.)

From the above examples you will note that:

(i)   In the perfect tense, the parts of the negative come before and after the auxiliary verb, for example:

Je ne suis jamais allé...

(ii)   Where there are pronouns preceding the verb, the negative 'ne' comes before the pronouns, for example:

Je ne le vois pas.

It is also worth noting that the 'ne' is very often omitted in everyday spoken French, though never in writing; for example, you might hear:

Je sais pas.   I don't know

(b)

The negative forms may also stand alone, for example:

rien   nothing
jamais   never

5.11 Interrogatives

(a) Ways of forming the interrogative (that is, putting questions)

(i)   The direct form of statement is used, and the question indicated by the rising intonation of the voice, for example:

Vous partez aujourd'hui?   Are you leaving today?

(ii)   The direct form of the statement is maintained but preceded by 'est-ce que...', for example:

Est-ce que vous partez aujourd'hui?

(iii) The verb and its subject are inverted, that is, the order is reversed, for example:

Partez-vous aujourd'hui?

Inversion of the verb is not now very widespread in everyday spoken French.

(iv) Note that in all the forms of questions given above, French can use both the noun and the pronoun, in a way which would never occur in English, for example:

Il est déjà parti, le garçon?
Est-ce qu'il est déjà parti, le garçon?   } Has the boy already left?
Le garçon, est-il déjà parti?

(b) Common interrogatives

combien?	how much? / how many?
quand?	when?
comment?	how?
où?	where?
pourquoi?	why?

All these words can be followed by 'est-ce que' or by inversion of the verb and subject, for example:

Pourquoi est-ce que vous partez? OR Pourquoi partez-vous?
Où est-ce que vous allez?   OR Où allez-vous?

(c) Negative interrogative

When putting questions in the negative, the usual pattern of forming the negative is followed, for example:

Est-ce que vous n'allez pas en France?

If the inverted form of the verb is used, the second part of the negative comes after the subject pronoun, for example:

N'allez-vous pas en France?

Note that when answering a negative question with a 'yes', French uses 'si' instead of 'oui', for example:

Vous n'allez pas en France cette année?	You're not going to France this year?
Mais si, j'y vais.	On the contrary, I am going there.

6 Adverbs

An adverb modifies a verb, an adjective or another adverb.

(a) Forms

(i) The most common way of forming adverbs is to add the ending '-ment' to the feminine form of the adjective, for example: 'heureusement' (happily).

(ii) Adjectives ending in '-ant' and '-ent' form adverbs in '-amment' and '-emment' respectively, for example:

> constant → constamment
> évident → évidemment

(iii) Certain adverbs add an acute accent to the feminine 'e' of the adjective, for example: 'énormément', 'profondément'.

(iv) There are a number of irregular adverbial formations, for example:

> bon   → bien
> gentil   → gentiment
> mauvais   → mal
> meilleur   → mieux
> petit   → peu

(b) Comparison of adverbs

This is carried out in the same way as with adjectives, for example: 'plus heureusement'. Note the irregular form 'mieux' (better), for example:

Il chante mieux que moi.   He sings better than I.

(c)

In a few cases, adjectives are used as adverbs, for example:

bref	in short	même	even
exprès	on purpose	soudain	suddenly
fort	loud(ly)	vite	quickly
juste	exactly		

(d) Position of the adverb

This can vary, but the main rule is that the adverb can never be placed between the subject and the verb as happens in English, for example:

Je le vois souvent.   I often see him.

7 Prepositions

7.1 Common prepositions

à	at; to	jusque	till; until
après	after	malgré	in spite of
avant	before (time)	par	by
avec	with	parmi	among
chez	at the house of	pendant	during
contre	against	pour	for
dans	in	sans	without
de	of; from	sauf	except
depuis	since	selon	according to
derrière	behind	sous	under
devant	in front of	sur	on
en	in	vers	towards
entre	between		

7.2 Idioms

It has been clear in previous explanations that prepositions can often not be translated by a single word, and that they are used differently in a wide variety of idioms. Below is a selection of such idioms, where translations of English prepositions could give problems.

about	De quoi parlent-ils?	What are they talking about?
	vers quatre heures	about four o'clock
	Il a environ 30 ans.	He's about 30.
above	avant tout	above all
at	Regardez l'heure.	Look at the time.
	chez moi	at my house
	au travail	at work
	enfin	at last
	de toute façon	at all events
	surpris de	surprised at
by	près de moi	by me; by my side
	par hasard	by chance
	à propos	by the way
for	par exemple	for example
in	s'intéresser à	to take an interest in
	à temps	in time
	au printemps	in spring
	à l'avenir	in future
	à la campagne	in the country
	au mois de mai	in May
	au lit	in bed
	au soleil	in the sun
	à Caen	in Caen

	dans quelques minutes	in a few minutes
	en France	in France
	à six heures du matin	at six o'clock in the morning
	le matin	in the morning
	l'après-midi	in the afternoon
on	à bicyclette	on a bicycle
	à pied	on foot
	au contraire	on the contrary
	en voyage	on a journey
	en vente	on sale
	en grève	on strike
	en route	on the way
	en vacances	on holiday
	le onze mai	on the eleventh of May
to	écouter la radio	to listen to the radio
	trois heures moins dix	ten minutes to three
with	être content de	to be pleased with
	fâché contre	annoyed with

8 Conjunctions

8.1 Conjunctions of co-ordination

The following conjunctions have a linking or co-ordinating function in the sentence:

mais	but	alors	then; so
ou	or	ou bien	or else
et	and	puis	then
donc	therefore	aussi	also
		ensuite	next

8.2 Conjunctions of subordination

The following conjunctions introduce a subordinate clause:

comme	as; like	quand	when
parce que	because	pendant que	while

(Note the difference between 'pendant' as a preposition, for example: 'pendant votre séjour', and 'pendant que' as a conjunction, for example: 'pendant que vous êtes à Caen'.)

9 Miscellaneous

9.1 Numerals

(a) Cardinal numbers

1	un, une	40	quarante
2	deux	50	cinquante
3	trois	60	soixante
4	quatre	70	soixante-dix
5	cinq	71	soixante et onze
6	six	72	soixante-douze
7	sept	73	soixante-treize
8	huit	74	soixante-quatorze
9	neuf	75	soixante-quinze
10	dix	76	soixante-seize
11	onze	77	soixante-dix-sept
12	douze	78	soixante-dix-huit
13	treize	79	soixante-dix-neuf
14	quatorze	80	quatre-vingts
15	quinze	81	quatre-vingt-un (une)
16	seize	82	quatre-vingt-deux
17	dix-sept	90	quatre-vingt-dix
18	dix-huit	91	quatre-vingt-onze
19	dix-neuf	92	quatre-vingt-douze
20	vingt	100	cent
21	vingt et un (une)	101	cent un (une)
22	vingt-deux	200	deux cents
23	vingt-trois	201	deux cent un (une)
30	trente	1000	mille
31	trente et un (une)	2000	deux mille
32	trente-deux	1,000,000	un million

(b) Ordinal numbers

first	premier (première)	seventh	septième
second	deuxième	eighth	huitième
third	troisième	ninth	neuvième
fourth	quatrième	tenth	dixième
fifth	cinquième	eleventh	onzième
sixth	sixième	twelfth	douzième
		thirteenth	treizième

Note that 'onze', 'douze', 'treize', lose their final '-e' when adding '-ième'. All the ordinal numbers then follow this pattern, but note that in compound numbers such as 'twenty-first', 'premier' is not used, for example: 'vingt-et-unième'.

9.2 Dates and times

(a) Days of the week

lundi	Monday	vendredi	Friday
mardi	Tuesday	samedi	Saturday
mercredi	Wednesday	dimanche	Sunday
jeudi	Thursday		

All days of the week are masculine. They are written in French with a small letter, unless they begin a sentence.

(b) Months of the year

janvier	January	juillet	July
février	February	août	August
mars	March	septembre	September
avril	April	octobre	October
mai	May	novembre	November
juin	June	décembre	December

All the names of months are written with a small letter in French. When saying 'in January', 'in May' and so on, you may either say 'en janvier', 'en mai', or 'au mois de janvier', 'au mois de mai'.

(c) Dates

(i) The first day of the month is referred to by the ordinal, that is, 'le premier juin' (the first of June). Other dates make use of the cardinal numbers in French, for example: 'le deux janvier', 'le cinq avril', and so on.

(ii) The year may be expressed in hundreds, for example, 1982 is 'dix-neuf cent quatre-vingt-deux'; alternatively the word 'mil' may be used, for example: 'mil neuf cent quatre-vingt-deux'. (Note that 'mille' is never used in dates.)

(d) Seasons

le printemps	spring	au printemps	in spring
l'été	summer	en été	in summer
l'automne	autumn	en automne	in autumn
l'hiver	winter	en hiver	in winter

(e) Times

		Quelle heure est-il?	What time is it?
(i)	Hour:	il est une heure	it is 1 o'clock
		il est deux heures	it is 2 o'clock
		il est midi	it is midday
		il est minuit	it is midnight
(ii)	½ hour	une heure et demie	half past one
		midi et demi	half past midday
(iii)	¼ hour	une heure et quart	1.15
		deux heures et quart	2.15
		midi et quart	12.15 pm

(iv) ¾ hour: une heure moins le quart   12.45
               deux heures moins le quart   1.45
               midi moins le quart   11.45 am
(v) Minutes: une heure vingt   1.20
               trois heures vingt-cinq   3.25
               quatre heures moins cinq   3.55
               cinq heures moins vingt   4.40
(vi) Am/pm: the 24-hour clock is used extensively to avoid ambiguity, particularly with timetables and opening times. Otherwise 'am' is expressed by 'du matin', and 'pm' by 'de l'après-midi' or 'du soir'. Thus, 4.30 pm might be expressed as 'seize heures trente' or as 'quatre heures et demie de l'après-midi'.

(f) 'Jour' / 'journée'; 'matin' / 'matinée'; 'soir' / 'soirée'; 'an' / 'année'
In the dialogues of the book you will have noticed that the French equivalents of the words for 'day', 'morning', 'evening' and 'year' come in pairs. You say 'Bonjour', but 'Nous passons une journée à Paris'.

The explanation for these pairs is that the simple form (given first in the pairs above) is used if you want to refer only to the unit of time, whereas the second form (journée, etc.) is used when you are thinking more about the activities and events which occupy that time. You can see why 'soir' means 'evening', but 'soirée' means 'party'. You can also see why, when you wish someone a Happy New Year in French, you say 'Bonne année!'.

Look at the following examples:

Je vais passer trois jours à Paris.   I'm going to spend three days in Paris.
Nous avons passé une journée   We spent an interesting day in Paris.
intéressante à Paris.

On s'est couché tard, alors on va   We went to bed late, so we are going
faire la grasse matinée.   to have a long lie-in.
Ce matin, je vais faire des courses.   This morning, I am going to do some
                                         shopping.

9.3 The alphabet

When spelling names and so on, it is necessary to know how the letters of the alphabet are pronounced in French. (See *guide to pronunciation* for information on the pronunciation of these sounds.)

The French names for the letters of the alphabet are as follows:

a	a	j	ji	s	ess
b	bé	k	ka	t	té
c	cé	l	el	u	u
d	dé	m	em	v	vé
e	e	n	en	w	double vé
f	ef	o	ô	x	iks
g	gé	p	pé	y	i grec
h	âche	q	ku	z	zed
i	i	r	er		

9.4 Common abbreviations

Cie	compagnie	company
dl	décilitre(s)	decilitre(s)
F	franc(s)	franc(s)
g	gramme(s)	gram(s)
h	heure	o'clock
l	litre(s)	litre(s)
M	monsieur	Mr
Mlle	mademoiselle	Miss
MM	messieurs	gentlemen
Mme	madame	Mrs
N^o	numéro	number
P et T	Postes et Télécommunications	Post Office and Telecom
qn	quelqu'un	someone
qch	quelque chose	something
RATP	Réseau Autonome des Transports Parisiens	Paris public transport
RER	Réseau Express Régional	Parisian suburban rail network
RSVP	répondez s'il vous plaît	please send a reply
SNCF	Société Nationale des Chemins de Fer Français	French Railways
TDF	Télédiffusion de France	umbrella authority for French TV
TGV	Train à Grande Vitesse	French high-speed train
TSVP	tournez s'il vous plaît	PTO (please turn over)
TVA	Taxe à Valeur Ajoutée	VAT

Guide to pronunciation

It should be stressed that the following summary of rules for French pronunciation can only be a rough guide. The way to get a good French accent is to listen to the sounds and copy them, especially when they occur in sentences and phrases. This is because the rhythm and intonation of French phrases are quite different from the English. So you have to approach the pronunciation at two levels; firstly the way in which the separate vowels and consonants are pronounced; secondly the pattern of intonation in the whole phrase or sentence.

Spelling

The spelling of French, like the spelling of English, has not changed significantly over the centuries, while pronunciation has altered in many ways. The written form of the language therefore looks very different from the spoken form, and each sound can be spelt in a number of ways. In the table below, each sound is given its approximate value compared with English, and a summary of the ways in which you might expect to find it written. It should be stressed that the English comparison can only be approximate, and only listening to examples of spoken French will give you the exact sound.

Vowels

The main characteristic of French vowels is that each sound is pure, and does not 'slide' as happens in standard English. Compare the vowel sound in the words 'boat' and 'grass' as pronounced in BBC English and in North Country accents. The latter are pure in the sense that the vowel has a single sound. You would hear the same differences between the English word 'bow' and the French 'beau'. French vowels are all pronounced with more energy than English vowels, and more exactness – English vowels sound rather lazy in comparison. It is also the case that French vowels almost always keep their full value wherever they occur in the word. In the English word 'magnificent', for example, the stress falls heavily on the 'if' syllable, whereas the other vowels are much less prominent. The French equivalent 'magnifique' gives each vowel its full value. (See more about this in the paragraph on stress and intonation.) Because of these differences, the suggestions in the table below for English sounds which are equivalent to French sounds are bound to be only rough approximations.

Approximate sound	Written forms in French	Examples
• like 'a' in 'made' (but shorter and 'tighter')	1. **é, ée, és, ées**	été; écrire
	2. **ez**	allez; chez
	3. **er** at the end of a word	aller (an exception is 'cher', pronounced like 'share')
	4. **ed, eds**	pied; assieds-toi
	5. **ef**	clef
	6. **es, et** in monosyllables	les; mes; des; et
• like 'e' in 'bed'	1. **è, ê**	père; tête
	2. **ai, ei**	palais; reine
• like 'e' in 'perhaps' (but very much shorter)	**e** in unstressed position and in monosyllables with no other letter following	le; te; de; que; boulevard; avenue; médecin

(Note that this vowel is the only exception to the statement made earlier that French vowels are given their full value. Often, when it occurs between two consonants, it disappears completely in pronunciation. The pronunciation of the examples above is therefore 'boul'vard', 'av'nue', 'méd'cin'.)

• like 'a' in 'rack'	1. **a**	cheval; ami
	2. **emm**	femme
• like 'a' in 'father'	1. **â**	château; âge
	2. **as**	pas; gras
	3. **ase**	phrase
	4. **able**	aimable
• like 'o' in 'hope'	1. **o** at the end of a word when final consonant not pronounced	dos; trop
	2. **au, eau, aux**	autre; auto; beau
	3. **ô**	côté
	4. **o** followed by '-se', '-sse', '-tion'	chose; grosse; émotion
• like 'o' in 'lot'	**o** followed by pronounced consonant	robe; comme; bonne
• like 'u' in 'true'	**ou**	vous; toujours
• like 'ee' in keen	**i, î**	fini; dîner

There are some vowels for which not even an approximate pronunciation can be given because they do not exist in English. They are as follows:

(i) 'u' – put your lips into position to pronounce 'oo' in English 'pool'. Now, keep your lips in that position and try to pronounce the sound of 'ee' in English 'peel'. You will produce a sound which must not be allowed to slip into the English 'oo' sound, or the sound of the French 'ou' listed above. Practise with 'sur', 'vue', 'plus'.

(ii) 'eu' – when followed by 'r' this sound is a little like 'ur' in English 'murder' (as in 'sœur', 'peur'). When not followed by 'r' it is a very similar sound, but much shorter (as in 'feu', 'peu', 'deux').

Nasal vowels

One of the most marked characteristics of French is the nasal vowel. Whereas with all English vowels the sound is produced by a passage of air through the mouth, in nasal vowels some of the air comes through the nose as well. Compare the word 'say' as pronounced in standard English and as pronounced by an American. American English is more nasalised than standard English. Once again, the only good advice is to listen to examples of spoken French. In written French the nasal sound is always indicated by an 'm' or 'n' after the vowel. This 'm' or 'n' is not pronounced. It stands there only as a sign that the preceding vowel is nasal.

Written form	Examples
in, im, ain, aim, ein	fin; main; faim
un, um	un; parfum; lundi
on, om	bon; mont; ombre
an, am, en, em	quand; camp;* lent; client

* Note that 'quand' and 'camp' are pronounced the same.

Notice that the nasal quality is lost when the 'n' is doubled (for example, 'bonne' is pronounced with the 'o' as in 'lot'), or when the 'n' is followed by a vowel (for example, in 'fini' both vowels are pronounced like English 'ee').

Semi-vowels

Approximate sound	Written forms in French	Examples
• like 'y' in 'yes'	1. **i** or **y** before a vowel	piano; pierre; yeux
	2. **ill** in the body of a word	briller; travailler; bouillon
	3. **il** or **ille** at the end of a word	travail; fille; feuille

(There are a small number of exceptions when the final 'l' is pronounced, for example, 'mille', 'ville', 'tranquille'.)

• like 'w' in 'wait'	1. **ou** before a vowel	oui; alouette
	2. **oi, oy** (pronounced 'wa')	oiseau; loi; voilà; trois
	3. **oin** is the same sound as **oi** but nasalised	coin

Consonants

The main characteristic to note is that the French consonants are not pronounced with such an escape of breath as the English ones. The 'p' in English 'pair' is pronounced with a puff of breath which does not occur in the French equivalent 'paire'. The French consonants are thus more tense and precise in their pronunciation. As far as the written language is concerned, you will already have noticed from the examples given when discussing vowels that the final consonants in French words are hardly ever pronounced, for example you have already met the words 'clef', 'trop', 'palais', 'pied', and so on. In the pronunciation of these words you can ignore the final consonant. But the consonant is sounded if the word ends with a consonant plus '-e'. Note the difference between 'vert' (pronounced as though the 't' wasn't there) and 'verte' (now the 't' is sounded).

In the list below, no further explanation is given for the consonants which are most similar to English (b, d, f, m, n, p, t, v), but even so you should remember that the sounds are not exactly as in English, and you should listen to and copy examples of spoken French.

Approximate sound	**Written forms in French**	**Examples**
• like 'c' in 'cat'	1. **c** (before 'a', 'o', 'u')	Cannes; cognac; curé
	2. **k**	képi
	3. **qu**	queue
• like 'g' in 'gate'	**g** (before 'a', 'o', 'u')	gare
• like 's' in 'pleasure'	**g, j** (before 'e', 'i')	plage; gentil; jour
• like 's' in 'save'	1. **s** (initial and after nasal 'n')	santé; service; danser
	2. **c** (before 'e', 'i')	ciel; ici
	3. **ç**	française
	4. **ss**	poisson
	5. **sc**	scène
	6. **ti** (in words ending '-tion')	émotion
• like 'z' in 'zoo'	1. **z**	gazon
	2. **s** when between two vowels	chaise; chose
• like 'sh' in 'shine'	**ch**	chéri
• like 'ni' in 'onion'	**gn**	gagner; magnifique

Among the other letters you will meet, note the following:

(i) 'h' is silent
(ii) 'th' is pronounced like 't' (for example 'thé')
(iii) 'x' is pronounced 'gs' before a vowel (for example, 'examen') and 'ks' before a consonant (for example, 'excuser')
(iv) 'w' only occurs in words of foreign origin and is pronounced like 'v' (for example, 'wagon')
(v) 'l' and 'r' offer particular difficulties:

'l' is a very different sound from the English 'l', as you can see if you compare the English 'bell' and the French 'belle'. In English the 'l' sound is pronounced with the tongue turned up and touching the ridge of the hard palate. In French the tongue is placed further forward so that it is touching the point at which the incisors meet the gums. Note also that 'l' is one of the consonants that is nearly always pronounced when it is final, for example: 'cheval'. (Note however that the final 'l' is not pronounced in the word 'gentil'.) For the pronunciation of 'il' and 'ill' see the section on semi-vowels.

'r' is perhaps the most characteristic sound of French, and the most difficult for foreigners to imitate. It is produced well back in the throat by bringing the soft palate down to meet the back of the tongue. The best way to explain it is to say that it is rather like the action of tongue and palate when gargling! Examples: 'jardin', 'grand', 'cri'.

Liaison

As was stated above, final consonants are generally silent in French. But when the following word begins with a vowel or with a silent 'h' the final consonant is usually pronounced together with the initial vowel which follows, for example: 'les‿enfants', 'très‿important', 'un petit‿homme', and so on. This process is called liaison. Note that there is no break of any kind between the words linked in this way. Each of the groups of words above sounds like a single word.

Although liaison is essential in the examples given, there are many cases where liaison might be expected but does not always occur in modern spoken French. For example, you may hear 'je veux‿aller' or 'je veux aller'.

Stress and intonation

It was pointed out earlier that English places a heavy stress on one syllable in a word (for example, 'magni*fi*cent'). French is characterised by a very even stress applied to each syllable, so that each vowel retains its full value wherever it occurs in the word. This is also true when words are grouped together, and it is also the case that the note of the voice is much more regular in French. To French ears, English has a sing-song accent, with lots of ups and downs of the voice. French retains an even accent and remains on a constant note until the voice drops at the end of the phrase. In Chapter 1, for example, you will find the statement: 'Vous‿avez une chambre pour ma famille' (You have a room for my family). The voice does not vary its note until it drops on the syllable '-mille'.

Bibliography and sources of information

1 Works of reference

1.1 Grammars
(a) J. E. Mansion, *A Grammar of Present-Day French* (Harrap and Co.)
(b) H. Ferrar, *A French Reference Grammar* (OUP)

1.2 Dictionaries
(a) *Harrap's Concise French and English Dictionary* (Harrap and Co.)
(b) *Collins-Robert French and English Dictionary* (Collins and Co.)
(c) *Oxford Concise French and English Dictionary* (OUP)

2 Opportunities for hearing French

2.1 Radio and television
Radio broadcasts from France may help to get the feel of the intonation and pronunciation of the language, but they will certainly be too difficult for learners at the early stages of French. The best source of opportunities for hearing French is the BBC, with programmes intended for adult listeners and for schools. Note particularly:

(i) 'The French Experience'
(ii) 'Get by in French'

2.2 Open University
The Open University course 'Ouverture' began TV transmission in February 1995 and comprises eight topics dealing with everyday contemporary French life.

3 Other sources of information about France or the French language

(a) Institut Français, Queensberry Place, South Kensington, London SW7
(b) French Government Tourist Office, Piccadilly, London
(c) French Railways, Piccadilly, London
(d) CILT (Centre for Information on Language Teaching and Research), 20 Bedfordbury, London WC2N 4LB. The Centre offers an information service on all aspects of language learning, course materials, and so on. There is also an extensive library where most current course materials – book, audio and video materials – may be consulted.
(e) Satellite TV: French programmes can now be accessed by satellite TV, but it is usually necessary to have a transformer to convert the French system for reception on English sets.

Supplementary vocabularies

1 La famille   The family

Masculine

le bébé	the baby
le cousin	cousin
le frère	brother
le grand-père	grandfather
un homme	man
le mariage	marriage
le neveu	nephew
un oncle	uncle
le père	father

Feminine

la cousine	cousin
la grand-mère	grandmother
la jeune fille	girl
la mère	mother
la nièce	niece
la sœur	sister
la tante	aunt

2 Les vêtements   Clothes

Masculine

le bouton	button
le chapeau	hat
les collants	tights
le costume	suit
le gant	glove
le jupon	petticoat
le mouchoir	handkerchief
le parapluie	umbrella
le pardessus	raincoat
le portefeuille	wallet
le sac à main	handbag
le short	shorts

Feminine

la boucle d'oreille	ear-ring
la ceinture	belt
la chaussette	sock
la chaussure	shoe
la cravate	tie
la jupe	skirt
les lunettes	spectacles
les lunettes de soleil	sunglasses
la montre	wristwatch
la poche	pocket
la robe	dress

3 Les parties du corps   Parts of the body

Masculine

le bras	arm
le cou	neck

Feminine

la barbe	beard
la bouche	mouth

le doigt	finger		la cheville	ankle
le dos	back		la dent	tooth
le front	forehead		la figure	face
le genou	knee		la jambe	leg
le nez	nose		la lèvre	lip
un œil	eye		la main	hand
le visage	face		une oreille	ear
les yeux	eyes		la poitrine	chest

4 La nourriture et la boisson   Food and drink

Masculine

un agneau	lamb
le bifteck	steak
le bœuf	beef
le foie	liver
le gigot	leg of mutton
le porc	pork
le riz	rice
le veau	veal
le vinaigre	vinegar

Feminine

la confiture	jam
la crêpe	pancake

5 Les fruits et les légumes   Fruit and vegetables

Masculine

un abricot	apricot
un ananas	pineapple
le chou	cabbage
un haricot vert	French bean
les petits-pois	green peas

Feminine

la banane	banana
la cerise	cherry
la framboise	raspberry
la pêche	peach
la poire	pear
la prune	plum

6 Les magasins et les métiers   Shops and professions

Masculine

un administrateur (une administratrice)	administrator
un agent de change	stockbroker
un agent immobilier	estate agent
un architecte	architect
un artiste (une artiste)	artist
un avocat (une avocate)	lawyer (barrister)
un avoué (une avouée)	solicitor
le banquier	banker
le boulanger (la boulangère)	baker
le charpentier	carpenter
le chirurgien (la chirurgienne)	surgeon

Feminine

la bijouterie	jeweller's
la boucherie	butcher's
la coiffeuse	hairdresser
la confiserie	confectioner's
la gendarmerie	police station
une horlogerie	watchmaker's
une infirmière	nurse
la librairie	bookshop
la ménagère	housewife
la modiste	milliner
la papeterie	stationer's
la pâtisserie	cake-shop
la poissonerie	fishmonger's
la quincaillerie	hardware store

le coiffeur (la coiffeuse)	hairdresser
le concierge (la concierge)	caretaker
le dentiste	dentist
un entrepreneur	builder/contractor
le facteur	postman
le fermier (la fermière)	farmer
le gérant (la gérante)	manager/manageress
un ingénieur	engineer
un inspecteur (une inspectrice)	inspector
le jardinier	gardener
le juge	judge
le marchand	merchant; shopkeeper
le notaire	solicitor
un ouvrier	workman
le patron	employer; boss
le pêcheur	fisherman
le plombier	plumber
le pompier	fireman
le rédacteur	newspaper editor
le serveur (la serveuse)	waiter (waitress)
le tabac	tobacconist's
le tailleur	tailor
le vendeur (la vendeuse)	salesperson
le vétérinaire	vet

● *For further information about the feminine of professions, see grammar reference section 2.1 (d).*

7 *L'automobilisme et le transport Motoring and transport*

Masculine

un avion	aeroplane
le camion	lorry
le capot	bonnet
le coffre	boot
le cric	jack
le démarreur	starter
un embrayage	clutch
le frein	brake
le kilomètre	kilometre
le moteur	engine
le pare-brise	windscreen
le pare-choc	bumper
le phare	headlight
le radiateur	radiator

Feminine

une autoroute	motorway
la bicyclette	bicycle
la crevaison	puncture
la moto	motorcycle
la pile	battery
la plaque	number-plate
la roue	wheel
la roue de rechange	spare wheel
la route nationale	A road

8 Le chemin de fer   Railway

Masculine		Feminine	
le chef de gare	station master	la consigne	left-luggage
le chef de train	guard		(office)
le compartiment	compartment	la correspondance	changing trains
le contrôleur	ticket inspector	la locomotive	engine
le filet	rack	la salle d'attente	waiting room
un indicateur	timetable	la sortie	way out
le passage souterrain	subway	la valise	suitcase
le porteur	porter		
le rapide	express		
le wagon	carriage		
le wagon-lit	sleeping car		

9 Les pays   Countries

The adjectives derived from the names of the countries are given in brackets.

Masculine		Feminine	
le Canada (canadien)	Canada	l'Afrique (africain)	Africa
le Danemark (danois)	Denmark	l'Allemagne (allemand)	Germany
les États-Unis (américain)	USA	l'Angleterre (anglais)	England
le Japon (japonais)	Japan	l'Australie (australien)	Australia
le Pays de Galles (gallois)	Wales	l'Autriche (autrichien)	Austria
le Portugal (portugais)	Portugal	la Belgique (belge)	Belgium
		la Chine (chinois)	China
		l'Écosse (écossais)	Scotland
		l'Espagne (espagnol)	Spain
		la Grèce (grec)	Greece
		la Hollande (hollandais)	Holland
		l'Irlande (irlandais)	Ireland
		l'Italie (italien)	Italy

Glossary of words introduced in this book

The number in italic refers to the chapter where the word is first introduced. SV refers to the *supplementary vocabularies*. Gender of nouns is indicated by *(m)* or *(f)* and plural is indicated by *(pl)*. Parts of verbs, numerals and pronouns are not included.

A

à   at *1*; to *3*
d'abord   at first *12*
abricot *(m)*   apricot (SV)
absent   absent *8*
absolument   absolutely *14*
accident *(m)*   accident *13*
d'accord   OK; agreed *9*
accueil *(m)*   welcome *18*
accueillir   to welcome *19*
acheter   to buy *5*
activité *(f)*   activity *10*
addition *(f)*   bill *2*
admettre   to admit *15*
adorer   to love; to adore *6*
adresse *(f)*   address *13*
adulte *(m)*   adult *3*
afin de   in order to *16*
africain   African (SV)
Afrique *(f)*   Africa (SV)
âge *(m)*   age *8*
âgé   aged *10*
agent *(m)*   policeman *1*
agneau *(m)*   lamb (SV)
agréable   pleasant *12*
agréer   to receive favourably *16*
agricole   agricultural *14*
agriculture *(f)*   farming; agriculture *14*
aider   to help *16*
ailleurs   elsewhere *17*
d'ailleurs   moreover *14*
aimable   nice; kind *3*

aimer   to like *5*
ajouter   to add *18*
alimentation *(f)*   food *6*
allée *(f)*   avenue; drive *10*
Allemagne *(f)*   Germany (SV)
allemand   German (SV)
aller   to go *3*
aller-retour *(m)*   return ticket *11*
allô   hello (on phone) *4*
alors   so; well *1*
allumettes *(f pl)*   matches *9*
s'améliorer   to improve *19*
américain   American (SV)
ami *(m)*   friend *16*
amical   friendly *19*
amusant   fun *10*
s'amuser   to enjoy oneself; to have a good time *5*
an *(m)*   year *8*
ancien   ancient *11*
anglais   English *2*
angle *(m)*   angle *12*
Angleterre   England *5*
animé   animated; lively *10*
année   year *8*
à part   except for *8*
à partir de   as from; with effect from *9*
apéritif *(m)*   aperitif *7*
à peu près   about; approximately *8*
appartenir   to belong *14*
s'appeler   to be called *1*
appétit *(m)*   appetite *5*
apporter   to bring *2*

apprendre   to learn *11*
apprentissage *(f)* (d'une langue)
    (language) learning *19*
après   after *5*
après-demain   the day after tomorrow *16*
après-midi *(m)*   afternoon *5*
arbre *(m)*   tree *11*
arc *(m)*   arch *10*
argent *(m)*   money; silver *2*
arrêt *(m)*   stop *3*
s'arrêter   to stop *13*
arrhes *(f pl)*   deposit *16*
arrière   back *17*
arriver   to arrive *8;* to happen *13*
article *(m)*   article *19*
ascension *(f)*   ascent *10*
aspirine *(f)*   aspirin *9*
s'asseoir   to sit down *7*
assez   quite *3;* enough *10*
assiette *(f)*   plate *7*
assurer   to assure; to ensure *18*
attirer   to attract *10*
attraper   to catch *17*
aucun   not a single one *17*
aujourd'hui   today *5*
aussi   also *2*
Australie *(f)*   Australia (sv)
australien   Australian (sv)
auto *(f)*   car *10*
autobus *(m)*   bus *3*
automne *(m)*   autumn *16*
autoroute *(f)*   motorway (sv)
autour de   around *14*
autre   other *12*
autrefois   in the old days *15*
autrement   otherwise *14*
Autriche *(f)*   Austria (sv)
autrichien   Austrian (sv)
avant   before *7*
avantage *(m)*   advantage *19*
avec   with *1*
aventureux   adventurous *15*
avenue *(f)*   avenue *5*
averse *(f)*   shower *16*
avion *(m)*   aeroplane (sv)
avis *(m)*   opinion *13*
avoir   to have *1*
avoir besoin   to need *13*
avoir lieu   to take place *16*
avoir raison   to be right *7*

B

bagages *(m pl)*   luggage *12*
baguette *(f)*   long, French loaf *9*
se baigner   to bathe; to swim *14*

balançoire *(f)*   swing *10*
balle *(f)*   ball *19*
banane *(f)*   banana (sv)
bancaire   bank *2*
banque *(f)*   bank *2*
banquier *(m)*   banker (sv)
barbe *(f)*   beard (sv)
basilique *(f)*   basilica *4*
bassin *(m)*   dock *3*
bateau *(m)*   boat *10*
bateau-mouche *(m)*   pleasure steamer *10*
bâtiment *(m)*   building *11*
bavaroise *(f)*   mousse *18*
beau (belle)   fine *5;* beautiful *6*
beaucoup   a lot; much *2*
bébé *(m)*   baby (sv)
belge   Belgian (sv)
Belgique *(f)*   Belgium (sv)
besoin *(m)*   need *13*
beurre *(m)*   butter *9*
bicyclette *(f)*   bicycle (sv)
bien   fine; well   *(1)*
bien des   many; a lot of *14*
bien que   although *16*
bière *(f)*   beer *9*
biftek *(m)*   steak (sv)
bijouterie *(f)*   jeweller's (sv)
billet *(m)*   ticket *3*
blanc   white *10*
bleu   blue *5*
bœuf *(m)*   beef (sv)
boire   to drink *9*
bois *(m)*   wood(s) *14*
boisson *(f)*   drink *7*
boîte *(f)*   box; tin *9*
bombardement *(m)*   bombing *15*
bon   good *1*
bordant   bordering *10*
bouche *(f)*   mouth (sv)
boucherie *(f)*   butcher's (sv)
boucle d'oreille *(f)*   ear-ring (sv)
bougie *(f)*   spark plug *18;* candle
bouillir   to boil *18*
bouillon *(m)*   stock (culinary) *18*
boulangerie *(f)*   bakery *17*
boulevard *(m)*   boulevard *10*
bouquiniste *(m)*   bookseller *12*
bouteille *(f)*   bottle *7*
boutique *(f)*   shop *10*
bouton *(m)*   button (sv)
bras *(m)*   arm (sv)
brasserie *(f)*   café-bar *12*
brûler   to burn *13*
buanderie *(f)*   laundry *9*
bus *(m)*   bus *12*

C

ça   this; that *1*
caennais   native to Caen *15*
café *(m)*   café; coffee *2*
cafétéria *(f)*   cafeteria *6*
caisse *(f)*   cash-desk *2*
calme   quiet; calm *2*
se calmer   to calm down; to quieten
   down *8*
camion *(m)*   lorry (SV)
campagne *(f)*   country *15*
camping *(m)*   camping (site) *8*
Canada *(m)*   Canada (SV)
canadien   Canadian (SV)
canard *(m)*   duck *7*
capable   capable; able *19*
capot *(m)*   bonnet (car) (SV)
caractéristique *(f)*   characteristic *15*
carrefour *(m)*   crossroads *13*
carte *(f)*   card *2*; map *11*
casserole *(f)*   saucepan *9*
cathédrale *(f)*   cathedral *11*
à cause de   because of *13*
ceinture *(f)*   belt (SV)
cela   this; that *5*
célèbre   famous *11*
centre *(m)*   centre *10*
cerfeuil *(m)*   chervil *18*
certain   certain *8*
certainement   certainly *2*
chaise *(f)*   chair *11*
chambre *(f)*   bedroom *1*
chance *(f)*   luck *5*
changer   to change *2*
chaos *(m)*   chaos *15*
chapeau *(m)*   hat (SV)
chaque   each *8*
charcuterie *(f)*   cold meats *7*
chargé   loaded; full *11*
charpentier *(m)*   carpenter (SV)
charte *(f)*   charter *19*
chasseur *(m)*   hunter *18*
château *(m)*   castle *3*
chaud   hot *5*
chaussette *(f)*   sock (SV)
chef de gare *(m)*   station-master (SV)
chef de train *(m)*   guard (SV)
chemise *(f)*   shirt *8*
chemisier *(m)*   shirt-blouse *12*
chèque *(m)*   cheque *2*
cher   dear *10*; expensive *14*
chercher   to look for *6*
chéri   dear; darling *7*
cheveux *(m pl)*   hair *8*
cheville *(f)*   ankle (SV)
chez   at the house of *1*

chic   smart *6*
chirurgien *(m)*   surgeon (SV)
choc *(m)*   collision; shock *13*
chocolat *(m)*   chocolate *2*
choisir   to choose *7*
choix *(m)*   choice *17*
chose *(f)*   thing *7*
chou *(m)*   cabbage (SV)
cidre *(m)*   cider *9*
ciel *(m)*   sky *6*
cigarette *(f)*   cigarette *9*
cinéma *(m)*   cinema *10*
circulation *(f)*   traffic *13*
cité *(f)*   city *11*
citron *(m)*   lemon *11*
classe *(f)*   class *19*
clef *(f)*   key *1*
climat *(m)*   climate *5*
code confidentiel *(m)*   personal number *2*
cœur *(m)*   heart *10*
coffre *(m)*   boot (car) (SV)
cognac *(m)*   brandy *12*
coiffeur *(m)*   hairdresser (SV)
coiffeuse *(f)*   hairdresser (SV)
collants *(m pl)*   tights (SV)
collègue *(m)*   colleague *8*
combien   how much?; how many? *6*
comme   like; as *5*
commencer   to begin *4*
comment   how? *1*
commerçant *(m)*   shopkeeper *6*
commissariat *(m)*   police station *16*
commun   common *15*
commune *(f)*   parish; commune *19*
compagnie *(f)*   company *15*
compartiment *(m)*   compartment (SV)
complet   full up *4*
compléter   to finish filling in (a form) *17*
comprendre   to understand *8*
comprimé *(m)*   tablet *17*
compris   included *2*
concernant   concerning *16*
concierge *(m)*   caretaker (SV)
conducteur *(m)*   driver *3*
confection *(f)*   clothing *6*
confiserie *(f)*   confectioner's (SV)
confiture *(f)*   jam (SV)
confortable   comfortable *11*
connaître   to know *5*
connaissance *(f)*   acquaintance *1*
connu   well-known *3*
conseiller   to advise; to recommend *7*
conserver   to preserve *15*
consigne *(f)*   left-luggage (office) (SV)
construction *(f)*   construction *14*
construit   built *14*
consultation *(f)*   consultation *17*

contact *(m)* contact *19*
contacter to contact *13*
content pleased *16*
contestataire argumentative *15*
contraire *(m)* opposite *12*
contrôleur *(m)* ticket-collector (SV)
copie *(f)* copy *16*
cordial cordial *19*
correct correct *16*
correspondance *(f)* changing trains (SV)
costume *(m)* suit (SV)
côte *(f)* coast *9*
côté *(m)* side *10*
à côté de beside; next to *11*
cou *(m)* neck (SV)
coucher to put to bed *12*
se coucher to go to bed *8*
couleur *(f)* colour *6*
coupe-vent *(m)* anorak *5*
cour *(f)* courtyard *10*
courir to run *14*
court short *8*
cousin *(m)* male cousin (SV)
cousine *(f)* female cousin (SV)
couteau *(m)* knife *9*
couvrir to cover *18*
cravate *(f)* tie (SV)
créer to create *19*
crème *(f)* cream *2*
crêpe *(f)* pancake (SV)
crevaison *(f)* puncture (SV)
cric *(m)* jack (SV)
critiquer to criticise *19*
croire to believe *5*
croissant *(m)* croissant *2*
croque-monsieur *(m)* cheese on toast *12*
cuillère *(f)* spoon *9*
cuillerée *(f)* spoonful *18*
cuire to cook *18*
cuisine *(f)* kitchen *9*
cuit cooked *7*
cultivateur *(m)* farmer *5*
culture *(f)* farming *19*; culture *14*

D

dame *(f)* lady *4*
Danemark *(m)* Denmark (SV)
danois Danish (SV)
dans in *2*
date *(f)* date *16*
davantage more *17*
de of; from *3*
débarquement *(m)* landing *4*
début *(m)* beginning *11*
déclaration *(f)* declaration *16*
décontracté relaxed *15*

découvrir to discover *16*
déjà already *2*
déjeuner *(m)* lunch *2*
déjeuner to have lunch; to have breakfast *2*
délicieux delicious *7*
demain tomorrow *9*
demander to ask *8*
démarreur *(m)* starter (SV)
demi half *2*
demi-heure *(f)* half an hour *3*
demi-tarif *(m)* half-price (ticket) *11*
dent *(f)* tooth (SV)
dentiste *(m)* dentist (SV)
départ *(m)* departure *14*
département *(m)* department *14*
dépendre de to depend on *6*
depuis since *8*
déranger to disturb *5*
descendre to go down *9*
description *(f)* description *8*
désirer to want *2*
désolé sorry *2*
dessert *(m)* dessert *7*
dessin *(m)* drawing *13*
détail *(m)* detail *16*
détaillé detailed *8*
se détendre to relax *14*
devant in front of *3*
devenir to become *15*
devoir to have to *15*; to owe *17*
dévoué devoted *16*
différence *(f)* difference *19*
différent different *14*
difficile difficult *15*
difficulté *(f)* difficulty *15*
dîner to have supper/dinner *1*
directement directly *14*
direction *(f)* direction *5*
discussion *(f)* discussion *15*
disposition *(f)* disposal; disposition *5*
disque *(m)* record *6*
distingué distinguished *16*
distributeur automatique *(m)* cashpoint *2*
docteur *(m)* doctor *17*
document *(m)* document *16*
doigt *(m)* finger (SV)
dôme *(m)* dome *10*
domicile *(m)* home address *16*
dommage *(m)* pity *4*
donc then; therefore *8*
donner to give *10*
dormir to sleep *12*
dos *(m)* back (SV)
douche *(f)* shower *9*
doute *(m)* doubt *10*
doux sweet *17*

droguerie *(f)* hardware and household goods 6
droit straight 3
droite right 3
dur hard 19
durer to last 17

E

eau *(f)* water 17
eau minérale *(f)* mineral water 7
échalote *(f)* shallot 18
échange *(m)* exchange 15
écharpe *(f)* scarf 19
école *(f)* school 8
écolier *(m)* schoolboy 15
écolière *(f)* schoolgirl 15
économie *(f)* economy 14
écossais Scottish (SV)
Écosse *(f)* Scotland (SV)
écouter to listen (to) 9
écrire to write 9
effort *(m)* effort 15
église *(f)* church 3
électroménager *(m)* household electrical goods 6
élément *(m)* element 19
s'élever to rise 14
embarcadère *(m)* landing-stage 10
embarquer to go on board 19
embarras *(m)* too much; too many 18
emboutir to crash into 16
embrayage *(m)* clutch (SV)
emporter to take away 17
employé *(m)* employee 2
en in 1
s'en aller to go away 8
enchanté delighted 1
encombré crowded 19
encore yet 4; again 5
endroit *(m)* place 8
énergie *(f)* energy 15
énergique energetic 15
enfant *(m)* child 1
enfin at last 9
ennuyer to bore 19
s'ennuyer to get bored 11
énorme enormous 6
enrhumé with a cold 17
enrichissement *(m)* enrichment 19
ensoleillé sunny 14
ensuite next 7
entente *(f)* understanding 19
entr'acte *(m)* interval 4
entre between 7
entrée *(f)* entrance 3
entrepreneur *(m)* builder; contractor (SV)

entreprise *(f)* firm; company 15
entrer to enter 1
environ approximately; about 3
envoyer to send 19
épicerie *(f)* grocer's 9
époque *(f)* period 15
épuisé exhausted 12
équivalent *(m)* equivalent 15
erreur *(f)* mistake 18
escalier *(m)* staircase; steps 9
escalope *(f)* cutlet 7
escargot *(m)* snail 7
espace *(m)* space 11
espérer to hope 10
essayer to try 6
Espagne *(f)* Spain (SV)
espagnol Spanish (SV)
estragon *(m)* tarragon 18
et and 1
États-Unis *(m pl)* USA (SV)
été *(m)* summer 5
étoile *(f)* star 9
étonner to astonish 13
étranger foreign 19
être to be 1
être en tort to be in the wrong; to be at fault 13
étude *(f)* study 15
étudiant *(m)* student 11
eurochèque *(m)* eurocheque 2
évacuer evacuate 15
évidemment evidently 10
évident evident 16
exact exact 6
exactement exactly 9
excellent excellent 7
excessivement excessively 15
excursion *(f)* excursion 8
exemple *(m)* example 14
expression *(f)* expression 16
extrait *(m)* extract 14

F

en face de opposite 11
facile easy 16
facilité *(f)* facility 9
façon *(f)* way 10
facteur *(m)* postman (SV)
faire to make; to do 1
faire des courses to go shopping 5
faire la cuisine to cook 9
faire le plein to fill up 18
fait *(m)* fact 13
falaise *(f)* cliff 9
falloir to be necessary 10
se familiariser to get to know 19

famille *(f)* family *1*
farine *(f)* flour *9*
fatigant tiring *12*
fatigué tired *10*
il faut it is necessary *3*
faute *(f)* fault *6*
faveur *(f)* favour *19*
femme *(f)* wife; woman *1*
fêter to celebrate *7*
feu *(m)* traffic light *13*; fire
feuille *(f)* leaf *18*
feuille *(f)* de sécurité sociale social
    security form *17*
fier proud *15*
fièvre *(f)* fever; temperature *17*
figure *(f)* face (SV)
filet *(m)* rack (SV)
fille *(f)* daughter *8*
fillette *(f)* little girl *6*
fils *(m)* son *8*
fin fine; refined; best *18*
fin *(f)* end *7*
finement finely *18*
fini finished *6*
finir to finish *15*
flamber to set light to; to set alight *18*
flâner to stroll *10*
flèche *(f)* spire *3*
flegmatique phlegmatic *15*
fleuve *(m)* river *10*
foie *(m)* liver (SV)
fois *(f)* time *3*
forêt *(f)* forest *14*
formidable terrific *12*
fort strong *7*
fougueux fiery; impetuous *15*
fourchette *(f)* fork *9*
fournir to supply *10*
foyer *(m)* home *19*
frais (fraîche) cool; fresh *17*
frais *(m pl)* expenses *19*
fraise *(f)* strawberry *2*
framboise *(f)* raspberry (SV)
franc *(m)* franc *2*
français French *8*
France *(f)* France *1*
frappant striking *15*
frein *(m)* brake (SV)
fréquent frequent *10*
fréquenter to frequent *10*
frère *(m)* brother (SV)
frites *(f pl)* chips *7*
froid cold *18*
fromage *(m)* cheese *7*
front *(m)* forehead (SV)
fruit *(m)* fruit *7*
fuite *(f)* leak *18*

G

gagner to earn; to win *18*
galerie *(f)* gallery *10*
gallois Welsh (SV)
gant *(m)* glove (SV)
garage *(m)* garage *18*
garagiste *(m)* garage owner *18*
garçon *(m)* boy *6*; waiter *7*
garder to keep *17*
gare *(f)* station *10*
garer to park *10*
gauche left *3*
gazeux sparkling *7*
gélatine *(f)* gelatine *18*
gendarmerie *(f)* police station (SV)
général general *8*
généralement generally *5*
genou *(m)* knee (SV)
gens *(m pl)* people *8*
gentil kind; nice *1*
gérant *(m)* manager (SV)
gigot *(m)* leg of mutton (SV)
glace *(f)* ice-cream *2*
gorge *(f)* throat *17*
goût *(m)* taste *17*
goûter to taste *7*
grand big; tall *3*
grand'chose a lot *12*
grandiose majestic *10*
grand-mère *(f)* grandmother (SV)
grand-père *(m)* grandfather (SV)
gras fat *12*
grave serious *2*
grec Greek (SV)
Grèce *(f)* Greece (SV)
grippe *(f)* 'flu *17*
gris grey *8*
guerre *(f)* war *15*
guichet *(m)* ticket-window *11*
guide *(m)* guide *3*

H

s'habiller to get dressed *14*
habitant *(m)* inhabitant *15*
habiter to live *15*
habitué à accustomed to *16*
hacher to chop up *18*
haricot vert *(m)* French bean (SV)
haut high *10*
hein? isn't it?; etc. *12*
hésiter to hesitate *7*
heure *(f)* hour *1*
heureusement luckily; happily *6*
heureux happy *1*
histoire *(f)* history *15*; story

historique historical *14*
hiver *(m)* winter *10*
hollandais Dutch (SV)
Hollande *(f)* Holland (SV)
homme *(m)* man *6*
honneur *(f)* honour *16*
horlogerie *(f)* watchmaker's (SV)
hors d'œuvre *(m)* hors d'œuvre; starter *7*
hot-dog *(m)* hot dog *12*
hôtel *(m)* hotel *1*
hôtelier *(m)* hotelier *1*
huile *(f)* oil *18*
huileux oily *18*
humain human *19*

I

ici here *3*
idée *(f)* idea *3*
île *(f)* island *11*
il y a there is *2*; ago *13*
immédiatement immediately *13*
imperméable *(m)* raincoat *6*
important important; large *3*
impression *(f)* impression *8*
inconnu unknown *8*
incorporer to mix in; to incorporate *18*
incroyable unbelievable *13*
industriel industrial *14*
infirmière *(f)* nurse (SV)
influence *(f)* influence *15*
ingénieur *(m)* engineer (SV)
inquiet worried *8*
intention *(f)* intention *8*
intéressant interesting *3*
intéresser to interest *10*
s'intéresser à to be interested in *15*
interviewer to interview *16*
invasion *(f)* invasion *15*
inverse opposite *13*
invitation *(f)* invitation *18*
inviter to invite *5*
irlandais Irish (SV)
Irlande *(f)* Ireland (SV)
Italie *(f)* Italy (SV)
italien Italian (SV)

J

jamais never *5*
jambe *(f)* leg (SV)
jambon *(m)* ham *9*
Japon *(m)* Japan (SV)
japonais Japanese (SV)
jardin *(m)* garden *3*
jardinier *(m)* gardener (SV)
jaune yellow *6*

jeu *(m)* game *9*
jeune young *15*
jeune fille *(f)* girl (SV)
joli pretty *6*
jongleur *(m)* juggler *10*
jouer to play *14*
jouet *(m)* toy *6*
jour *(m)* day *1*
journal *(m)* newspaper *13*
juge *(m)* judge (SV)
jupe *(f)* skirt (SV)
jupon *(m)* petticoat (SV)
jumelage *(m)* twinning *19*
jumelé twinned *14*
jus *(m)* juice *7*
juste just *17*
jusqu'à until *4*; as far as *10*

K

kilo *(m)* kilo(gram) *9*
kilomètre *(m)* kilometre *10*
kir *(m)* an aperitif (blackcurrant liqueur + white wine) *7*

L

là there *1*
là-bas over there *6*
laid ugly *16*
laisser to let; to permit *17*; to leave *18*
lait *(m)* milk *9*
langue *(f)* language *15*; tongue *17*
se laver to wash *8*
légume *(m)* vegetable *9*
lent slow *15*
lettre *(f)* letter *14*
se lever to get up *8*
lèvre *(f)* lip (SV)
librairie *(f)* bookshop (SV)
libre free *1*
se limiter to limit onself *17*
limonade *(f)* lemonade *9*
lire to read *14*
lit *(m)* bed *2*
litre *(m)* litre *9*
livre *(f)* pound (money) *2*; pound (weight) *9*
livre *(m)* book *12*
locomotive *(f)* engine (SV)
loger to stay; to put up at *8*
loin far *3*
long long *10*
longtemps a long time *11*
longueur *(f)* length *19*
lors de at the time of *19*
louer to hire; to let *9*

lourd   heavy *17*
lumière *(f)*   light *4*
lunettes *(f pl)* (de soleil)   (sun)glasses
 (sv)

M

magasin *(m)*   shop *12*
magnifique   magnificent *10*
maillot de bain *(m)*   bathing costume *6*
maintenant   now *2*
mais   but *2*
maison *(f)*   house *19*
majestueusement   majestically *14*
mal   bad *11*
mal *(m)*   ache; pain *17*
manger   to eat *7*
manque *(m)*   lack *17*
manquer   to miss; to be lacking *19*
marchand *(m)*   shopkeeper *17*
marché *(m)*   market *8*
marcher   to walk *10*
mari *(m)*   husband *6*
mariage *(m)*   marriage (sv)
marinier   marine *7*
maritime   maritime *5*
marquis *(m)*   marquis *14*
marronnier *(m)*   horse chestnut *10*
matériel *(m)*   equipment *9*
matin *(m)*   morning *4*
mauvais   bad *6*
médecin *(m)*   doctor *17*
médicament *(m)*   medicine *17*
se méfier   to beware *15*
meilleur   better *7*
mélanger   to mix; to blend *18*
même   same *4*
mémoire *(f)*   memory *19*
ménagère *(f)*   housewife (sv)
mener   to lead *11*
menu *(m)*   menu *7*
mer *(f)*   sea *5*
merci   thank you *1*
mériter   to deserve *14*
en mesure de   in a position to *16*
météo *(f)*   weather forecast *14*
mètre *(m)*   metre *3*
métro *(m)*   underground train *10*
mettre   to put *14*
mettre à la poste   to post *14*
midi *(m)*   midday *2*
Midi *(m)*   South of France *14*
mieux   better *17*
mime *(m)*   mime *10*
minuscule   tiny *6*
minute *(f)*   minute *2*
mode *(f)*   fashion *7*

moderne   modern *16*
modiste *(f)*   milliner (sv)
moins   less *4*
mois *(m)*   month *16*
moment *(m)*   moment *1*
monde *(m)*   world *4*; people *6*
monnaie *(f)*   (small) change *3*
monsieur *(m)*   man; gentleman *4*
mont *(m)*   mount *18*
montagne *(f)*   mountain; hill *18*
montée *(f)*   climb *10*
monter   to climb *10*
montre *(f)*   wristwatch (sv)
monument *(m)*   monument; public
 building *3*
mot *(m)*   word *19*
moteur *(m)*   engine of car (sv)
moto *(f)*   motorcycle (sv)
mouchoir *(m)*   handkerchief (sv)
moule *(f)*   mussel *7*
mouiller   to wet; to soak *18*
municipal   municipal *4*
municipalité *(f)*   municipality *8*
musée *(m)*   museum *4*

N

nager   to swim *14*
naissance *(f)*   birth *16*
national   national *15*
nationalité *(f)*   nationality *16*
neuf   (brand) new *11*
neveu *(m)*   nephew (sv)
nez *(m)*   nose (sv)
nièce *(f)*   niece (sv)
niveau *(m)*   level *18*
noir   black *19*
nom *(m)*   name *8*
nom de famille *(m)*   surname *8*
nombreux   numerous *10*
nord *(m)*   north *15*
normal   normal *6*
normand   Norman *7*
notaire *(m)*   solicitor (sv)
note *(f)*   bill *18*
nouveau   new *16*
nuit *(f)*   night *12*
numéro *(m)*   number *1*

O

oblitérer   to stamp; to cancel (ticket) *3*
obtenir   to obtain *2*
occuper   to occupy; to spend (time) *8*
œil *(m)* (les yeux *(pl)*)   eye (sv)
œuf *(m)*   egg *7*
officiel   official *3*
offrir   to offer *19*

oignon *(m)* onion *18*
omelette *(f)* omelette *7*
oncle *(m)* uncle (SV)
optimiste *(m)* optimist *5*
orage *(m)* storm *14*
orange *(f)* orange *7*
ordonnance *(f)* perscription *17*
ordre *(m)* order *18*
oreille *(f)* ear (SV)
origine *(f)* origin *11*
ou or *2*
où (?) where (?) *3*
oublier to forget *3*
oui yes *1*
ouvert open *4*
ouverture *(f)* opening *4*
ouvrier *(m)* workman (SV)

P

pain *(m)* bread *9*
paisible peaceful *15*
palais *(m)* palace *11*
panier *(m)* basket *17*
panne *(f)* breakdown *2*
panorama *(m)* panorama *10*
pantalon *(m)* trousers *8*
paquet *(m)* packet *9*
parapluie *(m)* umbrella (SV)
paraître to appear; to seem *14*
parce que because *2*
pardessus *(m)* overcoat (SV)
pardon excuse me *1*
pare-brise *(m)* windscreen (SV)
pare-choc *(m)* bumper (SV)
pareil similar *15*
parfait perfect *7*
parfois sometimes *10*
parfum *(m)* perfume; flavour *2*
parfumerie *(f)* perfumery *6*
parisien Parisian *10*
parler to speak *8*
partager to share *19*
partie *(f)* part *10*
partir to leave *10*
partout everywhere *15*
passage *(m)* clouté pedestrian crossing *13*
passage *(m)* souterrain subway (SV)
passager *(m)* passenger *17*
passeport *(m)* passport *1*
passer to pass *2*
passer (un examen) to take (an exam) *15*
se passer to happen *15*
pâté *(m)* pâté *7*
pâtisserie *(f)* pastry *7*; cake shop (SV)
patron *(m)* employer; boss (SV)
pâturage *(m)* pasture *14*

pauvre poor *17*
payer to pay *6*
pays *(m)* country *14*
Pays de Galles *(m)* Wales (SV)
paysage *(m)* landscape *10*
pêche *(f)* peach (SV)
pêcheur *(m)* fisherman (SV)
peine *(f)* trouble; worry *10*
pendant during *8*
se perdre to lose oneself *8*
perdu lost *8*
père *(m)* father *20*
période *(f)* period *15*
permettre to allow *17*
personne *(f)* person *9*; nobody *11*
personnel personal *16*
personnellement personally *13*
petit small; little *2*
petit déjeuner *(m)* breakfast *5*
petit pain *(m)* bread roll *17*
petits-pois *(m pl)* green peas (SV)
peu *(m)* (a) little *5*
peuple *(m)* people *19*
peut-être perhaps *5*
phare *(m)* headlight *15*
pharmacie *(f)* chemist's *17*
pièce *(f)* play *4*
pied *(m)* foot *3*
pile *(f)* battery (SV)
piquenique *(m)* picnic *17*
piscine *(f)* swimming pool *4*
place *(f)* square *3*; seat *4*
plage *(f)* beach *6*
se plaindre to complain *17*
plaine *(f)* plain *14*
plaisir *(m)* pleasure *1*
plan *(m)* plan *3*
plante *(f)* plant *3*
plaque *(f)* number-plate (SV)
plat *(m)* dish *7*
plateau *(m)* tray *7*
plein full *16*
pleuvoir to rain *5*
plombier *(m)* plumber (SV)
se plonger to immerse oneself *19*
plus more *5*
plusieurs several *14*
pneu *(m)* tyre *18*
poche *(f)* pocket (SV)
poisson *(m)* fish *18*
poissonnerie *(f)* fishmonger's (SV)
poitrine *(f)* chest (SV)
poivre *(m)* pepper *7*
poivrer to add pepper *18*
police *(f)* police *8*
pomme de terre *(f)* potato *9*
pommier *(m)* apple tree *14*

pompier *(m)* fireman (SV)
pont *(m)* bridge *10*; deck *19*
porc *(m)* pig; pork (SV)
port *(m)* port *3*
port *(m)* postage *19*
portefeuille *(m)* wallet (SV)
porter to wear *6*; to carry
porteur *(m)* porter (SV)
portugais Portuguese (SV)
Portugal *(m)* Portugal (SV)
poser to put (a question) *13*
possible possible *5*
possibilité *(f)* possibility *14*
postal postal *12*
poste *(f)* post office *14*
potage *(m)* soup *7*
poulet *(m)* chicken *18*
pour for *1*
pourquoi (?) why (?) *2*
poursuivre to pursue *15*
pouvoir to be able *1*
pré *(m)* meadow *(14)*
préfecture *(f)* police HQ *11*
préférable preferable *6*
préférer to prefer *2*
premier first *3*
prendre to take *2*
prénom *(m)* first name *8*
près near *3*
à présent now; at the present time *15*
présenter to introduce *1*; to present *2*
presque almost *12*
pressé in a hurry *8*; squeezed *11*
pression *(f)* pressure *18*
prêt ready *2*
prévenir to warn *13*
prévoir to have in mind *5*
prévu planned; foreseen *12*
prier to request *16*
primaire primary *15*
principal main; principal *3*
printemps *(m)* spring *17*
prix *(m)* price *17*
probablement probably *11*
problème *(m)* problem *2*
prochain next *11*
professeur *(m)* teacher *8*
profession *(f)* profession *8*
profiter to take advantage of *16*
promenade *(f)* walk; ride *10*
se promener to go for a walk; to go for a
    ride *8*
prononcer to pronounce *19*
proposer to suggest *14*
propre own *9*
provision *(f)* provision *17*
prune *(f)* plum (SV)

puis then *10*
pullover *(m)* pullover *6*

Q

quai *(m)* quay *5*; platform *20*
quand (?) when (?) *4*
quand même all the same; nevertheless *5*
quant à as for *19*
quart *(m)* quarter *4*
quartier *(m)* district *8*
quel? what? which? *2*
quelque(s) some *5*
quelque chose something *7*
quelquefois sometimes *5*
qu'est-ce que? what? *2*
question *(f)* question *8*
quincaillerie *(f)* hardware store (SV)
quitter to leave *15*

R

race *(f)* race *15*
raconter to relate *19*
raison *(f)* reason *13*
radiateur *(m)* radiator (SV)
rapide quick; swift *10*
rapide *(m)* express train (SV)
se rappeler to remember *15*
rapporter to take back *17*
ravi delighted *5*
rayon *(m)* department *6*
rebâtir to rebuild *15*
recevoir to receive *19*
recommander to recommend *14*
recommencer to begin again *16*
reconnaissant grateful *19*
reconnaître to recognise *15*
reconstruction *(f)* rebuilding *15*
rédacteur *(m)* newspaper editor (SV)
rédiger to draw up (a document) *16*
réfléchir to reflect *19*
regarder to look (at) *5*
région *(f)* region *7*
régional regional *15*
regretter to regret; to be sorry *2*
régulier regular *10*
rejoindre to rejoin *12*
rembourser to reimburse *17*
remercier to thank *8*
remettre to put back *19*
remonter to go up *10*
remplir to fill (in) *16*
rencontre *(f)* meeting *18*
rencontrer to meet *19*
se rendre dans to go to *19*
rendre service to do a favour *12*

rendre visite   to pay a visit 16
rentrée (f)   return; start of term 19
rentrer   to return (home) 8
rentrer dans   to collide with; to crash into 13
renseignements (m pl)   information 3
renvoyer   to send back 16
réparer   to repair 8
réparation (f)   repair 19
repas (m)   meal 7
répondre   to answer 8
se reposer   to rest 8
reprendre   to take again 12
représentation (f)   production (theatre) 4
représenter   to represent 19
réserver   to reserve 9
résister   to resist 12
ressembler   to resemble 14
restaurant (m)   restaurant 5
rester   to remain 1
retard (m)   delay 13
retour (m)   return 10
retourner   to come back; to return 7
se retrouver   to meet up 14
réussi   successful 18
réussite (f)   success 19
se réveiller   to wake up 8
révéler   to reveal 19
revenir   to return 10
revoir   to see again 1
rhume (m)   cold 17
rhythme (m)   rhythm 15
riche   rich 15
richesse (f)   wealth 18
rien   nothing 6
rivage (m)   bank (of river) 13
rivière (f)   river 5
riz (m)   rice 12
robe (f)   dress 12
roi (m)   king 7
Romain (m)   Roman 15
rond-point (m)   roundabout 10
roue (de rechange) (f)   (spare) wheel (SV)
rouge   red 6
rouler   to drive; to travel 14
route (f)   road 14
rue (f)   street 3
ruine (f)   ruin 15

S

sac (m)   bag 9
sac à main (m)   handbag (SV)
sacré   holy 10
saignant   bloody; rare 7
sale   dirty 18
saler   to salt 18

salle (f)   room 9
salle de bains (f)   bathroom 9
salon (m)   sitting room; lounge 8
sandwich (m)   sandwich 10
sans   without 12
santé (f)   health 18
satisfaction (f)   satisfaction 15
satisfaire   to satisfy 14
satisfait   satisfied 8
sauce (f)   sauce, gravy 18
saucisson (m)   salami-type sausage 9
sauf   except (for) 4
sauter   to fry and toss; to jump 18
savoir   to know 3
scolaire   educational 15
sec (sèche)   dry 17
secondaire   secondary 8
secrétaire (m) or (f)   secretary 1
section (f)   section 16
séjour (m)   stay 1
sel (m)   salt 18
selon   according to 13
semaine (f)   week 1
sens (m)   direction 13
sentiment (m)   feeling 16
se sentir   to feel 17
sérieux   serious 17
serveuse (f)   waitress 2
service (m)   service 2
seul   alone 8; one only 14
seulement   only 3
short (m)   shorts (SV)
si   if 2; yes 6
siècle (m)   century 14
siège (m)   seat 17
signaler   to point out 16
signature (f)   signature 16
signer   to sign 19
silhouette (f)   silhouette 10
similarité (f)   similarity 19
simplement   simply 7
sirop (m)   cough medicine 17
se situer   to be situated 11
snack (m)   snack 12
sobriété (f)   restraint; sobriety 14
sœur (f)   sister (SV)
soie (f)   silk 19
soin (m)   (medical) care 17
soir (m)   evening 1
soleil (m)   sun 6
sommet (m)   top; summit 10
sondage (m)   public opinion poll 8
sorte (f)   sort 9
sortir   to leave; to go out 13
soudain   suddenly 16
soufflé (m)   soufflé 18
soulager   to relieve; to comfort 17

soupe *(f)* soup *18*
sous under *11*
souvent often *8*
souvenir *(m)* souvenir *12*
se souvenir de to remember *18*
son *(m)* sound *4*
spécialité *(f)* speciality *7*
spectacle *(m)* show; performance *4*
steak *(m)* steak *7*
sucre *(m)* sugar *18*
sucré sweet *7*
sud *(m)* south *14*
Suisse *(f)* Switzerland *18*
suite *(f)* continuation *6*; sequel; result
    16
suivre to follow *3*
sujet *(m)* subject *15*
super *(m)* 4-star petrol *18*
supermarché *(m)* supermarket *17*
supposer to suppose *14*
sur on *3*
sûr sure *8*
sûrement surely; certainly *10*
surtout above all; especially *3*
symptôme *(m)* symptom *17*
syndicat d'initiative *(m)* tourist
    information centre *3*

T

taille *(f)* size *6*
tailleur *(m)* tailor (sv)
tante *(f)* aunt (sv)
tard late *5*
tapisserie *(f)* tapestry *14*
tarif *(m)* rate *14*; scale of charges *16*
taxe *(f)* tax *18*
téléphone *(m)* telephone *4*
télévision *(f)* television *9*
tellement so many *11*
témoin *(m)* witness *13*
temps *(m)* time *1*; weather *5*
tente *(f)* tent *9*
terminer to finish *18*
se terminer to come to an end *18*
terrasse *(f)* pavement café *2*
terre *(f)* earth *8*
tête *(f)* head *17*
thé *(m)* tea *9*
théâtre *(m)* theatre *4*
timbre *(m)* stamp *14*
tirer to pull *17*
tomate *(f)* tomato *18*
tomber to fall *18*
tort *(m)* wrong; fault *13*
toucher (un chèque) to cash (a cheque) *2*
toucher à to come to; to reach *16*

toujours always *8*
tour *(m)* tour, trip *6*
tour *(f)* tower *10*
tourisme *(m)* tourism *8*
touriste *(m)* tourist *11*
tout all; everything *2*
tous everybody *19*
tousser to cough *17*
toux *(f)* cough *17*
train *(m)* train *10*
trait *(m)* feature *15*
tranche *(f)* slice *9*
transport *(m)* transport *15*
traversée *(f)* crossing *19*
traverser to cross *3*
travail *(m)* work *16*
travailler to work *15*
très very *1*
triomphe *(m)* triumph *10*
tripes *(f pl)* tripe *7*
trop too *6*
trouver to find *6*
se trouver to be located *11*
truc *(m)* thing; whatsit *12*
typique typical *10*

U

unique unique, only *14*
universellement universally *10*
université *(f)* university *11*

V

vacances *(f pl)* holidays *8*
vache *(f)* cow *14*
vaissellerie *(f)* china department *6*
valise *(f)* suitcase (sv)
vallée *(f)* valley *18*
vanille *(f)* vanilla *2*
varié varied *14*
veau *(m)* calf; veal (sv)
vendeuse *(f)* sales assistant *6*
venir to come *4*
vent *(m)* wind *8*
vérifier to check *3*
verdure *(f)* greenery *14*
vers towards *6*; about *10*
vert green *6*
vêtements *(m pl)* clothes *5*
vétérinaire *(m)* vet (sv)
viande *(f)* meat *7*
vide empty *17*
vie *(f)* life *15*
vieux old *8*
village *(m)* village *14*
ville *(f)* town *3*

vin *(m)* wine 7
vinaigre *(m)* vinegar (SV)
violent violent 13
visage *(m)* face (SV)
visite *(f)* visit 4
visiter to visit 3
vite quick 5
vitesse *(f)* speed 16
vivre to live 19
voie *(f)* (railway) track 11
voilà here is, here are 1
voir to see 2
voiture *(f)* car 6
vouloir to want 3

vouloir dire to mean 18
voyage *(m)* journey 12
vrai true 5
vraiment really; truly 7
vue *(f)* view 10

W

wagon *(m)* carriage; cart (SV)
wagon-lit *(m)* sleeping car (SV)

Z

zone *(f)* zone 14

Grammar overview

Chapter 1

forms of address (monsieur, madame)
conversational extras (alors, eh bien)
gender
definite article (le, la, l', les)
plural of nouns
expressing possession (mon, ma, mes; notre, nos; votre, vos)
asking questions (intonation, est-ce que...?)

Chapter 2

present tense of regular verbs ending in '-er'
'pouvoir' (je peux...?, vous pouvez)
giving commands and instructions
negatives (ne...pas)
indefinite article (un, une, des)
asking and answering questions (qu'est-ce que...? pourquoi? parce que)

Chapter 3

asking the way
'à' and 'de'
position and agreement of adjectives
giving instructions (including negative commands)
asking and answering questions (qu'est-ce que c'est? c'est...)
'il y a' and 'voilà'

Chapter 4

telling the time
asking 'when?' (quand? à quelle heure?)
days of the week
'vouloir' (je veux, je voudrais)

Chapter 5

greetings and good wishes
using 'aller' + infinitive to talk about the future
'croire' (je crois que...)
talking about the weather
negatives (ne...jamais)
'si' after negative questions and statements

Chapter 6

likes and dislikes (aimer)
disjunctive pronouns (pour moi, avec lui)
present tense of 'être'
'on'
expressing possession (using 'de')
'c'est' (it is, this is)
negatives (ne...rien; ne...plus)
'tout'/'toute'
'y' and 'en'
more about adjectives

Chapter 7

present tense of regular verbs ending in '-ir'
making comparisons (comparative and superlative of adjectives)
'meilleur'
adjectives and adverbs
emphasising pronouns (moi, toi)
use of the definite article
verbs without a following preposition (chercher, attendre)

Chapter 8

reflexive verbs
common prepositions (en, à)
asking questions (quel...?; inversion)
'on'
'c'est'/'ce sont'
'il faut'
expressing age (using 'avoir')
definite article with countries and regions
singular or plural (les cheveux, le pantalon)?
'vieux'/'vieille'

Chapter 9

partitive article (du, de la, de l', des)
asking 'how much?', 'how many?' (combien (de)?)
irregular plurals

Chapter 10

future tense of regular verbs
future tense of irregular verbs
object pronouns
'connaître'/'savoir'
word order
expressing emphasis with 'bien'

Chapter 11

demonstrative adjectives (ce, cet, cette, ces)
ordinal numbers
duration of time (depuis, pour)
'se trouver'
nobody (ne...personne)

Chapter 12

perfect tense with 'avoir'
asking questions in the perfect tense
expressing the negative in the perfect tense
'pour aller à'

Chapter 13

perfect tense with 'être'
agreement of the past participle
perfect tense of reflexive verbs
position of object pronouns
use of verbs with a direct infinitive (aller, voir)
'avoir besoin de' and 'avoir raison'
'parce que'/'à cause de'
question tags (non?, hein?)
telephone numbers
'il y a' (ago)

Chapter 14

relative pronouns (qui, que)
indirect object pronouns
'y'
expressing quantity (bien des, plusieurs)

Chapter 15

imperfect tense
comparative and superlative of adjectives (aussi...que)

Chapter 16

writing letters
'devoir' (must, has to)
introduction to the subjunctive (bien que...; il faut que...)
relative pronouns (ce qui, ce que)

Chapter 17

reported speech
imperative + object pronouns
demonstrative pronouns (celle-ci, celui-là)
negatives (rien; ne...aucun)
'en'
'faire' + infinitive
'laisser' + infinitive
plurals ending in '-aux'
definite article with parts of the body

Chapter 18

conditional sentences
giving instructions using the infinitive
more about the subjunctive
'c'est' used for emphasis
'le soir où...'
'avant de' + infinitive

Chapter 19

pluperfect tense
conditional of 'devoir'
present participle
order of object pronouns
possessive pronouns (le mien, le nôtre)
'après' + past infinitive

Accounting
Advanced English Language
Advanced Pure Mathematics
Arabic
Banking
Basic Management
Biology
British Politics
Business Administration
Business Communication
Business Law
Business Microcomputing
C Programming
Chemistry
COBOL Programming
Commerce
Communication
Computers
Databases
Economic and Social History
Economics
Electrical Engineering
Electronic and Electrical Calculations
Electronics
English as a Foreign Language
English Grammar
English Language
English Literature
English Spelling
French

French 2
German
German 2
Human Biology
Italian
Italian 2
Japanese
Manufacturing
Marketing
Mathematics
Mathematics for Electrical and
    Electronic Engineering
Modern British History
Modern European History
Modern World History
Pascal Programming
Philosophy
Photography
Physics
Psychology
Science
Social Welfare
Sociology
Spanish
Spanish 2
Spreadsheets
Statistics
Study Skills
Word Processing